ON GENDERING TEXTS
Female and Male Voices in the Hebrew Bible

BIBLICAL INTERPRETATION SERIES

VOLUME 1

ON GENDERING TEXTS

Female and Male Voices in the Hebrew Bible

BY

ATHALYA BRENNER

AND

FOKKELIEN VAN DIJK-HEMMES

E.J. BRILL
LEIDEN · NEW YORK · KÖLN
1996

Previously published as a hardback edition (cloth with dustjacket), 1993, ISBN 90 04 09642 6.

The paper in this book meets the guidelines for permanence and durability of the Committee on Production Guidelines for Book Longevity of the Council on Library Resources.

ISSN   0928-0731
ISBN   90 04 10644 8

CONTENTS

III M Text Authority in Biblical Love Lyrics: The Case of Qoheleth 3.1-9 and Its Textual Relatives
Athalya Brenner

IV Divine Love and Prophetic Pornography

The Metaphorization of Woman in Prophetic Speech: An Analysis of Ezekiel 23
Fokkelien van Dijk-Hemmes

On "Jeremiah" and the Poetics of (Prophetic?) Pornography
Athalya Brenner

FOREWORD

One of the most productive catch-phrases of new literary criticism is Barbara Johnson's notion of "the difference within", which she used in her seminal 1987 book, *A World of Difference* (Baltimore: Johns Hopkins University Press). The present book shows why. Difference within, within the Hebrew Bible for example, makes room for interests other than the traditional preoccupations of scholarship, yet by exploring the internal dividedness of such an influential body of texts it also enables, explains, and thus helps along, the more traditional questions by providing them with more rather than less impact.

On Gendering Texts is a wonderful book in a field that demonstrates its maturity by this publication. It discusses the important and traditional issue of authorship. Whereas the idea of a unique and divinely inspired biblical author has long been abandoned, the issue of authorship itself has not. The criticism in line with "separation of sources" takes the Bible to be a patchwork of various strands, and its analytical procedures cannot solve the problem of mixture, blends, and other forms of diversity-within. The possibility that women might have contributed to the production of the Bible has not been taken seriously and yet the idea that everything is male unless otherwise proven is hardly acceptable. What can one do?

The two authors of this book shrewdly displace the question. Rather than worrying about unprovable historical authors, they consider gender-positions; authority; gendered textuality and attributions of gender within the text; voice; world-view and ideological content. Each of these issues is important, and the gesture of raising them in connection with that of authorship alone makes this book worthwhile. Thus they are able to lead a thorough discussion of the problem through to an attractive attempt at an answer. On the way, they discuss method and texts in parallel. Staying away from essentialist assumptions and from separationist cuts, they salvage the issue from the marginality it had been cast into, and from the mess any attempt to discuss it has so far led to.

This book is both unique and in line with a growing tradition; a climactic point in the developing area of feminist biblical study. There have been many contributions to biblical interpretation from

a feminist perspective, but as a whole the field of Biblical studies
remains largely male-dominated. Yet this is not due to lack of good-
will; I have noticed in my own vagaries in that field that Biblical
studies is more open than any other field I know of to the feminist
perspective. But the current generation of scholars has not had the
proper training to raise the right questions in this respect. Yet, as
a consequence of the tremendous interest and the excitement created
by feminist scholarship, the interest in feminist studies is growing so
rapidly that a good textbook is more than called for.

This is such a textbook. The interest in the Hebrew Bible is immense, and this book offers such a wide variety of analyses, covering
so many and such divergent texts, genres, and perspectives, that no
one studying the Bible can afford to ignore it. In terms of methodology, the book is not overburdened with jargon and theory, yet is ex-
emplarily explicit about its choices and procedures. Hence, even in
classes which study none of the texts chosen, the book has immense
value.

Early feminist criticism was hampered by a lack of theoretical
knowledge and an excess of religious and social zeal, focusing on an
audience of preachers more than scholars. Phyllis Trible's work, in
both its merits and its obvious limitations, marks the limit of how
far that takes one. If Trible's work has been extremely valuable in
getting the feminist study of the Bible started, this book demonstrates the definitive move beyond that start.

Others have followed the lead. Most of those held on to the divide
between ''positive'' views of the Bible (Trible) and ''negative'' ones
(the much-needed anger of Esther Fuchs comes to mind). The
latter's justified resentment tends to make scholars blind to
anachronistic projections, and blaming the Bible for today's problems is no help at all. This book is one of the few to move beyond
that division, and to strike the difficult balance between, in fact, *two*
divisions: between adherence and angry rejection on the one hand,
and between historical distance and contemporary ''use'' on the
other. This balance is characteristic of what I would call ''second
round'' feminist scholarship, the one that has matured and has been
integrated in most universities.

But that has not yet yielded a great deal of published work. This
book compares with, and usefully complements, the best work done
these days in this area. In New Testament studies, Elisabeth
S. Fiorenza and Bernadette Brooten have been leaders; their work

is addressed explicitly and, I think, rightly, in the methodological intermezzi this book offers. In Hebrew Bible/Old Testament, I think most highly of the work of someone like Cheryl Exum. A tradition is on its way to being established.

The present book can compete with the best work in the field in terms of thoroughness and inventiveness, while it beats all published work in the field I know of in range and methodological explicitness and innovation. It is still more widely useful than any of it. This book covers a wide range of genres and texts, and, while being on the highest level in terms of methodological subtlety, it is easy to read and, hence, more likely to conquer the classroom.

Students learn, not only from methodological guidelines, but equally, if not more, from seeing these applied. The combination of methodological discussion—also good examples to follow—and broad as well as in-depth analyses makes this book an ideal tool for teaching.

Feminist exegesis has a heavy burden to carry: it must make itself plausible in discussion with standard views, it must show competence even in the traditional skills, and it must integrate literary as well as biblical traditions with feminist philosophy. The danger is that unless it falls short of these high expectations, the heaviness of the load makes itself felt. I admire the skills with which this book has been kept readable—in a sense, light. For example, the systematic summing up of relevant points makes it easy to handle. Yet, in spite of its pedagogical accessibility, all the expertise is there, and explicitly so: feminist theory is presented and endorsed; literary theory is adopted; and Biblical scholarship gets its due. The book is obviously not separatist.

Several features make this book absolutely unique, and I attribute much of this uniqueness to the dual authorship. This book is about authorship, authority, and ideology, and the presentation contributes much to its persuasiveness in this respect. The way the authors have handled their own double authorship in a study on a revision of the very notion of authorship is impressive. One might argue with the decision to stay with the first person singular in the individual essays, where a "we" would have been smoother. But the "I" here and the "we" there, make for an honesty that has intellectual implications. No feminist book of this scope has been authored by two authors from respectively a Jewish and a Christian background and training. They agree on the basics and differ to some extent on details, and what is more realistic, and also, more constructive, than showing that overtly? I appreciate the way, for example, in which some of the issues raised by Van Dijk in Part I are taken up, in more detail, and with a somewhat different angle, by Brenner in Part II. Each author contributes her views on women's perspectives, and that fact emphasizes the diversity amongst feminists, much in need of emphasis. And Part IV is a mix of both authors' views on the issue of sexual oppression—there, when facing a common problem, they present a more unified front.

The book is equally unique in its combination of thoroughly historical considerations and contemporary concerns. The orchestration is masterfully effective. All through, the authors keep these two current but separate, and this leads to very fortunate emendations of previous attempts, as well as to very ingenious new interpretations. And then, dramatically, in the final part, where *The Story of O* serves as a direction for reading Jeremiah, the blend becomes so total that the reader must step back and think about what it means to do such a daring thing. My own conclusion is, then: why not? But if one wishes to distance oneself from this move, one is still burdened with the charge of defining the difference. Nothing is more illuminating. To end on such a provocative note is daring; it is also most stimulating, and I can imagine classroom assignments that will help students do the best thinking they have done so far.

The composition of the book shows the traces of the dual authorship, and given the above remarks, I mean that positively. It is surprising but innovative and good. First the authors present a combination of considerations of method and ''application'' of their preferred method to a large number of genres, with examples. This broadens the scope of the book usefully, and yet it shows enough of ''how to do this''. This first part (by Van Dijk) would make a useful book in and of itself. The examples demonstrate Van Dijk's long-standing expertise and experience as a teacher of this material. Her respectful attitude toward others, including opponents, sets a good example for students prone to show their cleverness by trashing predecessors. It also helps to bridge the gap between feminist and standard scholarship.

After this survey part, the second and third parts (by Brenner) go into more detail about one of the genres Van Dijk had outlined. This, too, helps the teacher and makes the general case more convincing. Even if one does not agree with every detail, one will still be encouraged to follow the lead and go into more detail on one of the other genres. And then, Part IV supplies a timely complement: after the search for traces of female positions, this final part rounds the discussion off with discussions of unambiguously male positions. To call this pornography may seem a bit strong to some readers, but it certainly clarifies things.

I consider this book a most valuable contribution to the field of feminist biblical studies, and *thereby* to biblical studies in general. This stems from the combination of interdisciplinary methodology, wide-ranging text choice, and the diversity of aspects (genre, particular genres, authorship, pornography) discussed.

March 1992
Mieke Bal

INTRODUCTION

This work grew out of two, initially separate, preoccupations. One of us (van Dijk-Hemmes) was searching for traces of women's culture in the Hebrew Bible; the other (Brenner) was looking for (presumably male) biblical literary paradigms of woman and their underlining social stereotypes. At first each of us argued for the merits of her respective approach. Then we came to realize that our individual programs overlapped to an extent and were certainly complementary. Thereby mutual criticism led to collaboration, and the present book evolved out of that collaboration.

Ultimately, each of us retains sole responsibility for her own personal contributions. However, because each has been intensely involved in the other's project for years, and because every critical move made by either of us was exchanged and ultimately thrashed out together, we regard this book not only as an assemblage of individually written pieces but, largely, as the product of a joint effort.

As we commenced, separately and together, we found that preconceptions, suppositions, presumptions, and sentiments that had generated our work had to be modified, altered, or discarded. Gradually our perspectives and objectives shifted and, throughout the stages of investigation and then writing, we had to continually reshape and reformulate both aims and methods. This Introduction, then, proceeds from an attempt to chart that process of an ongoing, gradual unfolding. We then present some of the basic premises and notions which inform our agendas. Short descriptions of the book's constituent parts follow.

On Gendering Biblical Texts: General Considerations

Feminist Bible scholarship is far from monolithic. The scholars who practise it follow diverse agendas. Some use their energy to unmask patriarchy (Fuchs). Some look for a women's subculture. Some try to rehabilitate women's images (Trible). Some are mainly interested in counter-reading and in the deconstructive properties attributable to biblical texts (Bal). The two of us started by pursuing twin strands: searching for women's texts within the Hebrew canon, and the means for differentiating them from men's texts.

We studied for our first degrees in different places, albeit roughly at the same time: one in Utrecht, the other in Haifa. We were both taught that the quest for biblical authorship was a legitimate pursuit, even though the question of gender authorship was seldom if ever broached. Later on, when awareness of gender matters and androcentrism and gender bias/oppression became heightened through feminist interest, it was—still is—commonly assumed that biblical texts were written exclusively or almost exclusively by males and for the consumption of males; and that whoever wanted to prove that a certain text is an exception to this generalization had to carry the burden of proof. An obvious response to this implicit challenge was to find, define and classify women's texts in contradistinction to men's texts.

A second and supplementary direction entailed having a closer look at gendering possible candidates for men's texts by attempting to redefine them as such, and by asking ourselves how those differed from texts classified as women's texts. We realize that we may come under fire here, mainly from feminists who object to the practice of covertly complying with androcentric standards by evaluating women's culture in accordance with dominant male culture. We therefore hasten to explain this point. We wanted to draw analogies between gendered texts by juxtaposition; our approach is informed by the understanding that a framework within which a text is embedded—and biblical texts of presumably female origin are indeed embedded—is meaningful, sometimes even fatally so, for whatever it envelops.

When looking for women's texts, one has to refer to two preliminary questions.

(a) Is it possible to gender a text or its author, that is, to define one or the other, or both, as a product of women's culture or men's culture? This, of course, is mainly a question of the adequacy of the methodology or methodologies employed.

(b) Is the gendering of texts important, and for whom? This is a question of validity and the contribution to literary and cultural knowledge that gendering texts might advance.

These questions will appear and reappear throughout the discussion. We shall try to relate to them by appealing to biblical scholarship, especially of feminist persuasions, as well as to literary criticism and related (feminist and other) disciplines.

Orality, Literacy, and Literariness

We started our investigation, then, by assuming—as we had been taught—that women's texts in the Bible, if there are any, are embedded in men's texts and framed by men's editing and redactional activities. Textual activities preserve but also change, distort, and recreate their subject matter (Ong 1982). Therefore, since women's traditions in the Bible in so far as they exist are preserved as written texts, one has to uncover the traditions behind and underneath the texts as well as relate to their embedding within their frames. We soon realized that in order to find women's traditions and trace their broken lines we had to consider orality, literacy and literariness, and the nature of the links between those concepts; and to apply these considerations to our search.

Ong (1982, 10) holds that the term "oral literature" is an unfortunate one. Since the word "literature" is etymologically derived from the Latin for "letter", "literature" and its semantic derivatives imply literacy (the ability to write) and therefore, by definition, preclude orality. That writing and textualization undoubtedly transform oral consciousness, unconsciousness, and traditions radically is beyond dispute. Nevertheless, we maintain, lack of literacy does not automatically preclude oral literariness (the ability to compose and transmit poetry/narrative). Etymology aside, the ability to write and record (even in a secondarily oral society, while we imagine biblical societies to still be primarily oral), is not necessarily a prerequisite for creative verbal activity.

The concept of orality has, certainly since Gunkel, been applied to biblical literature at large; therefore, it should and can be applied to the search for women's texts. This application emanates from a specific understanding: even if literacy was relatively scarce among women (like among men in the biblical world, but more about that later), this by itself does not preclude women's activities in literary composition and its performance in private and/or in public. In other words, although literariness and literacy overlap to an extent, the concept of oral literariness (perhaps for want of a more elegant term) is generally acknowledged in biblical studies. This tacit acknowledgement is important, for it is of great assistance in the quest for women's traditions that are transfixed in those texts.

S.D. Goitein (1988 [1957]) shows how the wealth of women's traditions is perhaps preserved, developed and enhanced precisely because of the need for mnemotechnical procedures. The problem of the eventual recording of those traditions is, of course, another matter entirely. Hence, we formulate the first premise which underlies and informs our investigation thus. Women's literary traditions were probably and by and large oral and were preserved and transmitted, at least in part, as the produce of collective efforts. We note in this regard that the relevant texts often introduce discourse attributed to women as oral performance (a song or recitation). While this mode of textual presentation can hardly point to an *actual* oral origin of those fragmentary traditions, it nevertheless attests to the orality which often underlines texts of literate, or partly literate, societies (Ong 1982, 157-160). In short, the notion of orality affects the evaluation of literary genres where women's verbal creativity is the most likely to have emerged (or been recorded). For instance, genres like victory poems for heroes and derisive poems about enemies must have evolved through orality before they were eventually reported in writing. Their *Sitz im Leben* (inside and outside the text) and presentation as oral must have facilitated their fictive preservation.

But who committed these presumably oral women's traditions to writing? Once more, it is widely assumed that men did. The notion of male supremacy in literacy cannot perhaps be challenged. We feel, however, that it can be modified somewhat.

Some scholars (notably Cross 1975, Millard 1985 and Naveh 1968; but see also Haran 1988) convincingly argue that, to judge by epigraphic finds, literacy became widespread in ancient Israel from the 8th century BCE onwards. There is no reason to assume that this important cultural development affected men's lives only. Furthermore, there is an abundance of extrabiblical Near Eastern evidence concerning women's literacy even from much earlier times (Hallo 1976, Fontaine 1989). Women's literacy and literariness was already to be found in Sumer: Enheduanna, daughter of Sargon, is but one example. Did those ancient women use professional scribes? Maybe, but so did their male counterparts. It seems safe to assume that ancient Israel did not differ substantially from its neighbours in regard to women's literacy, except for one important facility for advancing it—the existence of women-ministered goddess temples. And this difference, important as it is, appears less decisive when we take into account the forces of international cultural osmosis. For instance, Jezebel could write, and her juridical skill was more than adequate: this is not suppressed inspite of the negative portrayal she receives in the text (1 Kgs 21), hence we can probably regard it as reliable reporting. There is no need to assume that all or most women, of the upper classes but also of other classes, were excluded from the domain of written language, or from the domain of creative literary activity. It must be admitted, however, that there is no evidence for or against the existence of female *professional* scribes in ancient Israel; knowledge might exist without being exploited vocationally, especially where women are concerned. And, to return to this point, perhaps there were no female Israelite scribes because of the lack of female-run cultic centres. We have to accept, then, that in all probability women's traditions became texts, were recorded and transmitted (at least mostly), through the active agencies of male scribes and male editors.

A shift from oral creation to written text is always problematic. The transformation of women's orality into texts consigned to male scribes is, in addition, significantly more traumatic than indicated by the regular process. General problems which accompany the recording and transmitting stages are augmented by problems of inverted gender perspectives. The female character of original women's compositions may thus be obliterated or masked over in the process.[1] And this factor leads us back to the problematics of defining biblical authorship.

Author, Authority, Text, Voice

In modern literary theory the demise of the author often underlies critical theory (Barthes 1970, 1977), even though this notion is sometimes qualified (see Culler 1983, "Readers and Reading", 31-83). A modified "death of the author" notion (Foucault in Harari, 1979, 141-60) is useful when applied to contemporary texts but even more so when it is applied to ancient, largely anonymous, literatures. In fact, it is difficult not to subscribe to Gerald Bruns' opinion. To quote, "It is now hard to see how a notion of authorship can be applied to these texts [the Hebrew Bible] in any significant way." (Bruns 1984). This observation stems from, and is a reaction to, the preoccupation with The Author which has characterized biblical exegesis and scholarship for millennia.

---

[1] For the literacy and literariness of women in Greco-Roman times, and for the question of writing and dissemination of women's texts, cf. Kraemer and others in Levine (1991).

Attempts to identify authors of a largely anonymous collective literature of times past, such as the Bible, tend to be circular and highly speculative. Ultimately, the search for such Authors fails or, at best, remains vulnerable. Hence, in addition to the recognition of oral roots, we prefer to talk about *texts* rather than about the conjectured *persons* who might have composed those texts. It is the text rather than the person on which we focus. We are aware, however, that nevertheless, by force of habit and education, we keep looking for an author as a *subtext*. By that we mean that in our work, and to a certain extent despite ourselves, text and author are almost interchangeable (Culler 1983, "Stories of Reading", 64-83). For us the author is the creative imprint, the text as signature, the textual output as both literary prowess and reflection of human experience. And yet, in order to avoid acts of naming, we prefer to relate to a text and the voices within it rather than to a specificity of an identified (personal) authorship.

At this point, then, we reroute our initial quest—Where can we find women's texts in the Bible? How can they be differentiated from men's texts?—and redefine our objectives. What we wish to uncover are the gender positions entrenched in a text to the extent that its *authority* rather than its *authorship* can be gendered. In other words, we try to walk a tightrope of distinguishing between:

(a) Notions of women-authored texts, that is, texts that were actually composed and/or written by women.

(b) Textuality attributed to a woman or women in a text.

(c) The possibility of defining plausible, hence authoritative, women's *voices* which operate within and behind a text.

We start from a convinction that women composed literature in biblical times, a facility not rendered impossible by illiteracy. We add our recognition that the extent of female illiteracy has been rendered questionable by recent research into the popularization and democratization of literacy. We then link women's orality and (il)literacy with critical considerations concerning the author's status. Consequently, we have begun (contra positions adopted earlier) to find it more interesting to abandon acts of gendering texts by referring to the gender of their (conjectured) authors. Instead, in order to define a text as a women's text (or a men's text), we try to discern female (and later male) voices in them. In most cases we have therefore refrained from speculating upon the gender of a text's

actual *writer*—to distinguish from its oral composer, or trans-
mitter(s).

The concept of "voice" which we have finally arrived at merits
some articulation at this point. It indicates orality within writing,
the sum of speech acts assigned to a fictive person or the narrator
within a text. By implication, a voice's fictive owner has a privileged
position of power in the literary discourse within which it features.
If we want to use the language of visuality to describe the written
reproduction of this basically audial manifestation, we can define a
textual voice by turning to Bal's narratological model (Bal 1988b,
34-38). A voice belongs to her/him who holds the primary subject
position in a discourse (after that of the narrator but, quite often, as
the embodiment of the narrator's privileged albeit covert "voice").
The voice often belongs to and expresses the focalizer of the text.
When all or most of the affirmative answers to the questions, Who
speaks? Who focalizes the action? Whose viewpoint is dominant?—
converge on one and the same textual figure, then that figure em-
bodies the dominant voice of a passage, be it prose narrative or
poetic.

It seems worth noting yet again that the discursive "voices" discussed are textualized as well as fictionalized. Consequently, their
affinity with extra-literary discourses (the "real" world) is far from
simple, although both worlds reflect and reinforce each other. To
use Ong's phrases, writing is representational and referential and
context-bound to the non-literal world; however, it should be borne
in mind that the relationship between the two spheres is not a one-to-
one relationship (Ong, 166-7). Textualized voices are echoes only,
disembodied and removed from their extra-verbal situation.
Nevertheless, and paradoxically so, they remain grounded in "the
world".

Women's voices are further divorced from their presumed literary and non-literary origins by their having been contextualized into
male discourse. Thus we have come to realize by degrees that, while
interpreting women's textual discourse, it is hardly appropriate to
regard a voice as a woman's (or, for that matter, a man's) property:
the referential link between textual voice and the world outside is too
tenuous. Here we finally had to change our *terminology* so that it
would correspond to our changed perspective. Since the notion of
"textual voice" is an abstracted construct, we settled for a terminological abstraction. We came to symbolize traces of textualized
women's traditions as F (feminine/female) voices. By analogy,

men's texts were then perceived and symbolized as repositories of
M (masculine/male) voices. The work of Van Dijk-Hemmes documents the gradual process whereby the emphasis of inquiry shifts,
by stages, from notions of textual authorship toward the recognition
of F voices, a recognition which emerges at the end of her quest for
what, initially, had been styled "women's texts".

Reading and Women's Texts

A fundamental difficulty for gendering texts by the predominant
voices which operate in them is, how to separate F texts from M texts
(which are considered the literary "norm" unless proven otherwise). Elaine Showalter's (1986) "cultural model" is primarily concerned with the criticism of modern F literature. Van Dijk-Hemmes
has adopted this model for the purpose of uncovering women's texts
in the Hebrew Bible. This choice was motivated by two chief factors:

(a) The cultural model is inclusive; and it incorporates history
without allotting exclusive weight either to F experience or to (M)
chronological and spatial history.

(b) Its notions of women's "muted voice" and "double voice"
are useful parameters for gendering F texts.

To use Exum's phrases (1989), van Dijk-Hemmes searches for the
"submerged strains" of women's voices from underneath the male
"dominant world-view that also controls literary production"; and
"hopes to show how the female perspective, the female voice, cannot
be silenced...".

Fiction is in the eye of the beholder. Showalter (1986), Schweickart (1986), and Culler (1983) show that connecting with a text always entails either a covert or else an outspoken gender-motivated
stance. Now is the time to return to one of our initial questions,
namely, Whose readerly interests might the gendering of biblical
texts serve?

At this point we stop once more and draw together some of the
concepts that have informed our investigation—orality, voice rather
than author, group experience and group literary activity, the cultural model, diversity, the muting of F voices, the wish to distinguish between F and M voices, and the gendered nature of reading.
We can now reformulate in yet another way. Gendering texts depends to a large extent on the reader's membership of a gender.

Consequently, we allow that many biblical texts are potentially dual-gendered. F readers will listen to F voices emanating from those texts; M readers will hear themselves echoed in them. This is to say that, in many cases, two parallel readings are possible. In such cases, we feel, a presentation of both parallel readings is preferable to privileging any one of the two more than the other. In the case of other texts, however, the situation is more definitive genderwise this way or the other (although, even then, a dual sense of hearing can become a readerly advantage).

Now that the journey we took has been delineated, it seems appropriate to describe briefly what our agenda consists of.

Women's Texts and F Voices

In Part I van Dijk-Hemmes discusses women's texts classified according to literary genres. By the end of the discussion she has amassed and listed a classified *corpus* of F constituency, a literary body of F soundings or voices, in biblical "women's" texts. She thus continues Goitein's work on *Women as Creators of Biblical Genres* (1957 in Hebrew, translated 1988), which she uses as prooftext but modifies and enhances.

Although Van Dijk-Hemmes shares with Goitein basic concepts (such as the orality of so-called women's texts), her agenda and approach also differ from his. Some of these differences will be mentioned here by way of a prelude; others will become apparent upon reading her critique.

As indicated by the title of Goitein's work (and the rest of his book), when he relates women's voices within biblical texts to extra-literary "reality" he in fact discusses the notion of women's *authorship*. While he does not always state the authorship of particular texts, he certainly implies more than just "genre creativity" or "genre" authorship. His position is far from clear on yet another count for—and despite his occasional declarations to the contrary—he relies too heavily on the Bible's ascriptions of discourse to women. Although he does not claim that such ascriptions automatically guarantee women's authorship, he remains largely imprisoned by that notion. In contrast to Goitein, van Dijk-Hemmes regards such biblical ascriptions primarily as eye-catchers. The fact that an author/editor attributes a textual voice to a woman is helpful: it signifies that the voice might be read as such. However, it does not automatically mean that the voice in the text is an F voice unless and until it is more closely delineated by the parameters outlined above. Explicit biblical attributions of texts to women are used by her merely as an opening, as a possibility for counter-reading. The matter might be summarized as follows. Goitein looks for women creators and performers; he is not free from the authority traditionally invested in authorship and the naming of authors, and relates the findings of his literary investigations more or less directly to the world outside the biblical text. Van Dijk-Hemmes conducts a readerly search for F voices embedded in the text, and is more cautious in relating those to extraneous factors. As Ong states, "Writing. . . has been called 'autonomous discourse' by contrast with oral utterance, which is never autonomous but always embedded in non-verbal existence" (p. 160). When tracing text-bound orality, one must remember that the nature of the orality-literacy shift is much more complex than Goitein has it—not least because the extra-verbal context he visualizes does not account seriously for the transmutation of gender perspectives which, in the case of biblical texts, accompanies the orality-literacy shift.

Women's Discourse Embedded in Men's Discourse? An extended example

One of the genres which Goitein attributes to biblical women is the "rebuke song". According to him, and the analogies from Arabic poetry he cites, the genre conventionalizes a female rebuker (wife or mother) and the admonitions she metes out to her menfolk. In Part I van Dijk-Hemmes discusses Goitein's description of this genre in order to modify and qualify it. One of the points she deals with is the figure of the admonishing woman in Proverbs. In her discussion she raises the possibility that the fictive figure-at-the-window in Proverbs 7, universally interpreted as a representation of a male teacher posing as a father, can be read as the figure of the admonishing mother (I, 4.B). In Part II Brenner takes up this point and extends it to the first collection of Proverbs, Chapters 1-9, and to the Book of Proverbs as an editorial whole.

There has always been general consent in regard to this text. It is interpreted as an M discourse which is simultaneously attracted and repelled by women and their discourse. While it is obvious that F discourse is embedded in it, this discourse has always been judged as reflected discourse—not a reproduction of genuine F voices but a fitered image, mirrored through the literary convention of an M voice and delivered through the filters of M perspectives and perception of woman. Even feminist critics have agreed that F voices are here reproduced in a tendentious M manner (Newsom 1989) or, at the very least, within the textual envelope of M discourse (Camp 1985).

Brenner's reading reverses the tables. She asks, Can we read Proverbs 1-9 as a text in which a mother's voice, rather than a father's, occupies the central and privileged position of the speaking subject? Such a possibility seems worth exploring since (as Camp acutely observes) Proverbs is doubly framed at both ends by literary F figures—personified Wisdom together with her antitheses, the "strange" woman, and personified Folly, in the first collection; Lemuel's mother's instructions and the Worthy Woman (ʾešet ḥayil poem at the end of the Book (chapter 31). Brenner shows that the recognition, through F reading, of an F voice in these passages is helpful for dealing with their problematics, one of which is the superabundance of F discourse within an assumed M discourse. A byproduct of this gendered reading is the nuancing of the "female rebuker" genre and its qualification as "mother's instruction to son *and* to daughter", whereas Goitein's definition relates to menfolk only as the rebuke's textual target audience.

Desire and M Discourse

In Part I van Dijk-Hemmes discusses women's love poetry, as it is preserved in the Song of Songs, and the distinctive properties of the female voice which operate within those texts. In Part III Brenner illuminates the picture further by discussing biblical M love lyrics.

Brenner proceeds from an interpretation of Qoheleth 3.2-8 as a framed love poem. This passage has not been thematized by readers as such. Although the possibility that it indeed refers to love and sex (among other things) has been recognized from antiquity, the textual frame in which it is embedded (Qoh 3.1, 9) has influenced readers that its theme is human time. The poem does not overtly classify itself by genre, and the gender (M) attributed to its speaking voice is only implicitly inferred from the frame but not explicitly stated within it. Therefore, it is particularly interesting for our project. After the notion of the textual frame has been accepted, the poem itself can be dissociated from the textual assumptions implied by the frame,

and read afresh in order to find whose voice reverberates in it. It is
first classified by genre (poem of love/desire) and, then, gendered by
reference to its voice (M) and collated with other biblical instances
of men's voicings of love and desire.

Considered side by side, the corresponding F and M voices within
the same thematic field of love poetry (van Dijk-Hemmes on the
Song of Songs, Brenner on Qoheleth 3 and its textual relatives) form
a contrast which illuminates each text, and the gender positions textualized in them, by their mutual oppositions.

M Voices and Biblical Pornography

The definition of certain biblical texts, especially prophetic ones, as
verbal or literary pornography is not entirely new. Setel (1985) discusses it at length. Carroll (1986) applies it to passages in the Book
of Jeremiah. Van Dijk-Hemmes has written on pornography in
Hosea (1989b).

Like violence, pornography and its literal and visual (re)presenta-
tions is a key issue for feminists. Pornography attracts, for its subject
matter is human desire. It simultaneously fascinates and repels, for
it contains strong and often corrupting sadomasochistic elements. It
frightens, since its fantasy is the fantasy of power relations and, like
rape, it both expresses and reinforces gender roles and role models
in human society. In short: Like rape and violence, pornography relates to the deepest recesses of our psyches, hence it does not leave
us indifferent.

Biblical pornography has been utilized as an extremely effective
vehicle for the fossilization of gender roles because it carries a unique
authority even when not acknowledged as such. We therefore decid-
ed to include two pieces on biblical pornography in this book: Van
Dijk-Hemmes analyzes its form and function in Ezekiel 23 and
Brenner discusses its presence in Jeremiah 2-5.

The pornographic passages discussed clearly characterize themselves as soundings of M voices. Not simply because they are assigned to male speakers, even specifically to the supreme authority
of a male God; but, mainly, because they contain such fantasies
about and against women that—as corroborated by psychological
and psychiatric research—they must be classified as products of M
discourse. Nowhere in the Hebrew Bible is there a corresponding
pornographic vision assigned to an F voice.

We do not wish to claim that our work is exhaustive or comprehensive. More items can undoubtedly be added to the corpus of biblical women's voices here collected; many more texts can be gendered as F- or else M-voiced; more can and should be said about the methodology and advantages of gendering F and M texts and voices. Our aim has been to make a contribution to the ongoing quest for readerly alternatives, feminist style. We have constructed another model of reading which, we hope, will be taken up and expanded by others, so that our gender-motivated readings of the texts gendered will be regarded as openings. We also hope that our gender-motivated readings of the texts gendered will stimulate others to use the model here offered and to improve it; and that debates concerning gender, voices, and authority in biblical literature and biblical scholarship will eventually gain ascendancy over the more traditional debates concerning authors.

In our view, gendering texts is an invaluable step toward a reconstruction of ancient Israel's culture. Israelite culture, as it is reflected in the Hebrew Bible, is distorted by gender bias and M literary supremacy. It is so badly mutilated and falsified that, one fears, the cultural actualities of the quasi-historical construct fondly called "Biblical Israel" are, for us, beyond remembrance or recollection. One of the ways for dealing with this frustration is to dig for remnants in order to recall: the literary quest has obvious implications for history. By redefining biblical women's (and men's) voices we redefine not only individual texts, not only "women's culture". By so doing we redefine a human culture as a whole, for human societies are bi-gendered. The fact that our task is neither simple nor easily rewarding does not exempt us from dealing with it.

Athalya Brenner

PART I
TRACES OF WOMEN'S TEXTS IN THE HEBREW BIBLE

FOKKELIEN VAN DIJK – HEMMES

TRACES OF WOMEN'S TEXTS IN THE HEBREW BIBLE[1]

1. METHODOLOGICAL CONSIDERATIONS

Introduction

"The Old Testament is a collection of writings by males from a society dominated by males" (Bird 1974, 41). Phyllis Bird's much quoted statement has recently been subjected to further inquiry by Carol Meyers. In the methodological deliberations preceding her reconstruction of the daily life of women in ancient Israel, Meyers calls the Hebrew Bible the product of a "literate elite" emanating from "the male leadership circles of Jerusalem" (Meyers 1988, 11-12). With a view to its producers, the Hebrew Bible should thus be described as an "elitist, urban, male-oriented document" (Meyers 1987, 219). Clearly, such a document can be used as a historical source for the reconstruction of life of "the people from the land" with the greatest possible caution only. Caution should be exercised especially when an attempt at the reconstruction of women's daily life is concerned, as has been undertaken by Meyers. Because of her thorough methodical and interdisciplinary approach, Meyers manages to sketch a plausible image of the life, work and gender relations of the majority of "ancient Israel"—the women and men who inhabited the villages and hamlets of the highlands. Her study makes a new contribution to research into women's studies in the Hebrew Bible and the historical and sociological background thereof. This is a necessary supplement to earlier studies on the social (Brenner 1985), religious (Bird 1987, Winter 1987) and historical (Hacket 1985) rôles of women in ancient Israel, and to the exegetic research that is being carried out within the framework of women's studies. It is the latter investigation—exegesis in the sense of

---

[1] Earlier versions of this essay were published in Dutch (Van Dijk-Hemmes 1991 and 1992). They were written under the guidance of Prof. Dr. M. Bal and Prof. Dr. A. van der Kooij. In addition, I would also like to thank my colleagues, Drs. J. Bekkenkamp and Prof. Dr. A. Brenner, and my husband, Prof. Dr. H. van Dijk, for their support and valuable advice.

feminist or gender-nuanced reinterpretation of the Hebrew Bible—
that is emphasized in recent scholarship (Bal and others 1984; Bal
1987, 1988a, 1988b; Collins 1985; Russell 1985; Trible 1978, 1984;
Wacker 1987; and many others).
The question as to whether and to what extent traces of women's
texts are to be found in the Hebrew Bible, receives relatively little
attention in the critiques mentioned; precisely because of this relative neglect, that is the subject of my study. In view of the pregnant
manner in which the situation has been described in the quotes from
Bird and Meyers (above), it is hardly surprising that the problem of
traces of women's texts has scarcely been broached until quite recently. Indeed, at the outset the chance of positive findings seems
minimal. Why, then, should any attempt be made in that direction?
I think that two preliminary arguments for so doing can be considered at this stage.
1) Bird's and Meyers's remarks concerning the gender of the
Hebrew Bible authors do reflect a view generally held among Old
Testament scholars, and they make this explicit. At the same time
however, the fact that "those responsible for the actual editing of the
text did their best to obscure their identity" (Bruns 1984, 66), leaves
at least some room for the hypothesis that women could also be
found among the authors of the Bible.
This hypothesis would naturally gain in persuasion if we had any
details regarding the writing ability of women in ancient Israel. The
Bible mentions a woman's writing only twice: in 1 Kings 21.8,
where we read that Queen Jezebel writes letters in the name of
Ahab; and in Esther 9.29, where Esther writes a letter together with
Mordecai about the institution of the Purim festival. From this we
may probably deduce that, at the very least, women from higher circles were able to write and that they also made use of this ability in
practice. André Lemaire (1981, 58-59) thinks it probable that girls
from higher circles enjoyed a specific form of education. Meyers,
following Crenshaw (1985), comes to a much more radical conclusion. According to her, it was usual in many strata of Israelite society to teach both boys and girls to read and write, and it was part of
the educational task of *both* parents to ensure that the children possessed these abilities (Meyers 1988, 152-164). But even if this very
optimistic view were correct,[2] this still does not imply that women

---

[2] For another view concerning the diffusion of literacy in ancient Israel, see e.g.

were admitted into the circles in which various historical and religious traditions were committed to writing. According to Meyers and in view of her characterization of the Bible as a ''male-oriented document'' that was not, or hardly was, the case. Nowhere in the Bible is there mention of female professional writers (scribes). Women were by definition excluded from the communities of those who were predominantly responsible for the most important written traditions—the priests. Such an absolute exclusion may not have applied to other circles which were responsible for other written tradition. The action of the prophetess Huldah (2 Kgs 22.14-20) and the passage mentioned above concerning Queen Esther are pointers in that direction: Both women are represented as ''authenticators of written tradition'' (Camp 1985, 140-147). It was thus in any case *imaginable* that women made a contribution to written traditions.[3] This could indicate a practice occurring more often in prophetic and royal circles.[4]

2) My second argument arises from the fact that most of the biblical writings are products of a tradition that has, more or less, undergone a lengthy period of written transmission, but originated in an oral process. That women, in any case, must have made their contribution to the latter can be deduced from the biblical references to the songs sung by women. It is therefore obvious that a start should be made with these songs when searching for traces of women's texts in the Hebrew Bible. The question which immediately arises, however, is whether those songs attributed to women are indeed more or less literal ''quotations'' from the oral traditions of women; or else, are they actually texts composed by male authors and given

---

Smelik 1984. The importance of literacy for the establishment of (central) power is analyzed by T. Lemaire (1984).

[3] With Bal (1988b, 32-39), I am of the opinion that a text, and thus also a biblical text, is not so much to be seen as a ''transparent, immaterial medium, a window through which we can get a glimpse of reality'', but is rather a ''figuration of the reality that brought it forth and to which it responded''. With regard to the Bible this means, for example, that the grammatical or semantic phenomena which mark female personas as subjects and/or objects indicate which social possibilities were imaginable and (un)desirable for women. That is to say, imaginable and (un)desirable for the authors of the Bible.

[4] See also the spectacular hypothesis of Harold Bloom, according to whom the J layer of the Pentateuch must have been written by a woman, and a woman from David's court at that, at the time of King Rehobeam (922-915 BCE). Gabriel Josipovici's review in *TLS*, April 19 1991, pp. 3-5 convincingly shows, however, that Bloom's hypothesis is built on sand.

to the women-in-the-text to sing? In other words, we can conclude from biblical records that women have made a contribution to the oral "literature" of ancient Israel. The question, to what extent the Bible actually supplies a reliable picture on this point, remains open.

The possibility that a number of the songs reported in the Bible as being sung by women were in fact composed by women is specifically referred to in recent scholarship, and especially in Hebrew Bible feminist criticism. But very often the questioning is limited to the establishment of this possibility, whereas research into specific characteristics of these texts is lacking, as is research into the vision expressed therein.[5] And yet as early as 1957, in a critical assessment written by S.D. Goitein (in Hebrew), a very promising initiative was instituted for the undertaking of such literary investigation. In 1988 an English translation of this article appeared under the title "Women as Creators of Biblical Genres" (Goitein 1988). In my description of the search for traces of women's texts in the Hebrew Bible and for their specific characteristics, I shall be using this study by Goitein as a guideline.

I hope to have indicated by now why a search for texts by female authors in the Hebrew Bible—and by "authors" in this case I mean the creators of a particular written or oral tradition—is not a venture doomed to failure from the start. Nothing has yet been said, however, about the use and importance of such a quest. At the same time some questions arise concerning the methodological implications of such an undertaking. These questions will be dealt with next.

A. The Importance of the Search for Female Authors

What if it were indeed found practicable to highlight the possibility that a number of Old Testament texts were composed, spoken or perhaps even written by women? The New Testament scholar Elisabeth Schüssler Fiorenza summarizes her reservations in regard to the relevance of posing such hypotheses about New Testament texts thus,

---

[5] In 1986 I made a first attempt, together with J. Bekkenkamp, at this line of investigation within the framework of a symposium organised by the Department of Women's Studies, The National University of Utrecht on "Language, Culture and Female Future"; see Bekkenkamp and Van Dijk 1987.

In short, it seems helpful to conjecture female authorship for early Christian canonical writings in order to challenge the androcentric dogmatism that ascribes apostolic authorship only to men. However, the conjecture of female authorship does not in and by itself suggest a feminist perspective of the author. All early Christian writings, whether written by women or men, more or less share the androcentric mind-set and must be analyzed and tested critically as to how much they do so (Schüssler Fiorenza 1983, 61).

The reason Schüssler Fiorenza gives for her reservation deserves further investigation. She does not consider the sex of an author to be determinate for the *content*, or rather the *ideo-content* (Bal 1988b) of the text written by him or her. The writings of women, be they women of ancient times or contemporary women, are not necessarily written from a "woman-identified" point of view since women, like men, are socialized "into the same androcentric mind-set and culture".

> Only if one would claim a clearly definable innate feminine quality of cognition could one establish 'feminine' as essentially different from 'masculine' authorship. Yet such an attempt would only perpetuate the prejudices and sexual asymmetry created by the androcentric cultural mind-set (Schüssler Fiorenza 1983, 61).

From her conviction that the difference in sex is more often a sociologically than a biologically determined phenomenon,[6] Schüssler Fiorenza regards the search for specific characteristics in texts assumed to be written by women as an undesirable and even dangerous occupation. Prejudice with regard to a "feminine essence" innate in women could be confirmed and even exacerbated by such a search, with all the undesirable consequences this would entail.

Are Schüssler Fiorenza's considerations valid? Her proposition that texts written by women do not necessarily differ from, or state other values than, the work of male authors is doubtless correct. But is it not probable, in view of the *sociological* differences between women and men, that female authors are activated more often and to a greater extent in distancing themselves from delivering criticism on androcentric presuppositions, than are their male colleagues? That, thanks to the feminist movement, this is unmistakably the

---

[6] "Not 'biological' sex differences, but patriarchal household and marriage relationships generate the social-political inferiority and oppression of women" (Schüssler Fiorenza 1983, 86 *et passim*).

case in this day and age does not, of course, mean that the same naturally applies to women of antiquity. But if it were true, as Schüssler Fiorenza states, that the early Christian movement held attraction mainly for those on the fringe—women and slaves—through its practice of the "Discipleship of Equals" (Schüssler Fiorenza 1983, 140-151), then would not criticism of the patriarchal structures be likely to resound in their writings? In my opinion Schüssler Fiorenza, because of her resistance to a psychological explanation of sex differentials based solely on anatomy, foregoes the job of searching for women's texts somewhat too easily. Her reserved response to those who use the less androcentric character of some early Christian writings as an argument for female authorship of these writings is therefore not entirely convincing. Moreover, in her critical discussion she neglects the other argument mentioned by these scholars, namely that the "less androcentric" writings contain more information about women than do other comparable texts. Later in her book she nevertheless lets it surface that she does consider the latter argument valid for the possibility of recognizing female authorship.

In her discussion of the apocryphal writing *The Acts of Paul and Thecla*, Schüssler Fiorenza suggests the possibility that the story, with its striking portrait of a female missionary who received from Paul the command to teach "the word of God", may originally have sprung from a community of women. She writes that in its present form, in view of the clear traces of editorial treatment, it is probably the product of -

> male ecclesiastical writers who could tolerate women as ascetics persevering in contemplation and prayer but not as itinerant missionaries preaching the Gospel (Schüssler Fiorenza 1983, 175).

According to her this can be seen, for instance, by the way the author of *Acts* treats Priscilla. From the fact that she is here reduced to the "lady of the house of Aquila", Schüssler Fiorenza draws the following conclusion,

> It is not very likely that a woman author would have developed so little interest in the great missionary of Paul's time (Schüssler Fiorenza 1983, 175).

In her discussion of the question of the author of *Acts*, Schüssler Fiorenza uses exactly the same arguments which she criticised or ignored earlier. On the one hand she does interpret the explicit androcentric character of the editorial treatment to which, in her opinion, *Acts* has been subjected as an indication of the final author(s)' gender. On the other hand she shares the view, upon further consideration, that female authors' work contains more information about women than texts which have been written by men. She thus lets it be known implicitly, and in spite of the theoretical objections she has expressed earlier, that there can definitely be talk of a difference in content between the texts of female and male authors; and that these differences cannot be accounted for so much by an assumed ''feminine essence'' as by the specific social and religious interests of women.

For Bernadette Brooten the importance of the search for texts written by women is evident. She too is involved in reconstructing the history of women in early Christendom. Like Schüssler Fiorenza, Brooten resists the tendency—predominant in studies of women in the early Christian era—to focus on what men thought about women at that time instead of focusing on the women themselves.

> If we want to reconstruct the history of early Christian women, a shift of emphasis is therefore required. We will need to place women in the center of the frame. Placing women in the center means that the categories developed to understand the history of man may no longer be adequate, that the traditional historical periods and canons of literature may not be the proper framework, and that we will need to ask new types of questions and consider hitherto overlooked sources (Brooten 1985, 65).

Brooten sketches the picture conjectured by current writing on women's history in an illuminating manner. Women are deposited in the dynamic and active landscape of a male world as if they were static figurines made of clay; thus the rôle and position of ''women'' is studied.

> This clay-figurine method of the study of women is really based on the view that women are not active participants in history at all, but rather passive recipients of a role or roles given to them by men and a status allowed to them by men. Placing women in the center means that the clay figurines come alive. They begin to talk to each other, telling their experiences, their beliefs, their hopes, their theories and their opinions (Brooten 1985, 83).

The bringing to life of these static female figurines, especially when antiquity is studied, can naturally be realised only in a very limited manner. Lack of sources is a frustrating characteristic of women's history.[7]

> That we have been hindered from writing or forced to write anonymously or under a man's name, that male historians have considered women's lives unworthy of description, and that which women have written has usually been ignored by scholars or is no longer extant makes the writing on women's history qualitatively different from the writing of men's history (Brooten 1985, 66).

But if it is our aim to reconstruct the history of women and thus to discover what women themselves thought and did, then, according to Brooten, we must give the highest priority to the writings of women and to the texts which enjoyed popularity among women. And as an example of the latter she too mentions *The Acts of Paul and Thecla*.

This discussion of the views of Schüssler Fiorenza and Brooten raises a number of points which underline the importance of the search for female authors:

a) It can supply correctives to the self-evident view, made explicit by feminist scholars, that the Bible is exclusively the work of male authors.

b) In texts composed by female authors we are confronted by the views of women instead of the views of men on, among other things, women.

c) The information these texts contain about women is probably more extensive and possibly also more adequate than the information contained in men's texts.

d) The ideocontent of women's texts is unproblematically, conceivably less androcentric than that of the writings of male authors.

The points listed as c. and d. are assumptions about the *content* of texts which were probably engendered by women. They have been formulated in reply to the objections expressed by Schüssler Fiorenza concerning further study into women's texts, in the attempt to uncover specific characteristics of content. It has been mentioned above that, according to her, such a project would inevitably contribute to the view that women are *essentially* different from men. In my opinion any contents differences between texts of male and female authors need not necessarily be attributed to a specifically

---

[7] The same applies, of course, to the history of the "ordinary man".

female, or male, "nature". It is quite possible to explain these differences by the divergent *social* positions assigned to each gender and the particular gender interests this social distinction generates. In order to be able to include the social factors in the investigation into women's texts responsibly *and* to be able to analyze the views expressed in these texts as carefully as possible, an adequate interpretive frame of reference is required. Obviously, advice for such a project should be sought in feminist literary criticism, where a tradition of revaluation of women's literature has meanwhile been established.

B. *The Model of "Women's Culture"*

In an influential article, the literary scholar Elaine Showalter (1986) distinguishes between two types of feminist literary criticism. The first type, which she refers to as "revisionist", is engaged in reinterpretation of works from the literary canon and testifies to an "obsession with correcting, modifying, supplementing, revising, humanizing or even attacking male critical theory" (Showalter 1986, 246-47). By "male critical theory" she means,

> a notion of creativity, history of literature or interpretation of literature that is entirely based on the world of experience of men, but is presented as universally valid (Showalter 1986, 247).

The importance of this type of feminist literary criticism—and contemporary feminist exegesis is in many cases a variant of it!—is, according to Showalter, limited and does not lead to real theoretical renewal. The second type, which has literature written by women and women as writers as its subjects, does offer a possibility of renewal. Showalter introduces the term "gynocritics" for this form of feminist literary criticism which focuses on women as authors of textual import and on "history, themes, genres and structures of literature by women" (Showalter 1986, 248). Gynocritics is mainly concerned with the differences which determine the gender membership of women's literary work. Showalter discusses four models which are used for defining these differences: a biological model, a linguistic model, a psychoanalytical model and a cultural model. She considers the cultural model the most useful, since it incorporates the other models and the explanations they provide for gender differences, thus backing the cultural model up with the necessary contexts. The cultural model offers the possibility of interpreting ideas about women's body, language and psyche against the backdrop of the social context in which they develop:

> The opinions that women have about their own bodies and their sexual and reproductive functions are narrowly interwoven with the cultural sphere in which they find themselves. The psyche of woman can be analyzed as the product of cultural forces. Language is allocated a place in this too, if we look at the social dimensions and the determinants for the use of language, the forming of language behaviour by cultural ideas (Showalter 1986, 259).

Moreover, an important advantage of the cultural model is that the factors decisive for the differences between women—such as social class, race, nationality and history—are included within it.

The cultural model described by Showalter is based on the hypothesis of a women's culture. In recent years various forms of this hypothesis have been suggested by anthropologists, sociologists and socio-historians in order, in separation from prevailing androcentric theories and frameworks of interpretation, to be able to get into contact with the "primary cultural experience of women as expressed by themselves" (Showalter 1986, 260). With the aid of the "women's culture" concept a distinction can be made between the roles, activities, preferences and rules of behaviour *prescribed* for women and "those activities, patterns of behaviour and functions which arise from the life of women themselves" (Showalter 1986, 260). The most fruitful and enlightening elaboration of the idea of "women's culture" is, according to Showalter, that of the anthropologists Shirley and Edwin Ardener. They maintain (Ardener 1978) that women form "a *muted group*, the boundaries of whose culture and reality overlap, but are not wholly contained by, the *dominant (male) group*" (quoted in Showalter 1986, 261). Heleen Sancisi, who uses the Ardener theory in an article about the position of women in ancient Greece, gives the following instructive description of the "mutedness" concept:

> 'Muted'—gagged is perhaps the best interpretation—refers to those groups of whom the voice is not heard or may not be heard at the authoritative 'speech-making' level of society. The term is applicable to the position of women in many societies, but also to that of other minority groups whose activities do not take place at the dominant level, or whose presence there is not appreciated or even desired. *'Mutedness' certainly does not mean that the relevant group does not speak or is*

not heard, It means to a much greater extent that what they say is not heard or does not register; exclusion from dominant verbal communication (Sancisi 1986, 18; my italics, FvD).

Shown schematically, the relation between the dominant and the "muted" group is as follows:

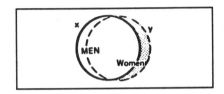

The figure illustrates how the culture of the "muted" group, in this case women, is made visible once more and should not be seen, or is seen to a more or less limited extent, as a separate world, cut off from the dominant culture. Rather, the "muted" culture forms the invisible background for the dominant culture. Within this subterranean women's culture, women (re)define "reality" from their own perspective. However, since they are also part of the dominant culture that marginalizes them, the language they speak is often "double-voiced, containing a dominant and a muted story" (Showalter 1986, 266). Literature written by women is also characterised by muteness and double voice. Hence, one implication of the cultural model for the interpretation of women's literary work is that it can help us to uncover the "muted story" alongside the "dominant" one.

With the aid of the cultural model championed by Showalter, I can now describe the search for traces of women's texts in the Hebrew Bible as follows. It is a search for the written remains of the traditions of "women's culture" in ancient Israel, with a view to a description of its identifiable characteristics. The "double voice" concept can be employed as a defining characteristic and, therefore, also as a key to the interpretation of the women's texts that are thus defined. Bal's focalization theory (1985), with the aid of which it is possible to check from which and from whose viewpont texts are presented, is a useful aid for my agenda.

One important advantage of using the cultural model is that it sheds fresh light on problems raised by Schüssler Fiorenza's work. The biological difference is not ignored in this model, but is placed in a broader context. Moreover, the concept of "women's culture"

can substantiate the notion that women's texts give more information about women and are less androcentric than comparable men's
texts. On the other hand, the model can also be utilized for clarifying
why these features do not always or automatically appear in
women's texts.

The way in which Showalter uses and applies the Ardener example of the overlapping dominant and "muted" cultures, deserves
further explanation on two counts. In the first place, it is important
to realise that neither the dominant nor the "muted" culture is a
homogeneous whole. The latter in particular usually consists of a
multitude of cultures which often relate to each other in a hierarchical manner, in addition to their collective affinity with the
dominant culture. Showalter mentions, in this connection, the position of black female authors in the United States. They not only belong to their women's culture, but also to the similarly "muted"
black culture (see also Meijer 1988, 316-344). As far as ancient
Israel is concerned the same consideration applies, for instance, to
female slaves. They are allotted a specific social status within their
women's culture because, in addition to being women, they are also
part of the "muted" slave group.

The fact that the dominant culture is not a constant, homogeneous whole either, is not further elaborated by Showalter. On this
point too some extra detailing is required. Shifts within the
dominant culture carry repercussions for the "muted" culture(s).
In other words, the relationship between the dominant and the
"muted" culture(s) is not static. A striking illustration of this point
is given by Ria Lemaire in her article, "Rethinking Literary History" (1987a). Building further on the work of Ong (1982) she
shows how, during the Middle Ages in Europe, the transition from
oral traditions to written culture led to an increased marginalization
of the cultural traditions of women.

> For men's culture a process of continuous growth, reinforcement and
> monopolization of written culture began. This movement is counter-
> balanced by the exclusion of women from written culture and by the
> progressive marginalization, deformation and obliteration of wom-
> en's oral traditions (R. Lemaire 1987a, 190).

It seems probable that a comparable process occurred in ancient
Israel. Religious traditions which originated with the male leadership elite of Jerusalem were written down and subsequently
canonized. This process was responsible for traces of the feminine

traditions and for their being largely erased en route. How can we uncover what is still left of these traditions, and which patterns can be seen if we decide to follow possible indications of it? As stated in the Introduction, I use Goitein's article, "Women as Creators of Biblical Genres", as a guideline in this quest. A discussion of the manner in which he sets to work is therefore in order at this point.

C. Goitein's Method

The study Goitein made of Yemenite immigrants who came to Israel through the "Magic Carpet" operation in 1949-50 inspired his biblical studies. These Yemenite Jews came mostly from small, uncharted villages and hamlets, where they had lived until then in accordance with centuries-old patterns. Songs and poetry played a large part in their life. Goitein points out that there obtained considerable differences between the poetic traditions of men and women:

> The men's songs are religious, though motifs from daily life do appear in them. The women's are secular, even though one genre does begin with the praise of God, and it is not unknown for the poetess to address the Creator of the world as in ordinary discourse. Men generally sing in Hebrew; only in a portion of their songs are Hebrew and Arabic rhymes intermingled, and very few are completely in Arabic. Women's poetry is always in colloquial Yemenite, and only rarely does some nugget of Hebrew appear. When men's poetry does employ Arabic, it is close to the literary language, though sometimes with a local flavor; but women's poetry is in the popular tongue (though by the nature of the poetry, the women, too, borrow here and there a passage from some literary source). Men do their singing from printed or handwritten books, or directly from an author's manuscript; women's poetry is entirely oral. Furthermore, the compositions a man sings are generally of famous bards who lived centuries ago; but a woman sings songs of recent vintage, most of them created at the moment they are uttered. That is, she combines familiar rhymes that come to her mind with ones she creates on the spot (Goitein 1988, 1).

The state of affairs Goitein describes is strikingly similar to that described by R. Lemaire concerning various oral traditions in Europe of the Middle Ages. Before written culture acquired supremacy there was also a male, in that case mainly epic, oral tradition and a female, mainly lyrical tradition. The two traditions coexisted and were more or less of equal value (R. Lemaire 1986, 1987a and 1987b). The difference in literary genres corresponded to gender-related division of labour (see also Bücher 1896 and Katona

1979). The different poetical traditions among Yemenite Jews were also rooted in the gender-related division of labour in effect there, and in the different cultural worlds men and women inhabited. That division meant that,

> (...) the world of the man, who had the developed culture of the religion of the book, and the world of the woman, who, despite her identification with the beliefs and opinions of the male, nonetheless nourished her spiritual life in great measure from the ancient culture of the village tribe's culture around her (Goitein 1988, 2-3).[8]

Goitein warns against linking the world of the Jewish community in Yemen too closely to the world of biblical Israel. In the latter the division between male and female worlds was much less definite. If we translate this observation which, as far as ancient Israel is concerned, matches the findings of Meyers (1988), into the terms of the cultural model, then we are able to describe the difference between the Jewish community in Yemen and the society in ancient Israel as a difference in the measure in which the male and female cultures overlapped.

The next characteristic of the poetic tradition of Jewish women from Yemen is considered by Goitein to be especially relevant to his biblical studies. This poetic tradition belonged specifically to the professional poetess, that is, one or at the very most two women per village or district, some of whom also achieved fame outside their own region. The songs and poems composed by these women were indeed limited to a number of specific subjects, but differed in regard to form and content. Recitation, accompanied by the beating of a drum, took place on special occasions. An important function of female poetry was to express public opinion by pronouncing comment on political occurrences. The verses composed within this framework often had satirical or at least humorous undertones.

Goitein states that the professional poetess phenomenon has parallels in many other ancient cultures. He refers to pre-Islamic Arab women's poetry. There too women specialised in particular genres, for instance lamentations and songs of mockery. It was the latter genre in particular which was "a weapon which the ancient

---

[8] This quoted passage indicates that the division between the men's world and women's world was not as decisive as he wishes us to believe. The women's identification with men's views here noted is a striking illustration of Ardener's cultural model (as adopted by Showalter).

Arabs feared more than the edge of the sword'' (Goitein 1988, 3). Another widespread subject of ancient female Arab poetry is the preaching of virtue to a man by his wife, and especially by his mother. An undertone of rancour toward a daughter-in-law is often found in the latter songs. Women's poetry sometimes also acquires the form of prophecy. A surprising characteristic of ancient Arabic poetry is that romantic love songs were composed exclusively by males. ''Woman was the object, not the author of love poetry'' (Goitein 1988, 3).

After pointing out that there are people among whom the profession of poetry is given over entirely into the hands of women,[9] Goitein delineates his methodolgy for finding women's literary traditions. Books which have women as subjects—for instance Esther, Ruth, or Judith—do not come within the framework of his project. As he says, there is no proof that books *about* women were also written *by* women. The opposite seems more obvious, since the praise of women is mostly done by men (see Prov 31.28). Moreover, nothing in the Books mentioned indicates that they were written by a woman.

Goitein's hypothesis necessitates a certain modification to be made to one of the hypotheses formulated in 1.A. above, namely that texts by female authors supply more information about women than male texts do. It now seems that texts about women do not necessarily contain more information about the life women actually led. The fact that a woman appears as the main character in a literary work is by itself no decisive argument for female authorship. Heroines like Esther and Judith fit perfectly into a man-made gallery of ideal femininity (Van Dijk-Hemmes 1983 and 1986). The notion that texts *about* women were also written *by* women is valid only if additional and different arguments can be advanced. There should, for example, be traces of a less androcentric intent; and/or of a (re)definition of ''reality'' from a women's point of view; and/or of a striking difference between the views of male and female characters-in-the-text. A couple of interesting examples for the latter can be gleaned from the Book of Ruth. This is why Ruth merits

---

9 ''A famous example of this in our own part of the world is the great nation of the Tuareg, who dwell in the Sahara. The wives of their nobles dedicate a large portion of their time to the study of poetry and its transmission to their daughters. They even write it in a special script, which serves them as a sort of code'' (Goitein 1988, 4).

further consideration along these lines, as indicated by Goitein in a footnote. I shall return to this point at the end of this study.

Goitein's search for traces of women's texts in the Hebrew Bible focuses on literary traditions practised by women. In his opinion the search should begin with the question, In which biblical passages are women explicitly mentioned as being active in a particular field of (oral) literature? Subsequently, one should find out whether remains of the relevant literary genre have been preserved as biblical texts. Such remains were not necessarily written down by women. Often they will have been preserved in the texts of male writers "who wrote about subjects and in a style which were traditional among Hebrew women." In view of this situation Goitein ceases to speak about women as "*authors*", and shifts to discussing them as "creators of biblical literary *genres*".

> It is in the nature of popular oral literature that it does not retain its original nature, but is poured from one vessel to another. Yet the original imprint is not erased. And thus it leaves a recognizable impression in literature which has reached us after many metamorphoses (Goitein 1988, 5).[10]

It seems to me that Goitein's method is a reliable point of departure for searching for traces of women's texts in the Hebrew Bible. In general, therefore, I shall largely follow his suggested lines of argument. I shall also juxtapose his view of the biblical texts he discusses with other interpretations. I shall appeal for support mainly to recently published studies that are written from the perspective of women's studies. Then I shall give my own interpretation of the texts under discussion. My own interpretation relies heavily on the cultural model introduced in the previous section and on Bal's focalization theory.

2. Victory Songs and Mockery Songs

A. *Victory Songs*

According to Goitein the most striking thing in biblical women's participation in public life is their involvement in the changing political situation of their country. The geographic situation of

---

[10] For a perceptive description of the transformations to which oral traditions are subject when they are written down see also Watson 1984, 66-86.

Israel dictated that national security and therefore wars were the most important issues of public life. Women did not, or only by great exception (Judg 4.9 and 9.53), take part in these wars. Their task was to welcome the warriors on their return home and to pay them homage. In their songs they expressed public opinion. The texts Goitein cites in this connection are the following,[11]

And it came to pass as they came
when David returned from slaying the Philistine
that the women came out of all the cities of Israel
singing and dancing to meet Saul the King
with tambourines with shouts of joy[12] and with triple stringed instruments
The dancing women sang to one another in answer and said
    Saul has slain his thousands,
    David his ten thousands (1 Sam 18.6-7).

Then Jephthah came to Mizpah to his house
And behold his daughter came out to meet him
with tambourines and dances (Judg 11.34a).

Then Miriam the Prophetess the sister of Aaron
took a tambourine in her hand
And all the women went out after her
with tambourines dancing
And Miriam answered them singing
    Sing for YHWH for high high is He elevated
    the horse and its charioteer He has thrown into the sea
(Ex 15.20-21).

The song in honour of Saul and David, in view of the anger it aroused in Saul from whom the greatest honour is denied, is connected by Goitein with the Song of Deborah. There too the honour is not given primarily to the military leader but in this instance to Deborah, the "spiritual leader":

Rural life came to a standstill
it came to a standstill
until I/you arose[13] Deborah
until I/you arose a mother in Israel (Judg 5.7).

---

[11] The translations from the Hebrew are mine. I have tried to remain as close as possible to the Hebrew text.

[12] According to Winter (1987, 30) *bśmḥh* in this case indicates "grell trillernden Freudenbezeugungen". See also Herzberg 1956.

[13] With regard to the ambiguity of this form of the verb see Bal 1988a, 112-115; Van Dijk-Hemmes 1989, 191-192.

And when both leaders are mentioned in this song, Deborah has precedence:

Awake awake Deborah
Awake awake utter a song
Arise Barak
and take your captives son of Abinoam (Judg 5.12).

In the Song of Miriam Moses, the leader of the people of Israel, is not even mentioned, and all the honour goes to YHWH. In short, a common characteristic of this genre of women's songs is, according to Goitein, the relativization or even total avoidance of honouring political and military leaders.

The Song in Honour of Saul and David
Goitein's discussion of the victory song genre deserves further consideration on a number of counts. His interpretation of the song in honour of Saul and David is grounded in the song's contextualization by subsequent verses of 1 Samuel 18. Those verses lend the song a scoffing force; such scoffing appears to be characteristic of the political songs sung by women of the Jewish community in Yemen too. With the aid of the cultural model, this phenomenon can be accounted for as follows. When women, who are marginal participants in the dominant culture, are given the opportunity to raise their voices in this dominant culture and to express public opinion, they often make use of this opportunity in order to express their own opinion through the ironic and sometimes subversive thrust of their songs.

It remains to be examined whether this phenomenon applies to the women's song in 1 Samuel 18 also. Does the text have a mocking ring to it? In that case, its structure should be regarded as antithetic parallelism: Saul has slain his thousands, *but* David his ten thousands. But is such an interpretation acceptable? Is it not preferable to view the parallelism here as synonymous or additional parallelism? In the latter case, the conjunction *w* would not have an adversative function but, rather, a subsidiary one: Saul has slain his thousands *and* David his ten thousands; in other words, Saul and David have slain the foe in great numbers together. The latter interpretation is strongly defended by Gevirtz (1963, 15-24). He points out that the word pair ''thousands''//''ten thousands'' is a fixed poetic formula, and that it should not be viewed as antithetical but as synonymous or synthetically parallel.[14] "And is it not furthermore incredible", he notes with regard to 1 Samuel 18.7,

> that the welcoming party of women—singing and dancing, obviously pleased and proud of the accomplishment of their men—should be thought to have seized this opportunity, his return from victory, to insult their king? The song contains no insult. It is a lavish praise of both Saul and David, utilizing the largest (single) equivalent numerals available in Syro-Palestinian poetic diction: the fixed pair "thousands"//"ten-thousands" (Gevirtz 1963, 24).

Let us assume for the time being that Gevirtz's presentation is acceptable. Then, the function attributed to the song in honour of Saul and David in 1 Samuel 18 becomes a striking example of the transformation an orally transmitted women's song can suffer in male written traditions. How does this occur in this case? The narrator places the responsibility for the antithetical reading of the song on Saul:

> Then Saul flew into a great rage
> This saying was evil in his eyes
> and he said
> They have attributed to David his ten thousands
> to me they have attributed thousands
> and what more is there for him but the kingship (1 Sam 18.8).

Saul's words stand in chiastic relation to the song. He expresses his displeasure in a pregnant manner. He thus imputes to the women great power: he transforms the "thousand" that he has slain into a *humiliating gift to himself*. It is humiliating, for it is totally eclipsed by what the women have attributed to David. The conclusion he draws from his "incorrect" interpretation of the song is, then, that the kingship is to pass to David too. Within the context of 1 Samuel, this is a prophetic conclusion which is by no means a surprise for readers. After all, they already know that David was secretly anointed as king in 1 Samuel 16. We can therefore deduce that the narrator is utilizing the women's song for showing Saul that David is a threat to his kingship. Furthermore, the song is subsequently quoted twice,

---

[14] Gevirtz cites a number of Ugaritic texts in this connection, and also Deut 32.30; Micah 6.7; Ps 91.6 and Dan 7.10. In regard to the function and meaning of "number parallelism" see also, for instance, Watson 1984, 144-149. On parallelism as a structural characteristic of Hebrew poetry see, in addition to Watson, Alter 1985; Berlin 1985; Kugel 1981; van de Meer & de Moor 1988.

in 1 Samuel 21.12 and 29.5. Thus it acquires an important function in the service of the story's message, namely that David is the true king of Israel.

To summarize the implications of Gevirtz's reading. A subversive meaning is wrongly attributed by Saul to the women's song, originally intended to be an "innocent" song. Hence, Saul attributes to the women great power. This power also seems to be completely in the service of the narrator's message. By endowing the song with a function totally different from that originally intended, the narrator renders the women—whom he so deliberately allows to speak—"muted". He takes away from their song the meaning that they themselves have given it.

This reconstructed reading is based on the non-antithetical interpretation of the song, as suggested by Gevirtz. However, when directing attention to the pair "thousands"//"ten thousands" which he regards as equivalent parallels, Gevirtz overlooks an important point: the change of subject from the first to the second colon. The reading of the song as if it contained synonymous parallelism is thus rendered impossible. Had the song had synonymous structure, it should have read as follows: Saul has slain his thousands, the king his ten thousands. A complementary reading might look like a possibillity too. However, the change of subject indicates both a comparative structure, and an oppositional force for the second half of the verse. Saul *and* David have together slain great numbers *but*, of the two, David has slain the greater number. In other words, the song of the women does not reflect purely uncritical pride of the "accomplishment of their men" only, as Gevirtz would so gladly have us believe. It really does have a subversive undertone. One explanation for this is to be found, to begin with, in the text *preceding* the song.

In the light of these verses (1 Sam 18.1-5) the women's words function as a continuation of the manifestations of increasing love and esteem for David. He gets it from Jonathan, from Saul, from "all the people" and from Saul's servants. The women express this increasing appreciation in their song, which is overtly linked by the narrator to what occurred in 1 Samuel 17 ("when David returned from slaying the Philistine", 1 Sam 18.6a). In this way the narrator gives us the chance to interpret the appreciation and the preference the women express for David as follows. The women express their preference for a hero who does not belong, to the same extent that they themselves do not belong, to the dominant circle of men waging war but who has, nonetheless, played a decisive and critical role in it by refusing the military equipment offered to him; and by beating the enemy with the aid of his shepherd's equipment.

I do not pretend to have revealed in this interpretation the "original meaning" of the song honouring Saul and David. In contrast to Gevirtz, I do not assume that this is possible or even desirable. Goitein is right in pointing out that orally transmitted literature loses much of its original character when it is written down. We know the women's victory song in the form in which it has come down to us in 1 Samuel only. It probably is a (fragment of a) verbatim "quotation" from oral tradition; there is no certainty, however, that this is indeed so. At most we can state that it is "imaginable" that this song expresses a women's view. For the interpretation of this view we are dependent on the context in which it is embedded, or to which it was adapted. Saul's reaction to the women's song serves as a significant guideline for the interpreter. But interpretations which limit themselves to the *Wirkungsgeschichte* of the thus determined reaction to the song have no ear for the "double voice" which can be distinguished therein. A more complete interpretation of the women's song and its subversive import is then obtained by paying attention to its contextualization by the portions of text preceding it.

The Dance of Jephthah's Daughter
The second text which Goitein cites in his discussion of the genre of victory songs, illustrates how significant the context is for the way the songs are or are not quoted. In Judges 11 the reference to the genre of victory songs acts as a narrative element only. After the announcement that Jephthah's daughter goes out "with timbrels and dances" to meet her father (Judg 11.34a), we expect to hear the words she sings; instead, we get the narrator's announcement,

> She was his only child
> beside her he had neither son nor daughter (Judg 11.34b).

The words used by the narrator to replace/drown the song of the daughter underline the gruesomeness of the fate that this daughter has to meet. In advancing to meet her father, she advances towards her death and her murderer. Her father had indeed made a vow in which he had promised YHWH, "whoever comes forth from the

doors of my house to meet me shall be offered as a burnt sacrifice''
(Judg 11.31). The "muting" of the daughter in verse 34 is thus
highly significant. It points in advance to her actual death (Bal
1988b, 41-69; Exum 1989; Trible 1984, 93-116).[15]

The Song of Miriam

The song that Miriam and the women sing after the crossing of the
Sea (Ex 15.20-21) is presented as an answer to the song of Moses and
the Sons of Israel (Ex 15.1-18). According to Goitein we should not
be misled, however, by the sequence of the presentation. In his
opinion the song of Miriam came first and was "the root from which
the entire song at the Sea sprouted" (Goitein 1988, 7). This viewpoint, for which Goitein supplies no further substantiation, can be
defended by reference to the song's text. The beginning of the song
of Moses, apart from the opening words, is exactly identical to that
of Miriam's. The introduction of Moses' song, "I will sing", can
be understood as an answer to the imperative "Sing", with which
Miriam starts her song. In other words, the song of Moses and the
Sons of Israel is in fact an exhaustive answer to the song of Miriam
and the women. But if this were indeed the case, why has/have the
author/s of Exodus 15 reversed the sequence of the songs? Or,
should we perhaps read the words which introduce the song of
Miriam as, "And Miriam sang them this refrain"?[16]

Athalya Brenner (1985) disputes this suggestion. She gives the following explanation for the problematic relationship between the two
songs. To begin with, Miriam was considered the original author-
ess/singer of the song by the Sea (Ex 15.1-18). Gradually, a tradition
evolved whereby this song was attributed to Moses. Confronted
with this dual tradition the author of Exodus 15 solved the problem
by bringing both traditions into agreement, "thus making Moses
the author and Miriam his female echo" (Brenner 1985, 52). Additional support for this hypothesis is found by Brenner in Numbers
12, where again traces can be found of two traditions which oppose
each other: a tradition according to which Miriam was as important
a leading figure as Moses was (see also Micah 6.4!), and a tradition
in which Moses' unique position is emphasized. Brenner argues

---

[15] I return to Jephtah's daughter below in the section about laments.
[16] For this view see, for instance, Cassuto 1967.

further that Miriam, like Deborah, fits the literary model of the "ideal leader" from pre-monarchical Israel.

> Miriam's and Deborah's names are linked, as co-performers or co-authors together with a male figure, to two great victory poems. Evidence derived from defining the literary model of the Ideal Leader before the time of King Solomon suggests that oratorical and literary skills are an important component of the leader's inventory of abilities. There is no reason to confine these features to male leaders alone. Therefore both women—the greatest female leaders in pre-monarchical Israel—were probably conceived of by some traditions as more independent and autonomous than they were by the mainstream of the Hebrew Bible (Brenner 1985, 56).

Brenner's reconstruction of the almost "muted" Miriam tradition "within the present, male-orientated framework of the text" would have been more convincing if she had also paid attention to the verse previous to the one which describes Miriam and the women. Phyllis Trible (1989) points out how strange it is that the song of Moses is followed by a narrative text, Exodus 15.19, in which the story of the passage through the Sea is retold in a nutshell. Together with the song of Miriam this verse now forms a second conclusion to the story of the passage through the Sea and, as such, is an anticlimax, "no more than an afterthought, a token of the female presence" (Trible 1989, 19). Trible refers to Cross and Freedman (1955) and ascribes Exodus 15.19 to an editorial intervention, which was necessary since those adapting the song of the Sea which was originally Miriam's eventually put it into Moses' mouth.

> Thus they construed an ending for the Exodus story that contradicted the older tradition. Unable to squelch the Miriamic tradition altogether, the redactors appended it in truncated form (Ex 15.20-21) to their preferred Mosaic version. So they gave us two endings: their preferred Mosaic version (Ex 15.1-18) and their truncated version (Ex 15.20-21) of the original Miriamic conclusion. To separate these two endings (as well as to introduce the Miriamic section) the redactors placed between them a narrative that recapitulated the struggle at the sea (Trible 1989, 19-20).

How plausible are the reconstructions suggested by Brenner and Trible, according to which Miriam's voice was reduced by the author(s)/redactor(s) of Exodus 15 in an almost evil manner to an echo of Moses' voice? Both are based on the assumption that the song of the Sea—which was errroneously attributed to Moses—is the most original and therefore the oldest, whereas Miriam's song was derived from it as a later addition. According to Cross and Freedman (1955), the song of the Sea is indeed very old. Sound arguments can be advanced, however, for a (much) later dating of the latter (see for instance Alter 1985, 50; Wagenaar 1986). Is it not, then, more illuminating to assume that Miriam's song belongs to a more ancient tradition, and that the song of the Sea is a later expansion of it?[17] Trible's statement that the "redactors (editors) who were intent upon elevating Moses took the song right out of her [Miriam's] mouth and gave it to him" should therefore be rephrased as follows. By introducing the song of the Sea into the story about the Exodus, and by putting it in Moses' mouth, the redactors of Exodus 15 created a situation whereby the song of Miriam and the women was shouted down by that of Moses and the Sons of Israel.

In spite of this authorial/editorial intervention, the passage containing Miriam's song has been preserved. The tradition that it was she who, after the Exodus, raised a hymn of victory together with the women of Israel was thus ineradicable. That does not mean that the song of Miriam, in contrast to the song of Moses, was authentically hers. There can be absolutely no certainty about this. By referring to the passage which has been handed down about her, we can note only that there was a living tradition about Miriam, "the prophetess", who led the women in a dance and voiced public opinion in a song. As I indicated above, this tradition was probably more ancient than the tradition that Moses and the Sons of Israel were the first to sing praises of YHWH after the Exodus. That the song of Moses, a premature answer to its successor, is positioned before Miriam's song can and must almost certainly be explained by androcentric motives. In addition, considerations of composition might have also played a part in this inverted order. Miriam's song concludes the story of the Exodus from Egypt. In Exodus 15.22 the passage through the desert is begun. Thus women's performance determines both the beginning (Ex 1, 2.1-10) and the end of the Exodus story (Trible 1989, 20).

The text of the victory song ascribed to Miriam has the formal characteristics of a hymn (Anderson 1987, 288). After the call to sing

---

[17] According to Noth (1965) and Ohler (1987), the Song of Miriam is very old indeed: the "älteste biblische Zeugnis vom Auszug aus Agypten" (Ohler 1987, 74).

unto YHWH, the motivation for so doing follows: "for high, high is He elevated".[18] The elevation of YHWH is then specified further in the description of His deed: "The horse and his charioteer He has thrown into the sea". Just as in the case of the song in honour of Saul and David, this song too summarizes preceding events in a pithy manner while, at the same time, giving a specific vision of them. Egyptian military supremacy is strikingly personified as "man and horse". The liberation from the tyrant's hands is expressed in a "mythical-poetical" manner (Coats 1967, 13) as being the work of YHWH, who triumphs by lifting Himself up like the sea into which He throws "the horse and his charioteer". Thus,

> The hymn wrought by the poet makes the world. Had there been no poet, the world offered would not have been this particular world. The "root experience" (i.e. the liberation from Egypt as fundamental experience for the belief of Israel, FvD) is not only a happening in public purview, but the "root experience" is a poem which shapes, decides and nuances what happens. And one may well wonder why these world-creating poems that run from Miriam to Mary are preserved in the tradition of the speech of women, who then are the "world-makers" in Israel. Perhaps in that society they are the only ones free enough from the "known world" to have the capacity to speak of an alternative world (Brueggemann 1987, 299).

Even without adopting the last suggestion uncritically we are able, with the assistance of this quotation from Brueggemann, to introduce a correction to Goitein's view, namely, that women's victory songs reflect public opinion. It is better to state that these songs *reshape* public opinion and lend it specificity. Moreover, women could act, as in the case of the song ascribed to Miriam, as a source of inspiration for new poetic work.

In conclusion we could say that in Exodus 15 Miriam stands out as the founder of the tradition that certain types of songs were sung by women. Through the action of the daughter of Jephthah (Judg 11.34) and of the women in 1 Samuel 18.6-7,

> (...) the musical legacy of Miriam passes into liturgical traditions. Though rejected by the priesthood, this woman nevertheless resounds in the cultic experience of the people (Trible 1989, 34).

---

[18] Alter translates the *figura etymologica g'h g'h* by "Who surged, oh surged" in order "to retain the clear suggestion in the Hebrew of a rising tide of water" (Alter 1985, 50 and 52).

Trible refers also to Psalm 68.25, where the "procession of God" is described as follows: "the singers in front, the minstrels last, between them maidens playing timbrels"; and to Psalms 81.2, 149.3-4, and 150.4. The memory of Miriam is kept alive in prophetic tradition too. In Jeremiah 31, where the liberation of Israel from the Babylonian exile is described as a new Exodus, YHWH addresses His people as a woman, like Miriam, "Again you shall adorn yourself with timbrels and go forth in the dance of the merrymakers" (Jer 31.4, see Anderson 1987, 294; Trible 1989, 25). But this positive conclusion about the presentation of Miriam does not of course obliterate the fact that her performance in Exodus 15 is placed in the shadow of Moses'. Like in the "solemn procession of God" (Ps 68.25), the (male) singers are in front. They sing the song of the Sea. The "maidens playing timbrels" (and see Meyers 1991) join in with the chorus.

The Song of Deborah

To what extent does the song of Deborah fit into the tradition of the victory songs sung by women? It is not introduced with the formula stating that the women went out to dance, but with the words "Deborah sang and Barak the son of Abinoam on that day" (Judg 5.1). Just like the song of Moses and the Sons of Israel, this song is represented as an immediate and extensive reaction to victory. Deborah plays an important part in this. It is expected of her (Judg 5.12) that, by uttering a song, she will awaken to the fight the military commander, the people and YHWH himself:

> Then they marched down to the gates the people of YHWH
>   Awake awake Deborah
>   Awake awake utter a song
> Arise Barak
> and capture your captives son of Abinoam
> Then now march down you that remain
> with the nobles O people
> YHWH come down to me with the warriors (Judg 5.11c-13).

According to Goitein, Deborah's song is a "distillation of the poems which were written in that decisive period of Israel's strengthening its hold upon its land" (Goitein 1988, 7). We hear in it, so he states, the echoes of public opinion expressed by the dancing women. He discusses portions of the poem within his examination of the genre of mockery songs. Since I have discussed the song of Deborah in detail elsewhere (Van Dijk-Hemmes 1989), I would here limit myself to the quotation of just two passages from the poem.

For the loosening of locks in Israel[19]
for a people that volunteered
bless YHWH
Hear O kings
give ear O princes
I to YHWH I will sing
I will make melody for YHWH the God of Israel
YHWH when you went forth from Seir
when you marched from Edom's field
The earth trembled
the heavens dropped also
even the clouds dropped water
Mountains quaked from the face of YHWH
Sinai itself from the face of YHWH
the God of Israel (Judg 5.2-5).

Kings came and fought
they fought there the kings of Canaan
at Taanach by the waters of Megiddo
Spoils of silver they did not take
From heaven fought the stars
from their highways they fought against Sisera
The torrent Kishon swept them away
the ancient torrent the torrent Kishon
Go forth my soul with might
Then the hooves of the horses hammered
the galloping galloping of his stallions (Judg 5.19-22).

In these passages elements which feature in the song of Miriam are used once more, albeit with further elaboration. The praise of YHWH and the downfall of the enemy are the themes developed in the poem. The hypothesis that it contains echoes of women's views from Israel's pre-monarchical era seems justified (Bal 1988a; Brenner 1990; Van Dijk-Hemmes 1989; Globe 1974; Smith 1912).

B. Mockery Songs

The singing of victory songs in the ancient Near East was often accompanied by mockery of the enemy. That this genre also belongs to the repertoire of the women of ancient Israel can, according to Goitein, be illustrated by the following texts.

---

[19] Scilicet: in a vow of war (BDB, 828).

Tell it[20] not in Gath
publish it not in the streets of Askelon
lest the daughters of the Philistines rejoice
lest the daughters of the uncircumcised exult (2 Sam 1.20).

She despises you she scorns you
The young woman the daughter of Zion
behind you(r back) she wags her head in derision
The daughter of Jerusalem (Isa 37.22b = 2 Kgs 19.21).

In the latter text Jerusalem is metaphorically presented as one of her inhabitants who fulfils her task of scoffing at the enemy, in this case Sennacherib king of Assyria. The metaphor points to a mockery song which the "daughters of Jerusalem" have sung about this king. A "quotation" from it may be found, according to Goitein, in the following section of the text, where the intentions, expectations and tyranny of Sennacherib are given in "his own" words:

Through your servants you have reviled my Lord
and said
    I with the multitude of my chariots
    I ascend the heights of the mountains
    the sides of Lebanon
    I fell its stately cedars
    the choicest of its cypresses
    and I come to the height of its summit
    to its luxuriant orchard
    I I dig and drink water
    and I dry up with the sole of my feet
    all the tributaries of the Nile in Egypt (Isa 37.24-25; cf. 2 Kgs 19.23-24).

The mockery song at the end of Deborah's song strikingly reconstructs the false expectations entertained by the foe.

Through the window she peered and lamented
the mother of Sisera through the bars
    Why does his chariot tarry in coming
    Why does the clatter of his chariots linger
The wise ones among her prominent women answered her
she herself responded to her words
    Are they not finding and dividing the spoil
    a maiden two maidens for a warrior's head
    plunder of dyed cloth for Sisera
    plunder of dyed cloth embroidered
    a dyed embroidered cloth for my neck as spoil
(Judg 5.28-30).

---

[20] The deaths of Saul and Jonathan.

It appears from the preceding verses, the poem in praise of Jael which "is interleaved with satire at the expense of the army commander Sisera" (Goitein 1988, 8), that the expectations of this mother of the enemy are not to be fulfilled.

> Blessed above women be Jael
> the wife of Heber the Kenite
> Blessed above the women in the tent
> He asked for water
> she gave him milk
> she offered him cream in a lordly bowl
> She stretched her hand to the tent peg
> her right hand to the workmen's hammer
> She hammered Sisera, smashed his head
> she struck, pierced his throat
> Between her feet he kneels falls lies
> between her feet he kneels falls
> Where he kneels down
> there he falls destroyed (Judg 5.24-27).

In addition to mockery of the enemy, the women's mockery may also target on the people of their own side who refused to "come to the help of YHWH". The text of the Song of Deborah, to which Goitein refers in this respect, is a good example.

> Curse Meroz
> says the messenger of YHWH
> Curse yea curse those who (continued) to sit there
> for they did not come to the help of YHWH
> to the help of YHWH among the warriors (Judg 5.23).

As a second example of this type of satirical song Goitein refers to the mockery of the tribes who refused to do battle with Sisera, once again from the Song of Deborah:

> In the divisions of Reuben
> great were the searchings of heart
> Why did you continue to sit among the burdens
> To hear the piping of the flocks
> In the divisions of Reuben
> great were the scrutinies of heart
> Gilead stayed camped across the Jordan
> and Dan why did he stay on the ships
> Asher sat on the coast of the seas
> in his bays he stayed camped (Judg 5.15c-17).

Goitein considers Jeremiah 38.22 an explicit indication for the practice of women's performance of this specific genre, satirical songs.

> Behold all the women who are left behind in the palace of the king of Judah
> are led away to the superintendents of the king of Babylon
> And behold they are saying
>   They have misled and overwhelmed you
>   the men you trusted as friends
>   Now that your feet are sunk in the mire
>   they turn their backs on you (Jer 38.22).

Here the prophet has the women say what he himself has said many times to King Zedekiah, namely, that his political advisors are totally unreliable and will cause his downfall. Goitein claims that these biblical instances teach us, "that the ancient Hebrews were accustomed to hear advice and warning from women just as they did from the prophets" (Goitein 1988, 9).

I agree with Goitein's analysis of the mockery songs genre but consider it of importance to add another dimension to it by asking, What function does the singing of these songs have for the women themselves? In my treatment of the song in honour of Saul and David I have pointed out that women, because of their marginal position in any dominant culture, tend to view with criticism events which occur in that culture. Practising the genre of mockery songs gives them the best opportunity for expressing criticism. What is the vision expressed in these songs? What is the motivation which informs them? What interest do women have in making the enemy laughable? What interest will they have in mocking, or even cursing, unwilling members of their own people or party?

We discover answers to these questions in the two songs of mockery which conclude Deborah's Song (Judg 5.24-27 and 28-30). These passages do not express the joy of the *people* about the downfall of the *enemy* only, but also the joy of *women* at the destruction of a *man* who is perceived as extremely threatening to them. In the passage where Sisera's mother appears at the front of the stage (Judg 5.28-30), the fact that her son and his men have still failed to return is attributed to their activity of distributing the spoils of war: "a maiden, two maidens for a warrior's head". The description, couched in "manly" terms and depicting the expected fate of the vanquished people's women, contextualizes the song of Jael (Judg

5.24-27) as an extremely humiliating satirical song about Sisera. The murder of this enemy chieftain is depicted as a rape scene, and this is done with vengeful joy (Bal 1988a, 127-134; Van Dijk-Hemmes 1989, 204). In other words, the enemy who would doubtless manifest himself as a rapist after his triumph (see v. 30) is, thanks to Jael the "blessed above women", himself the victim of the humiliation he has planned to inflict upon the womenfolk of the other side.

With the help of the insights the mockery songs at the end of Deborah's Song give us into women's vision of and interest in military affairs, we can now explain the other songs of satire mentioned by Goitein. The women from king Zedekiah's harem that are mentioned in Jeremiah's speech (Jer 38.22) can expect the inevitable fate of women during a war: "(...) they are led out to endure the lot of women wherever men gain complete power over them. (...) rape, concubinage, abuse and exploitation" (Carroll 1986, 687). The poem ostensibly sung by the women, in which Zedekiah is mocked for his false trust in his political friends and in which they deride him and his fate, acquires a still more cynical and bitter tone against this backdrop. The mockery of their own people in Deborah's Song because they refuse to "come to the help of YHWH" becomes even more understandable in this light. The women are critical of the *refusniks* not only for communal reasons but, also, because their own safety as women is jeopardized by the refusal of their own people to fight for them. The satirical song about Sennacherib (Isa 37.24-25) acquires a pregnant meaning too when we read it, like Goitein, as a song of the women of Jerusalem. Sennacherib is not only presented and reviled in his capacity as a power-crazy enemy, but also and above all because of his tyrannical masculinity.

This last observation touches a significant issue. It will have become clear from my discussion of victory songs that it is by no means certain that those songs ascribed to women were indeed "quotations" from women's (oral) traditions. The same applies to mockery songs discussed in this section. The poem that is ascribed to the women in Jeremiah 38 and the satirical song about Sennacherib, acquire an explicit gender-nuanced, or gender-motivated meaning *due to the fact that they are presented or read as women's texts*. Perhaps it would be better to state that the gender meaning of these texts is thus revealed. The songs of satire at the end of Deborah's Song direct us toward this gender-motivated meaning. That is not to say that the latter songs are indubitably the work of (a) female author(s). They too draw their gender meaning from their context, from the fact that they form part of the song that is known as Deborah's Song. This offers the reader the possibility of reading this text as a women's song (Van Dijk-Hemmes 1989, 207). The passages where Sisera and his mother are introduced consecutively do *not* allow themselves to be read only as songs of satire about a vanquished foe. Thus contextualized, they are to be read as "muted" women's songs that deal with the fate to which women are exposed in times of war, the vindictiveness this arouses in them, and their joy if and when they are spared.

3. WISDOM AND WARNING DISCOURSE

A. Wisdom Speeches

Women's practice of the victory song genre and the mockery song genre is usually presented to us as collective activity, whether it is subsumed under the leadership of a prominent woman or otherwise. However, we sometimes come across women who raise their voices within the dominant culture as individuals. The "wise" women in 2 Samuel 14 (the wise woman of Tekoah) and 20.16-20 (the wise woman of Abel-Beth-Maacah) are pertinent examples. Goitein points out that the wisdom of these women is more than an innate talent.

> It is the complete ensemble of traits and training by which a woman acquires leadership among women, and sometimes among the public in general. In Jer. 9:16 we find wise women as professional mourners; in the Mishnah, Shabbat 18:3 and Rosh Hashana 2:5, as midwives (like the French *sage-femme*)[21] She who excels in a handicraft is also called "wise of heart" (Ex 35.25) (Goitein 1988, 10).[22]

From the title "mother in Israel" (Judg 5.7) we can deduce that the wise women's field of activity is not always limited to their own district, as in the case of the wise women of Tekoah and Abel-Beth-

---

[21] A biblical representation of wise midwives can be found, according to Goitein, in Exodus 1.

[22] Brenner (1985, 38) claims that the expression *ḥkmt lb* here does not denote "wise of heart" but rather "expert", "skilled". The "wisdom" of these women is their skill in spinning and weaving.

Maacah, but can also cover the whole country. Thus a wise woman is "a woman to whose voice the entire nation pays heed as children listen to the instruction of their mother" (Goitein 1988, 10). Wise women spoke in a unique manner: both the form of their words, and the choice of words and images, were unusual. They spoke "in the language of hints and riddles" through which a proverb might be woven, and their language "was notable for its particular descriptiveness" (Goitein 1988, 11). Although we do not possess the sources of the wise women of ancient Israel as written by themselves, we can deduce this from the texts in which they feature. The authors put into their mouths "what a reader in Israel expected to hear from such a woman" (Goitein 1988, 10).

I now wish to illuminate further a number of specific characteristics which define women's wisdom. While so doing I shall rely heavily on the studies of Claudia V. Camp (1981 and 1985), who has studied the phenomenon of feminine wisdom in the Bible in depth.

The Wise Women of Tekoah and of Abel

> The woman said
> Why then have you planned such things against the people of God
> Since the king has said this he is guilty
> since the king himself will not let his banished one return home
> For we must die we must die
> like water spilt on the ground
> which cannot be gathered up
> But would God not set Himself[23]
> to making the plans in order not to keep the banished one banished from him
> Now the reason I have come
> to speak this word to the king my lord
> is that the people have made me afraid
> Your handmaid said then
>> Let me speak to the king in any case
>> It may be that the king will act according to the words of his handmaid
>> For the king will hear
>> and deliver his handmaid from the hand of the man who intends to destroy me and my son together from the inheritance of God
> And your handmaid said
>> May the word of my lord the king set me at rest

---

[23] For this translation of $n\check{s}$' $np\check{s}$ see Hoftijzer 1970, 434-437.

For like a messenger of God so is my lord the king
in hearing what is good and what is evil
YHWH, your God be with you.

(From the speech of the wise woman from Tekoah in which she, at
Joab's instigation, successfully persuades David to make an end to
the exile of his son Absalom; 2 Sam 14.13-17.)

She said
In olden times it was said
    They ask for counsel counsel in Abel
    and so they settle a matter
I
    (belong to) the peaceloving the faithful in Israel
You
    seek to kill a city a mother in Israel
Why will you destroy the inheritance of the Lord.

(The speech of the wise woman from Abel-Beth-Maacah, in which
she successfully persuades Joab to leave her city alone; 2 Sam
20.18-19.)

Both women are designated by the adjective "wise" and the name
of the place where they lived in only. This, in Camp's opinion,
indicates

> that the audience who heard these accounts must have had some prior
> image of these two nameless figures who stand so boldly before a king
> and a general; that when the words *ʾšh ḥkmh* were used, features of
> a culturally stereotyped character arose in the hearer's mind, thus ob-
> viating the need for further description (Camp 1981, 17).

Camp then goes on to discuss two characteristics of such women's
actions, which are often associated with the notion of "wise". In the
first place, both women speak with authority. The wise woman from
Tekoah perhaps starts the tale that Joab had whispered to her (2 Sam
14.1-12), whose purpose is to invite David to lift the banishment of
his son Absalom, in a modest manner, but "her accusing rhetorical
question in 14.13 is spoken by one who seems accustomed to making
and delivering such judgment" (Camp 1981, 17). The authority of
the wise woman from Abel-Beth-Maacah is not apparent from her
words to Joab (quoted above) only, but also in the description of her
return to her people after her successful intervention. "The woman
came to the whole people with her wisdom", upon which the people
immediately carry out what she promised to Joab, "they cut off the

head of Sheba the son of Bichri[24] and threw it out to Joab" (2 Sam 20.22a).

The second characteristic that is usually associated with "wisdom" is, according to Camp, the use of proverbial sayings (see also Goitein 1988, 11). The wise woman from Abel carries on her confrontation with Joab with "what might be described as a classical application of the wisdom of the ages as a basis for authority" (Camp 1981, 19): she "quotes" a proverb about the reputation of Abel as a source of wise advice. Having pointed out with authority the authoritative reputation of her city, she makes an urgent request to Joab to renounce his intention of destroying this city.

> A saying (. . .) is employed by a wise person for a particular purpose, possibly to educate another (which always involves some implicit directing as to what is "right" or "wrong") or, as in this case, to exert influence over another's action in a way that carries some authority. Thus the proverb about Abel, when spoken by this wise woman, constitutes a directive to Joab that to attack the city would certainly be a wrongful deed. She is a wise person utilizing the art of wisdom speech to an end often associated with ancient Near Eastern wisdom literature, viz., the persuasion of the ruler by a soft tongue in a delicate situation (cf. Prov 25.15; 15.1) (Camp 1981, 19).

As a follow-up for her accusation of David, the wise woman of Tekoah adds a proverb-like saying: "We must all die, we are like water spilt on the ground, which cannot be gathered up again" (2 Sam 14.14). Within the framework of her plea the saying's function is to convince David of her point of view. Its meaning is, probably deliberately so, ambiguous. The wise woman, like the prophet Nathan in 2 Samuel 12, involves David in her own imaginary story in order to open his eyes by degrees to the many lives which have been involved in his erroneous behaviour.

In addition, Camp mentions a third common characteristic for the action and speech of the women as *wise*, i.e. in conformity with a wisdom tradition. This last characteristic applies to the women's action and speech as wise *women*. Motherhood plays a major role in both texts. The wise woman from Tekoah presents herself as a mother. The wise woman from Abel speaks of her city as a "mother in Israel". For Camp, this demonstrates a vision in which mother-

---

[24] The man because of whom Joab threatened to destroy the city.

hood is an important source of female wisdom. In the pleas of both women this "motherly" wisdom is related to and acquires concrete form in the concern and care for the "inheritance of YHWH (or God)". The plea of the wise woman-and-mother from Tekoah reveals not only concern for the continuity of kingship, but also and particularly concern for the maintenance of family name and the protection of widows and orphans against the destruction of "the inheritance of God" (2 Sam 14.16).

> (. . .) her return to the mother-role (14.15-16) *after* her mask-removing accusation of David (v. 13) suggests her larger concern as village leader for the protection of widow, orphan and inheritance ("the heritage of God", v. 16) under the new monarchical government (Camp 1985, 122).

The wise woman from Abel subsequently identifies her city, which she has named "a mother in Israel", in a parallel phrase as "the inheritance of YHWH", which should not be swallowed up. In the plea for the integrity of "the inheritance of YHWH" she shows herself as the personification of her city and thus as a "mother in Israel" (Van Dijk-Hemmes 1985; Fokkelman 1981, 334). In doing so she is akin to that other "mother in Israel", Deborah, "a creator and hence a symbol of the unity that bound Israel together under one God, YHWH" (Camp 1981, 28).

Abigail
Although she is not designated by the phrase a "wise woman" Abigail, wife of Nabal the "fool" speaks (see Goitein) the language of wise women (1 Sam 25). She is successful in persuading David to renounce his planned revenge on the house of Nabal:

> (. . .)
> If ever a person arises to pursue you
> and to seek your soul
> Then the soul of my lord will be a bundle
> in the bundle of those living with YHWH your God
> And the soul of your enemies H/he shall throw away
> from the middle of the sling
> And then it will come about
> if YHWH does to my lord all the good
> that he has spoken concerning you
> and appoint you a ruler over Israel
> Then this will not be an obstacle to you
> nor an offence to the heart of my lord

(Namely) that you had shed blood unnecessarily
and that my lord would have saved himself
And when YHWH has dealt favourably with my lord
remember then your handmaid (2 Sam 25.29-31).

Abigail does indeed have the gift of eloquence, and a talent for
manipulation which wise women have. She too knows how to avoid
unnecessary bloodshed. Still, her action differs on a number of
counts from that of the professional wise women discussed above.
Brenner regards it as decisive in this connection that

> (. . .) her scope is limited to her own affairs and does not extend to
> public affairs. Perhaps the differentiation is hinted at in the choice of
> (Hebrew) adjective which describes her: Abigail is a woman of "good
> sense" (*twbt śkl*), but not "wise" (*ḥkmh*) (Brenner 1985, 41).

The following features mentioned by Camp are missing in Abigail's
performance: she does not speak with authority and she is not
associated with "motherly" wisdom.[25] In her discussion of biblical
literary models which were used as sources of inspiration for the construction of Lady Wisdom in Proverbs 1-9, Camp counts Abigail
among the literary types of the "wife as counsellor". As such Camp
considers Abigail one of the literary examples for the presentation
of wisdom as a woman (Camp 1985, 89-90). The wise women of
Tekoah and Abel, as "representatives of a non-regular but recurrent leadership role for women in pre-monarchical Israel", are not
just literary models but, possibly, also the historical models for the
metaphorical Lady Wisdom of Proverbs (Camp 1985, 120-121).

Lady Wisdom
If Camp is correct in her assumption that a link exists between the
wisdom tradition of wise women from pre-monarchical and early
monarchical Israel, and the presentation of Wisdom as a woman,
then it goes without saying that traces of this oral tradition of the wisdom of women can also be found in Proverbs 1-9. These traces
perhaps resound in the following words of Lady Wisdom,

I have advice and deliberation
I am wisdom I have strength
By me kings practise their kingship

---

[25] It is nonetheless true that her address probably includes a proverb or saying,
see v. 29.

and princes determine what is just
Through me leaders practise their leadership
and nobles all those who exert justice (Prov 8.14-16).

In any case, we can assume with Camp that the stories of 2 Samuel
about wise women offer a cultural context for this proud
self-presentation of Lady Wisdom, and thus also for Israel's "theological appropriation of a female Wisdom" (Camp 1985, 123).
Goitein too ends his section about the "wise" woman with a similar
conclusion:

> And who knows whether the image of Wisdom in the form of a woman
> who stands "at the topmost heights, by the wayside, at the crossroads,
> near the gates at the city entrance, at the entryways" (Prov 8.2-3), or
> who prepares the feast, pours the wine, sets the table and sends her
> girls throughout the city to invite anyone who so desires to enjoy her
> hospitality (Prov 9.2-5)—who knows whether this allegorical descrip-
> tion did not originate with the actual wise women whom we have
> found in the earliest history of Israel in such varied circumstances?
> (Goitein 1988, 11).

This attractive and plausible hypothesis does not, however, remove
the fact that only *men* are addressed in Proverbs. There, Lady Wisdom and her opposite number Lady Folly symbolise good and evil
that a man, a young man of the upper class (Bird 1974, 59), who is
addressed in the text as "my son", can meet on his life's path and
between which he must make a choice (Bekkenkamp and Van Dijk
1987, 103-104; Newsom 1989). The transformation of the "wise"
woman into the metaphorical Lady Wisdom in post-exilic Israel occurred within an exclusive androcentric framework and with a view
to men's welfare. We can therefore state that although, in Lady Wisdom's phrases, the echoes of a wise women's tradition can probably
still be heard, this wisdom tradition is "muted". It is "muted" because it is fixated as a metaphorical figure created for men's use in
the service of their wisdom ideals. Hence, by a ruse, women's wisdom in the Lady Wisdom figure is divorced from its original milieu
and enlisted for androcentric ends. It is not only "muted", but undergoes a transformation that enrolls her as advertiser for the
dominant male culture.

B. Warning Speeches

Motherhood functioned, as we have seen, as an important source of
the wisdom of "wise" women in ancient Israel. The role played by

the mother in the upbringing of her children was considered, as we can glean from various indications in the Bible, equal to that of the father. The fifth commandment demands respect for "your father and your mother" (Ex 20.12). In Proverbs the "son" is urged to take to heart the commandment or discipline of his father and the instruction of his mother (Prov 1:8 and 6:20). Goitein thinks it rather striking that in Deuteronomy 21.18-21 *both* parents are told which measures they should take in regard to a rebellious son. The stories about Rebekah and Jacob (Gen 27) and Micah and his mother (Judg 17) generate an outline of the kind of authority mothers enjoyed. The possibility that during the era of the monarchy the position of the king's mother was superior to, and often much more superior than, that of his wife may serve as corroboration for the privileged status of Israelite mothers.

> Given the particularly lofty position of the queen-mother—which has a parallel in Assyria—it is understandable that she became *the literary representative of the mother rebuking her child.* (Goitein 1988, 12)

In the last chapter of Proverbs there is an example of this kind of literary genre—the instruction of a son, the (otherwise unknown) king Lemuel by his mother. We shall turn to this passage now.

The Mother of Lemuel

> The words to king Lemuel
> The proverb with which his mother admonished him
>   What my son yes what son of my womb
>   yes what son of my vow (shall I say to you)
>   Give your strength/wealth[26] not to women
>   nor your ways[27] for (female) destroyers[28] of kings
>   It is not fitting for kings Lemuel
>   it is not fitting for kings to drink wine
>   nor for princes to desire intoxicating liquor[29]
>   Otherwise he drinks and forgets what is prescribed
>   and perverts the right of all the oppressed
>   Give intoxicating drink to the one that perishes
>   and wine to those who are bitter of soul
>   Let him drink and forget his poverty

---

[26] *ḥyl* means strength, virility and riches.
[27] The BHS (ed. Fichtner) suggests reading here *wyrkyk*, "your loins".
[28] Cf. BHS to read *lmhwt* as a f. plural part.
[29] Cf. BHS to read *'wh* instead of *'w*.

and think no more on his misery
Open your mouth for the dumb
for the right of all the weak[30]
Open your mouth and judge justly
and protect the right of the oppressed and the needy
(Prov 31.1-9).

The beginning of this speech illustrates the validity of Schüssler Fiorenza's proposition (see under 1.A): Women's views are not by definition more well-disposed toward women than men's views. Lemuel's mother speaks about women in a manner that is comparable to the pronouncement of Sisera's mother in the Song of Deborah (Judg 5.30; see 2.B.), phrases which constitute an aggression toward women. Sisera's mother views women as the deserved lot of her victorious son; Lemuel's mother shows them to be a threat to the virility and riches of the son-king, yes, even "destroyers of kings". The possibility that these phrases have been attributed to Lemuel's mother by a male author does not necessarily mean that they could not represent the views of many mothers in ancient Israel. Mothers who advance the interests of their sons, and identify themselves with them, enjoy recognition and are assured of a respected position in a patriarchal society. Moreover, the mother's view fits excellently into the androcentric framework of the Bible as a whole and of Proverbs in particular. Therefore, it is not surprising that the "words to King Lemuel" which have come down to us as the "proverb whereby his mother admonished him" have been given a place in Proverbs, a document which is a product of the dominant culture of the post-exilic period.

Lemuel's mother is a parent who rebukes a son. As such, she represents the positive image of woman in Proverbs—woman as a wise and sound adviser, thanks to whom the son or husband is successful. By means of introducing women into her discourse, and by letting them enter her plea, she underlines her own positive role while, simultaneously, teaching her son to distinguish between "good" and "bad" women. The threat women represent for the strength and power of her son is comparable to the risk of alcohol and its detrimental effect for the execution of his task as king. Alcohol hinders the king's ability to judge, and that comes at the cost of the oppressed. The surprising advice to give people drink when they

---

[30] Cf. BHS to read ḥly instead of ḥlwp.

are without prospects, does not absolve the king from his duty to dispense justice. It is perhaps significant that, in the following passage of this last chapter of Proverbs (31.20), this same royal task of dispensing justice is performed by the earthly counterpart of Lady Wisdom, the "woman of strength" (*'št ḥyl*) (Camp 1985, 279). It would seem that women can govern justly: neither females nor alcohol will cloud their judgement.

The I persona in Proverbs 7

Goitein considers it possible that the warnings against temptations of "strange" women in Proverbs 5-7 and against the drinking of wine formed part of the repertory of the Hebrew female "rebuker". He thinks that the passage concerning the dangers of wine and strong drink in Proverbs 23.29-35 can, in view of its final verse ("As soon as I awake, I seek it again" [i.e. the drink]), be read as a parody on this type of warning.

If by "parody" Goitein means a *male* parody, his hypothesis would gain force if there were indications that in Proverbs 5-7 a female voice was speaking. It is generally accepted that the I persona speaking in Proverbs 1-9 is that of a wisdom teacher who speaks to his student son or sons like a father does. I have, however, shown above that in Proverbs texts delivered by the I persona are characterized not only as "the command of your father" (*mṣwt 'byk*), but also as "the instruction of your mother" (*twrt 'mmk*) (see Prov 1.8 and 6.20). The speaker in certain parts of Proverbs 1-9 could therefore be a woman, a teacher of wisdom or female "rebuker" who exhorts her son, thus exercising her prerogative as a mother. In my opinion the hypothesis of a female speaker is unavoidable, particularly so in view of Proverbs 7. After the summons to the "son" to keep the commandments and beware of the "strange" woman, the I persona introduces him/herself with the words,

> For through the window of my house
> through the bars I looked out (Prov 7.6).

In the Bible looking through the window (with the exception of Genesis 26.8, where Abimelech looks out of his window at Isaac and Rebeka "playing"), is an activity that is mostly practised by women. So do Michal (2 Sam 6.16), Jezebel (2 Kgs 9.30), and Sisera's mother (Judg 5.28). The similarity between Proverbs 7.6 and the last passage cited is particularly strong. It is said of Sisera's

mother too that she looked out of the window, through the bars
(Judg 5.28). These details indicate to the intended reader, who is
addressed through the textual figure of the "son", a traditional motif.[31] The "son"/reader who heeds it is expected to regard Proverbs
7 as the rebuking instruction of a woman. She continues as follows:

> And I saw among the inexperienced
> I noticed among the sons a young man without heart/willpower
> He passed by in the street at her corner
> he turned into the way to her house
> in the twilight at the eve of the day
> in the *pupil* of night and darkness
> And behold a woman comes to meet him
> dressed as a prostitute and the heart on guard
> Restless is she and rebellious
> her feet do not stay in her house
> A step in the street a step in the squares
> besides every corner she skulks
> She grabs him and she kisses him
> with a hard face she says to him
>> Peace offerings I have to bring
>> today I am to fulfill[32] my vows
>> That is why I have come out to meet you
>> to seek your face and I have found you
>> I have spread my couch with covers
>> with coloured linen from Egypt
>> I have sprinkled my bed
>> with myrrh aloes and cinnamon
>> Come let us revel in love till morning
>> let us delight in each other's embraces
>> For the man is not in his house
>> he has gone away far away
>> The bag with silver money he has taken with him
>> he will come home on the day of the full moon
> She distracts him with her great persuasiveness
> she seduces him with the smoothness of her lips
> All at once he follows her
> as a bull goes to the slaughter
> like a handcuffed fool to the punishment
> until an arrow pierces his liver

---

[31] See also the frequent portrayal of "the woman at the window" in ancient
Near East art. This specifically concerns "phönizische Elfenbeinreliefs, auf denen
der Kopf der Göttin bzw. derjenige ihrer Repräsentantin über einer Balustrade in
einer gerahmten Fenster erscheint" (Winter 1983, 296).
[32] For this translation cf. van der Toorn 1989, 198.

like a bird rushes to the snare
and does not know that it will cost him his life

Now then sons listen to me
and attend to the words of my mouth
Do not let your heart stray into her ways
do not wander into her paths
For many are the slain whom she has felled
and very many are they that have been killed by her
Ways to the kingdom of the dead her house
going down to the halls of death

This warning, addressed to the inexperienced young men, is a good example of the use of graphic description in education. The I persona has spent her time at the window well. She paints the dangerous attraction that "strange" women have for unsuspecting young men in a compelling manner. She lets her audience experience, through the figure of a young man "without willpower", how a person can become a victim of a dangerous woman who does not know that her proper place is inside the house, and who watches out for her victim like a beast of prey. The meeting between both personas is described as the beginning of a rape scene. After being "grabbed", however, the victim is not overpowered like Dinah (Gen 34.2), or Tamar (2 Sam 13.14), but only kissed and then seduced by the "smoothness of her lips". Language is an important weapon in the battle waged by the seducer. The contrast with the behaviour of the male seducers or rapists of Genesis 34 and 2 Samuel 13 is remarkable indeed[33]. Shechem does not say a word before he rapes Dinah, Amnon utters short commands only. This contrast is rooted in the difference in physical strength and social power between men and women, a difference which is exemplified most distressingly in the arena of sexuality. The physically more powerful, the rapist, does not need language in order to achieve his aim. For the less mighty, the temptress, language is a necessary expedient.

Camp, like Aletti (1977), points out the misleading character of the language that the "strange woman" speaks in Proverbs 7.

---

[33] This counts a fortiori for the action of the rapists in Judges 19. For an interpretation of this "tale of terror" see Trible 1984, 64-91 and, particularly, Bal 1988b, 147-161. For an analysis of 2 Samuel 13 see van Dijk-Hemmes 1989e.

(...) the significance of the seduction of the Strange Woman is that it is carried out in language that separates deed from consequence. In Proverbs 7, for example, the woman does not seek to convince her prey that adultery is right, but only that they can get away with it because her husband is not home. Using language, she creates a false sense of security, seemingly insulating the perpetrator of wrongdoing from any negative outcome. Language here throws up a smoke screen, blinding its listeners to the effect of their actions upon themselves and society. In this manner, not only is morality threatened, but the use of language is perverted, its relationship to what the sages considered reality sundered, and the discourse of the sage, on which the intellectual endeavor depends, thus rendered suspect (Camp 1987, 51-52).

Camp's analysis accords with the message of the I persona in Proverbs 7, hence is merely a paraphrase of it. The I persona exposes the words of the seducer as "persuasiveness" and thus misleading language too. The gripping and horrifying pictures with which she ends her story bring her listeners back to "reality" with a shock. In the final passage, where her moral sermon to the "son" acquires a universally valid character with the switch from "son" to "sons", she summons her listeners to be attentive to "the words of my mouth". At this point her imagery acquires a more threatening character as she sketches the destructive power of women in a penetrating manner, a thing done by Lemuel's mother too. He who pursues the advances of a "strange" woman further does not only risk his fortune, but also takes his life in his hands, "for many are the slain whom she has felled".

The message of Proverbs 7, stated with such conviction, gives the reader who does not allow herself to be addressed as a matter of course by the sons-in-the-text every reason for asking a number of questions. Is Camp's analysis applicable to Proverbs 7 as a whole? And, on second thoughts, is her analysis of the "strange" woman's language really convincing?

Let me take up the latter question first. It should be recognized that the "strange" woman gives a correct and clear picture of her situation and her intentions. She is no professional prostitute, but probably a married woman[34] who needs money in order to pay her

---

[34] The "strange woman" does not speak of "my husband" in any case in verse 19 but of "the man". This can mean that she, in her capacity as temptress of the young man "without willpower", only wishes to speak of her husband in detached terms. It can also mean that she refers to the man responsible for her. In that case

vows (van der Toorn 1989). She cannot get any help from her husband since he has gone on a journey, taking the money with him.
In short, the language the "strange" woman uses is certainly seductive, but not necessarily misleading. She does not allow the young
man to entertain any misapprehension or misconceptions as to what
it is all about.

It therefore seems that the language of the I persona-in-the-text
deserves further consideration. If we apply Camp's analysis to it,
then the words of this textual persona, rather than those of the
"strange" woman, are themselves exposed as "persuasiveness", as
misleading language which "throws up a smoke screen". The reality sketched in this text, and in which the man is represented as a
defenseless victim who will not survive if a woman exercises her sexuality upon him for her own ends (Bekkenkamp and others 1985),
is after all a totally one-sided figuration of social reality, where the
reverse usually obtains. The language of the I persona blinds the
readers, who are addressed through the "sons", to this reality,
which is, in the Bible, presented in literary form. The stories
referred to above about the rape of Dinah (Gen 34), and Tamar
(2 Sam 13), and the nameless wife of the Levite (Judg 19), indicate
that a different kind of moral lesson for young men would have
deserved priority. In these stories, the women "go out" at their own
peril; they endanger themselves; their sexuality is abused. No trace
of a moral lesson to (young) men which takes such situations into account is, however, to be found here or elsewhere in the Book of
Proverbs. The vision that is presented in this Book, in contrast to
conclusions that can be drawn from the rape stories, pays no attention to the dangers to which women and their sexuality are subject
to in a patriarchal society.

It is precisely because Camp's analysis of the language of the
"strange" woman agrees with its evaluation by the I persona-in-
the-text that she does not go far enough. Camp herself remains a
prisoner of the text's rhetoric. It escapes her that here it is not so
much the young man "without willpower" who is led astray and
blinded, but rather the reader addressed through the "sons" and,
alas, especially the female reader addressed through the "sons".
And yet, the male or female reader addressed thus could have been

---

her father or brother, or another male protector, is invoked. Therefore it is not
certain that 'ʃ here actually refers to a husband, and that the woman is married.

warned. The I persona sitting at the window can be associated with certain intertexts. Those call to mind negatively presented biblical female figures such as Michal, Jezebel and Sisera's mother. It is above all the last figure who is generally seen as a woman who is brought into action against women. The sexual associations form a pointer for the male or female reader to react with at least some scepticism to the view of the woman-at-the-window who speaks with such "persuasiveness" in Proverbs 7.

The voices of admonishing and rebuking women which can be heard in Proverbs, are not in disagreement with this androcentric discourse. They are the voices of women who have internalized this discourse. And yet, the woman's voice in Proverbs 7, because of the associations it evokes, deconstructs its own position. It does not ring true, and this—given the framework—is not without irony. The story of the woman who knows how to reproduce the dominant discourse perfectly—first by calling on the voice of another woman who is qualified as "strange", then by "muting" it—is, in keeping with the laws of that same discourse, hardly an example of reliable instruction.

4. Prophecy and Soothsaying

A. Prophecy

The word *nby'*, "prophet", appears 309 times in the Hebrew Bible; the female form *nby'h*, "prophetess", 6 times. The first woman who is called a prophetess was, as we have already seen, Miriam (Ex 15.20). The "mother in Israel" Deborah is also given this title (Judg 4.4). The other prophetesses mentioned are Huldah (2 Kgs 22.14 and 2 Chron 34.22), Noadiah (Neh 6.14) and the namelessly presented wife of the prophet Isaiah (Isa 8.3). Does such a relatively small number indicate that prophetesses were an unusual phenomenon in ancient Israel? According to Goitein that is not the case. Miriam's activity marks the beginning of the era of prophecy, whereas that of Noadiah stands at the end of it. Therefore we can deduce that "the whole time there were prophets in Israel, prophetesses were active as well" (Goitein 1988, 13. See also Brenner 1985, 66; van der Toorn 1987, 125). Another indication that this was the actual state of affairs is the way the narrators refer to the appearance of the prophetesses mentioned. The references are so unproblematic that their appearance neither constitutes an unusual event, nor requires further explanation.

In order to ascertain what was characteristic of the prophetesses' speech, we are forced to limit ourselves to the words of Miriam, Deborah and Huldah. Noadiah and the unnamed prophetess in Isaiah are not presented as speaking. Miriam and Deborah, the two oldest prophetesses, are mainly shown as singers. (The songs attributed to them are discussed above, in 2.A.) Hence, Goitein accepts that poetry was the original medium of female prophecy.[35] Deborah's call to rise and fight, delivered by song (Judg 5.12), also signifies that the actual power ascribed to a prophetess' words was as great and decisive as that ascribed to the appearance of a military leader.[36]

> During Israel's formative period, which was full of wars, the inspiring poetry of the prophetess took on special importance. No doubt, if the ancient collection of poetry such as the "Book of Jashar" (i.e. of the "hero" like Jeshurun, 2 Sam 1.18) or the "Book of the Wars of the Lord" (Num 21.14) had come down to us, we would know still more about the poetry of the Israelite prophetess of the ancient days (Goitein 1988, 13-14; see also Bekkenkamp and Van Dijk 1987, 94).

Of the prophetesses of the era of classical prophecy, only the words of Huldah have come down to us. This prophetess was consulted at the command of king Josiah, in connection with the discovery of the book of the law in the Temple (2 Kgs 22.1-13 = 2 Chron 34.1-21). The formula with which she introduces her prophecy—"Say to the man who sent you to me" (2 Kgs 22.15)—is, according to Goitein, probably characteristic of the oracle of a prophetess. The amazement expressed from time immemorial by commentators about the fact that the prophetess Huldah, who was actually a contemporary of Jeremiah, was given such a crucial role in the history of Israel is not shared by Goitein. He concludes from the fact that people asked her for advice that,

> (...) Huldah was the chief prophet at that time, just as Noadiah was the most influential of the prophets during Nehemiah's day (Goitein 1988, 14).

---

[35] The same also applies to male prophecy; see, for example, Freedman 1975.

[36] The same also applies to the prophets Elijah and Elisha (cf. 2 Kgs 2.12; 13.14).

Huldah and Deborah

Goitein limits his discussion of Miriam and Deborah to a reference to their songs, which he has discussed earlier. From Huldah's message he extracts only the opening formula, in an (in my view) forced attempt to find something that would be representative of the speech of prophetesses. In so doing he implies that those phrases of the prophetesses which are preserved in prose contain barely echoes of female prophetic tradition. This, it seems to me, is a correct assumption for Hulda's prophecy. In a discussion of this passage Marie Theres Wacker rightly points out the typically Deuteronomistic character of Huldah's prophecy. Wacker's conclusion is that Huldah "unter der deuteronomistichen Bearbeitung (...) als historisch greifbares Individuum fast völlig ausgelöscht [wird]" (Wacker 1988, 95). She regards it as remarkable that the memory of Huldah's appearance has been preserved in the "so frauenkritisch, ja häufig geradezu frauenfeindlichen deuteronomistischen Tradition" (Wacker 1988, 95).[37]

Duane Christensen makes an interesting statement about the inclusion of the story of Huldah in 2 Kings. He shows that the appearances of Deborah in Judges 4 and of Huldah in 2 Kings 22 frame the Deuteronomistic history of life in the promised land (from Judges up to and including Kings) on both sides, thus forming an inclusio. In that way these two prophetesses, together with their opposite numbers Queen Jezebel (1 Kgs 16.31—2 Kgs 9.37) and Queen Athaliah (2 Kgs 11), acted as female examples of the theme so important in the Deuteronomistic history—the conflict and tension between prophet and king. Shown schematically,

A – Deborah: a "Prophetess" of YHWH alongside Barak (Israel)
B – Jezebel: a Royal Advocate of Baal in Israel
B' – Athaliah: a Royal Advocate of Baal in Judah
A' – Huldah: a Prophetess of YHWH alongside Josiah (Judah)
(Christensen 1984, 402).[38]

---

[37] Brenner (1985, 60), in contrast to Wacker, does not consider it out of the question that the second part of Huldah's prophecy is authentic. She considers the fact that this prophecy to Josiah is not fulfilled an important argument for its historicity. Van der Toorn has rightly pointed out, however, that Huldah's prophecy in regard to Josiah *was*, strictly speaking, fulfilled. Huldah certainly does not say that Josiah will die on the battlefield (2 Kgs 23.29-39); and he is "buried with his fathers" as Huldah prophesied. Brenner's argument about the authenticity of this passage is thus not acceptable.

[38] Christensen, in contrast to Wacker, explains the prominent role of these four women in the Deuteronomistic history by a pro-female motive.

It seems probable that the Deborah in Judges 4 who, like Hulda, may or may not be a historical figure, should be considered first and foremost a literary creation inspired by the song of Deborah. In her words the voice of the female prophetic tradition is barely distinguishable. She, like Huldah, is shown as the model of the true prophet, as sketched in Deuteronomy 18.18-20. She too answers to the criteria formulated there: she speaks on behalf of YHWH and her prophecies are fulfilled. Her prophecy to Barak in Judges 4.9 is of an explicitly gender-motivated nature. This could be an indication that a reminiscence of the oral tradition of female prophecy can be heard in it. To Barak's provisional undertaking to go to war against Sisera—he will only do so if Deborah goes with him—Deborah replies,

> Go yes I will go with you
> Only there will be no fame for you on the road you go
> YHWH will sell/deliver Sisera into the hand of a woman.

This utterance, as is often the case with prophetic oracles, is somewhat ambiguous. Deborah does not say whether by "a woman" she means herself or another woman. Moreover, her oracle can also be read as "double voiced". Both a dominant and a "muted" story can be uncovered in it. The dominant story becomes visible in the light of the texts of women's rebuke discussed above. Deborah's pronouncement fits into this literary convention since she too represents woman as a threat to man, in this case particularly to his honour. The "muted" story becomes visible when we place Deborah's words in the tradition of those mockery songs in which the lack of men's effort to guarantee safety is censured by (the women of) their own party. And, in addition to the anger concerning Barak's conditional pledge, a desire for a reversal of socially prescribed gender roles and their division is evident in Deborah's words too (see also Rasmussen 1989).

Miriam

The anger which can be heard in Deborah's utterance, according to the afore mentioned interpretation, can be compared with that of Miriam in Numbers 12.

> Miriam and Aaron spoke to Moses concerning the Cushite woman
> that he had taken
> For he had taken a Cushite woman

They said
   Has YHWH only spoken through Moses
   Has he not also spoken through us (Num 12.1-2).

Miriam, together with Aaron, contests a certain division of role and task. It is she who takes the initiative in this respect. The phrase which introduces the words of Miriam and Aaron has given rise to many speculations. The connection between the reason given for speaking to Moses (v. 1) and the spoken text that follows is far from obvious. Many interpreters claim that two stories have been interwoven here in a somewhat unfortunate manner. Trible (1989) imagines that a more extensive story must have been introduced by verse 1, a story in which Moses is challenged about his priestly function. The ritual purity required for that function had been damaged by his marriage to a foreign woman. In the present version of the story this criticism is paired off with an originally different tradition, according to which Miriam and Aaron attack Moses' unique authority as a prophet. In the follow-up (further in Num 12) YHWH, who acts as Moses' advocate, reacts in two ways to this combined attack on Moses' authority. To the second attack, the criticism of Miriam and Aaron on Moses' unique position as prophet, YHWH responds verbally. Without discounting the fact that Miriam and Aaron are themselves prophets, He emphasizes the unusual relationship between Him and Moses and addresses Miriam and Aaron in a reproving manner (vv. 4-8). Their first point of contention, not "quoted" by the narrator, regarding Moses' ritual purity is answered by YHWH with an act which damages Miriam's ritual purity profoundly. Like a father who spits humiliatingly in the face of his rebellious daughter (v. 14), YHWH punishes Miriam with a skin desease (leprosy?). The intervention of Aaron with Moses and subsequently, of Moses with YHWH, thanks to which Miriam's "leprosy" is limited to seven days (vv. 11-14), illustrates and confirms the hierarchical relationship between the three leaders which has just been proclaimed by YHWH.

   The plea initiated by Miriam for shared responsibility and equal prophetic authority (Brenner 1985, 53) functions in Numbers 12 as an excuse for confirming the unique position of Moses once more. As such, this story fits into the description of the the role of Moses (discussed in 2.A. above in connection with Exodus 15). There too a tradition which increased Moses' role at the expense of Aaron and, particularly, Miriam's is probably secondary and later. The way

Miriam is "muted" in the Numbers story is a striking example of the male historiographic practice of reducing women's traditions to silence through recourse to the assistance of a male God.

B. Soothsaying

In addition to the prophetesses discussed above, we also come across another mention of "prophesying women" in Ezekiel 13.17 (*mtnb'wt*).The text denies that these women speak to or in the name of YHWH; they prophesy "from their own heart/view". It is against such self-generated forms of prophecy that Ezekiel has to place his own prophecy, which is in YHWH's name.

> Woe to the women who sew bands over all the joints of the hand
> and who make veils for the head of each figure
> in order to hunt for souls
> Are you hunting the souls of my people
> to keep souls alive for you
> You desecrate Me among My people
> for a couple of handfuls of barley
> and for a couple of pieces of bread
> to let souls die which should not die
> and to bring souls to life that should not live
> Because you lie to My people
> those who listen to lies (Ezek 13.18-19).

From this complaint we can deduce that it concerns women who made a living as professional necromancers and soothsayers (see Ezek 13.23). The picture that this text sketches of their prophetic activity is that of "a seance, in which a group of soothsayers, with the help of secret cords and veils, try to get in touch with the 'spirits of the dead'" (van der Toorn 1987, 117). People imagined the souls of the dead as "fluttering (birds)" (*lprḥwt*), as can be gleaned from Ezekiel 13.20. For this reason, perhaps, the speech of the spirits of the dead, or of spirit raisers, in two passages in Isaiah (8.19 and 29.4) is characterized as "chirping" (*spsp*) and "cooing", or "murmuring" (*hgh*) (TWAT 1, 144).

Over and against this "prophetic" (re)presentation of affairs stands the story in 1 Samuel 28. The impression this story generates of the appearance and speech behaviour of soothsayers who specialized in raising spirits is quite different. There is no mention of the magical aids and rituals listed in Ezekiel 13.17-23. Those probably reflect a later practice which developed under the influence of

Babylonian usage (Brenner 1985, 74-75, Zimmerli 1969, 281-299). There is no talk of ''chirping'' and of ''cooing''; and the spirit of the dead (*'wb*) appealed to actually materializes but is visible only to the woman who ''causes him to rise'' as an old man ''wrapped in a mantle''. The sober narrative style used in 1 Samuel 28 activates the suspicion that this text supplies a highly stylized, thus hardly trustworthy, picture of the phenomenon of raising spirits. Perhaps this sobriety can be construed as polemic, incorporated in the narrative text, against this phenomenon (Beuken 1978). Goitein does not concur. He considers it very probable, at least in part on the grounds of his study of the necromancer (*musafileh*) among Yemenite Jews, that the story about the raiser of spirits (*bᶜlt ʾwb*) from Endor is a sample presentation of the performance and, particularly, of the speech style of this kind of woman, who was to be found in ancient Israel regularly (see also TWAT I, 145).

> The story of the witch of Endor has always surprised me by the *prosaicness* of its style. The witch does not speak in hints or riddles or poetic meter, as we might expect from one who gives oracles in the name of a dead seer. As far as I am aware, most scholars see here a later literary hand. And yet the sheer factuality which distinguishes the style of the witch of Endor is found in the oracles of the modern *musafileh*. She is asked what she sees and what the dead person told her, and she answers in simple prose and with a straightforwardness which admits of no ambiguity. It seems to me that this comparison gives us a proper appreciation of the meaning of the received text (Goitein 1988, 15).

In order to illustrate and evaluate the ''*prosaicness*'' of which Goitein speaks as characteristic of the language of soothayers, I shall now reproduce in translation the dialogue between king Saul and the raiser of spirits from Endor. Saul, in the greatest despair and unrecognizably disguised, has arranged to have recourse to her.

> He said
>> Tell me through the spirit of a dead person (*'wb*)
>> and raise for me whom I shall tell you
> The woman said to him
>> See, you know yourself what Saul has done
>> how he has turned out all the spirit raisers (*'bwt*)
>> and the Soothsayers from the face of the earth
>> Why are you setting a snare for my soul to kill me
> Saul swore to her by YHWH
>> As truly as YHWH lives
>> Blame for this affair will certainly not attach to you
> The woman said

Who shall I raise for you
He said
   Raise Samuel for me
The woman saw Samuel and she cried with a loud voice
The woman said to Saul
   Why have you cheated me
   You are Saul
The king said to her
   Do not fear but what do you see
The woman said to Saul
   A godly being see I coming up from the earth
He said to her
   What is his appearance
She said
   An old man comes up
   and he is wrapped in a mantle
Then Saul knew that it was Samuel
and he knelt with his face to the ground and bowed himself
(1 Sam 28.8b-14).

After the conversation Saul has with Samuel without the intermediacy of the woman, a conversation which has disastrous consequences for Saul, the woman offers him a meal so that he can regain his strength. The tone in which she speaks to her ''client'', meanwhile unmasked as the king, is then different. As a ''wise woman'' who is giving her king advice, she now refers to herself with the polite formula, ''your servant''.

The woman came to Saul
and saw that he was frightened to death[39]
She said to him
   Behold your servant has listened to your voice
   I have placed my soul in the palm of my hand[40]
   and listened to the words you spoke to me
   Now therefore listen to the voice of your handmaid
   I shall set a morsel of bread before you
   Eat so that there may be strength in you
   as you go on your way
(1 Sam 28.21-22).

---

[39] For this translation of *nbhl m'd*, literally: ''(was) terrified'', see Beuken 1978, 12. ''The root of the verb *bhl* can indeed refer to the fright with which people react when an unexpected event enters their life, but often, more seriously, it marks their reaction to a sudden confrontation with death; in a word, that fright in which the grip of death on man becomes visible (Ex 15.15; Lev 26.16; Isa 13.8; 21.9; 65.23; Ps 30.8; 78.33; 104.29)''.

[40] I.e. ''I have risked my life''.

Quite apart from the question as to whether or not there is here "a representative presentation" of affairs, the way in which the soothayer-necromancer from Endor is shown in this story strengthens our respect for those practising the profession (Brenner 1985, 73-74; *contra* Beuken 1978). The negative perspective which informs the prophetic texts mentioned above thus acquires a valuable complement. The words the woman speaks demonstrate her professional competence, businesslike approach and considerate manner. They also afford a penetrating image of the fear the practise of this profession, reviled by the prophets of YHWH and forbidden by the Law, could bring with it for those who practised it.

To avoid misunderstandings, the form of prophecy known as "fortune telling" or "soothsaying" was not the realm of women only.[41] Nonetheless, it seems legitimate to suspect that women practised this and related activities, such as wizardry, on a relatively large scale. One explanation is, that men probably had greater possibilities for carrying out such activities in a setting recognized as legitimate. Brenner states that a number of magical practices were incorporated into Israelite religion and became the duty of priest and prophet. This endowed men with much more scope than women to carry out magical tasks within the framework of institutionalized religion (Brenner 1985, 70). Van der Toorn also derives the relatively broader participation of women in activities like sorcery and soothsaying from their extremely marginal position in official religion. He uses the phrase "popular religion" in his discussion of these phenomena. Popular religion is formed as a reaction to and compensation for what is permitted or not permitted by official religion. It consists of

> (...) intuitions and convictions, sometimes laid down in stories and teachings, experiences regarded as religious, and a number of religious rituals performed in groups (van der Toorn 1987, 106).

In terms of Showalter's cultural model, we can represent van den Toorn's description of the link between official (institutionalized)

---

[41] In Leviticus 20.27 both male and female necromancer or soothsayer are threatened with death. In Deuteronomy 18.9-14 those who practise all sorts of magical activities are addressed solely in male terms and condemned. The same applies to Leviticus 19.31 and 20.6. From Ezekiel 13.17-23 and 1 Samuel 28 it can be assumed, however, that a certain form of spirit-raising was particularly, or maybe exclusively, practised by women (Goitein 1988, 15).

religion and popular religion in ancient Israel as follows. Both religious strata relate to one other as a dominant to a "muted" culture. The dominant religion officially condemned popular religion, to the point of sometimes literally "muting" it. In practice, however, the latter was mostly, albeit secretly, tolerated. Thus Popular religion which flourished in the shadow of official religion offered many women possibilities for developing their abilities, possibilities that were denied to them in official religion (see also Rollin 1983). The Soothsayer/necromancer from Endor supplies us with an illustration of the way in which women exploited this narrow escape.

5. LOVE SONGS AND SONGS OF HARLOTS

A. Love Songs

In spite of women's marginal position within institutional religion and their *"complete exclusion from the Temple cult"* (Goitein 1988, 15),[42] there is a biblical reference to a festival in honour of YHWH, in which women played a prominent part.

> They said
>   Behold there is a festival for YHWH in Shiloh every year
> (. . .)
> And they commanded the sons of Benjamin
>   Go and lie in wait in the vineyards
>   Watch
>   and behold when the daughters of Shiloh come out
>   to dance in dances
>   Then come out of the vineyards
>   and abduct for yourself every man his woman from the daughters of Shiloh
>   and go to the land of Benjamin (Judg 21.19-21).

Symbolically, our quest for traces of women's traditions in the Hebrew Bible reveals that the only explicit mention of a women's annually repeated festival is framed by, and embedded within, a story about the violent kidnapping of maidens. With a view to an attempt to reconstructing the normal state of affairs during this

---

[42] We can probably infer that there might have been some room for women on the fringes of the temple cult from the passages about "the women who served at the entrance to the tabernacle of the congregation" (Ex 38.8 and 1 Sam 2.22). See also Bird 1987, 406 and 419; Winter 1987, 56-65.

festival, Goitein first connects the details of the text in Judges with a passage from the Mishna (M. Ta'anit 4.8). There is a description therein of how the girls of Jerusalem went out annually on the fifteenth day of the month Ab and on the Day of Atonement to dance and sing in the vineyards, inviting young men to "make their choice" (see also De Vaux 1961, II, 447). Texts like Jeremiah 31.3-4, Hosea 2.17 and Isaiah 5.1 are, in Goitein's view, biblical references to the festival mentioned in Judges 21.19. We can conclude from those prophetic traditions that the maidens' dance round the vineyards was traditionally accompanied by the singing of love songs.

> I give her her vineyards from there
> And the valley of Achor shall be an entrance of hope
> And she sings there in answer as in the days of her youth
> as on the day of her coming up out of the land of Egypt
> (Hos 2.17/15).

> Let me sing for my beloved
> a song of my beloved about his vineyard (Isa 5.1).

By connecting these passages with a text from the Song of Songs, Goitein arrives at the following reconstruction of the course of events during this "feast for YHWH" in ancient Israel:

> If the dance of the maidens on the day of the Lord is intended to glorify the fruitfulness of the orchards—and perhaps also to assist in their growth, like the synagogue prayers for rain—then the "dance of the camps" (Songs 7:1/6:13) which comes after it, the camp of the girls on the one side and that of the young men on the other, served the eternal social purpose of finding a mate (Goitein 1988, 19).

The creation of the Song of Songs, "or more exactly, [the creation of] those chapters of it in which the woman is the speaker, the thinker and the actor" (Goitein 1988, 19) is due to this centuries-old tradition, . In other words women in ancient Israel, just as in Sumer and Egypt and in contrast to Arabia, were "*creator[s] of love poetry*". The important role which nature plays in Hebrew love songs finds its origin in the vineyard songs. One innovation worth noting is that, although the maidens come out in groups for the "feast of YHWH", the I persona in the love songs in the Song of Songs dreams that she wanders *alone* with her beloved through the fields and the vineyards (see, for instance, SoS 7.10-13).

Goitein further states that other songs from the Song of Songs can be classified as "formal wedding songs". Examples of this genre are the songs, probably a parody on the "female matchmaker's exaggerated, overpraising description of the proposed mate" (Goitein 1988, 20), in which a woman's body is praised (SoS 4.1-7; 6.4-10 and 7.2-10/1-9); and the same applies to the summons to the bridesmaids, as for example in the Song of Songs 3.11. The singing of this and other love songs during the preparation for a wedding and the celebration of the wedding itself, which lasted for seven days (see Judg 14.12), served for women as time fillers and a time structuring device. Meanwhile males acted similarly: "At the wedding of Samson the 'friends' spent the time solving riddles" (Goitein 1988, 20).

The Dream Sequences

If Goitein is right in his assumption that (a great number of) the songs from the Song of Songs are the creations of women, then we are here confronted for the first time with a collection of texts which reflect women's views in a relatively direct and expansive way. Moreover, there are in the Song of Songs regular occurrences of a dialogue between women—the I persona and the daughters of Jerusalem. Can the Song of Songs be interpreted as a relatively undamaged product of Israelite women's culture? Such a hypothesis stands in opposition to prevailing interpretations of the Song of Songs, according to which this text need not necessarily be ascribed to Solomon (see SoS 1:1) but is, nevertheless, attributed to (a) male poet(s).[43] In recent years various scholars have engaged in a renewed search for female authorship of the Song of Songs. Brenner (1985, 46-50) originally takes up an extremely careful position in respect to this possibility. She suggests that the markedly large number of texts in which a woman's voice is speaking could indicate that the final author/editor of the Song of Songs must have been a woman. But since no further proofs can be advanced for such a hypothesis, she limits herself to the question of to what extent certain poems

> (. . .) are not only spoken by a woman or women, but also reflect a woman's emotions and world in such a manner that no man is likely to have written them (Brenner 1985, 49).

She thinks that the two "dream sequences" (SoS 3.1-4 and 5.1-7)

---

[43] For an excellent survey of the various theories concerning the authorship and the date of the Song of Songs, see Pope 1977.

can be considered examples of such texts. In these poems the female I persona dreams that she searches for her beloved. In the first poem she is successful, in the second her search is in vain.

> Upon my bed by night
> I sought him whom my soul loves
> I sought him but I found him not
> Let me arise now and go round about the city
> in streets and in squares
> I will seek him whom my soul loves
> I sought him but I found him not
> They found me the watchmen
> who go round about the city
> He whom my soul loves have you seen him
> Scarcely had I passed them
> when I found him whom my soul loves
> I grasped him and would not let him go
> until I had brought him into my mother's house
> into the room of her who was pregnant with me (SoS 3.1-4).

> I sleep but my heart is awake.
> The voice of my beloved he knocks
>   Open up to me my sister my friend
>   my dove my perfect one
>   for my head is full of dew
>   my locks (full of) drops of the night
> I have taken off my garment
> how should I put it on again
> I have bathed my feet
> how should I soil them again
> My beloved put his hand through the hole
> My innermost being was excited for him
> I arose to open up for my beloved
> My hands dripped with myrrh
> my fingers with liquid myrrh
> upon the handles of the bolt
> I opened up for my beloved
> but my beloved had turned and gone
> My soul went out to his word
> I sought him but I found him not
> I called him but he gave no answer
> They found me the watchmen who go round about the city
> they beat me they wounded me
> they took off my wrap
> the watchmen of the walls (SoS 5.2-7).

With an appeal to Pusin (quoted in Pope 1977, 133-134), according to whom the conflicts which figure in these poems, the contents and

the symbols are typically female, Brenner too is of the opinion that
the dream scenes express female desires and fears. The second poem
exemplifies the inner conflicts and concrete dangers which patriarchal emphasis on virginity causes women. Passages such as Song of
Songs 1.2-6 and 5.10-16 are, according to her, "so essentially female that a male could hardly imitate their tone and texture successfully" (Brenner 1985, 50). For her one important difference between the male and the female view of love, as expressed in the Song
of Songs, is not so much the openness with which sexuality and
erotic desire are discussed—both lovers excel in that—as the lack of
"humour" which is characteristic of the female-attributed texts. By
"humour" she means the "rather hilarious male ribaldry" of the
Song of Songs 7.1-10, in which men sing to the dancing Shulam-
mite. Such "humour" is absent from Song of Songs passages which
are asigned to a woman's voice or women's voices. These texts assigned to females impart the impression that, for women, love is a
serious emotion. Brenner explains this difference by citing the
stereotypic notion that, for women, love is a "*raison d'être*", whereas
men busy themselves with other matters as well. If this explanation,
which Brenner herself puts into perspective in later publications (see
below), were valid then the term "essentially female" (Brenner
1985, 50) should be discarded entirely. Ultimately, there is every
reason to view the difference indicated as a social (gender) construct
rather than a symptom of a constitutional sex difference.

A Dialogue Between Women

Jonneke Bekkenkamp's hypothesis (1984; 1986; Bekkenkamp and
van Dijk 1987) concerning the (original) authorship of the Song of
Songs concurs, albeit for other arguments, with Goitein's. She
postulates, through a comparison with mediaeval female poetry and
specifically the Portuguese "Cantigas de amigo" investigated by
Lemaire (R.Lemaire 1981a, 1981b, 1986; 1987b), that the Song of
Songs as a whole is a women's song. A woman converses therein
with other women, the daughters of Jerusalem, about her absent
love and her desire for him.

> In the cantigas the beloved is often absent. The desire for him and the
> dream of seeing him again, or the fact that they were together in the
> past, is central. The beloved is also absent in the Song of Songs. Take,
> for example, the first part of Song of Songs 5: in the woman's dream
> he is practically, physically present, but once she gets up he is gone.

The looking forward to seeing him again can be heard for instance in
   Hear! my beloved!
   See! there he comes!... SoS 2.8;
and the dream of a previous occasion when they were together [can
be heard] in passages like SoS 2.6/8.3,
   His left hand is under my head
   his right hand embraces me ...
The song in which she sings of his beauty, the second part of the Song
of Songs 5, in contrast to the songs in which he sings of her beauty,
is therefore also in indirect speech (Bekkenkamp 1986, 73-74).

Other similarities between the female European lyric and the Song
of Songs, pointed out by Bekkenkamp, include themes like the dying
of love, or being sick with love (SoS 2.5); sleeplessness (SoS 3.1-2,
5.2); the continual presence of eroticism; the woman's blackness
(SoS 1.5-6); the frequent (seven times!) mention of the mother as
against the fact that the father is not even mentioned once; the
prevalence of woman's initiative; and the mutuality, enhanced by
an absence of power struggle, of the lovers' relationship.

Bekkenkamp's study can be compared with Rabin's (1973-74), to
which it shows conspicuous similarities. Rabin draws an extensive
analogy between the Song of Songs which, according to him, was
composed at the time of King Solomon, and the Šangam poetry of
the Tamils (of the same period). In both forms of poetry -

a. The woman is the main character, and she expresses her desire
for the beloved quite openly.

b. Nature plays a considerable role in the imagery of the songs.
There are recurrent references to phenomena of growth and renewal, which constitute the background against which the emotional
life of the lovers is realized.

c. The beloved—a person or a dream figure—speaks with male
aggression, whereas the woman readily expresses her desire. She
longs for her beloved, who is a long way off and comes near her in
her dreams only. She is aware of the fact that her desire is at odds
with social norms, giving rise to contempt or even agressiveness
(SoS 8.1; 5.7).

d. The theme of conflict between the world of men and the world
of women is much in evidence. In the Song of Songs the world of
men is represented by "King Solomon", who is surrounded by his
soldiers and is afraid of the night (SoS 3.7-8), who has many women
and concubines (SoS 6.8), and is involved in economic affairs (SoS
8.11). These values of Solomon's are disputed or mocked at: his

military power is of less value that the crown his mother (!) places on his head on his wedding day. The queens and concubines must give way to the heroine of the Song (SoS 6.8-9), who says to Solomon disdainfully that he can keep his money for himself (SoS 8.12).

e. The girl in love speaks to other women. In Tamil love poetry she speaks to her confidant and her mother; in the Song of Songs— to the "daughters of Jerusalem" and, in addition, she mentions her mother or her beloved's mother more than once.

It would therefore appear, for Rabin too, that the male beloved is largely absent (as a subject) from the Song of Songs (see c. above). He infers this from passages like the Song of Songs 2.17, 4.6-8 and 8.14. The biblical text, then, bears the hallmarks of a "woman's fantasy". It is striking, for example, that the woman-in-the-text not only regularly speaks of her beloved, but also presents him as speaking within her imagination (see, for example, SoS 2.10 et seq.; 5.2), whereas the reverse does not occur.

> A case could be made out for the theory that everything the lover says is imagined by her, even if this is not expressly stated (Rabin 1973-74, 219).

And yet, Rabin does not regard the Song of Songs as a creation of (a) female poet(s). On the grounds of the similarities he perceives between Tamil love poetry and the Song of Songs, he ascribes the composition of the Song of Songs to a male author. During his caravan travels to Southern Arabia and Southern India this presumed male author would have become acquainted with the love songs composed by Tamil women. Their songs reflect a society in which young men are presumably required to leave their homee in search of fortune, whereas the women are left behind. Inspired by the desire of Tamil women, which can be heard in the songs and which he regarded as exemplary of human desire for God, the male poet Rabin postulates transported this poetic model from the secular sphere into the Song of Songs. Thus, the Song of Songs has been composed—its model notwithstanding—as a contribution to the religious wisdom literature of Israel.

In spite of Rabin's less than plausible attempt to preserve the view, current from ancient times, concerning the male authorship of the Song of Songs and its allegorical meaning, his analysis, like Bekkenkamp's, contains a number of interesting observations. The interpretation of the Song of Songs in the light of other products of women's culture opens one's eyes to specific characteristics of this poetry, and one's ears to the voices of the women-in-the-text; voices that, in the prevailing interpretations, have so often been "muted".[44]

Unconventional Imagery

One of the unique features of the Song of Songs, to which Meyers (1986) draws attention, is the unconventional imagery of the woman in a number of passages. We come across female images from the military male world like, for instance, Song of Songs 4.4, where a woman's neck is compared to a well-protected defence tower (see also SoS 7.4 and 8.9-10), alongside associations which link women with wild animals like lions and leopards (SoS 4.8). Meyers postulates that such reversal of traditional sex stereotypes fits into the world evoked in the Song of Songs. This world, in contrast to the rest of the Hebrew Bible where an androcentric perspective predominates, can be characterized as gynocentric. This is apparent not only from the prominent role women play in this text. The fact that there is talk of the "house of my mother" twice (SoS 3.4 and 8.2) can also be regarded as significant in this respect.

> In the light of the importance of the concept of "father's house" in Israelite society and the frequent use of that phrase in the Hebrew Bible, the appearance of "mother's house" startles the reader. The normal masculine-oriented terminology for family and/or household derives from lineage concerns, from descent and property transmission reckoned along patriarchal lines. But here in the Song we encounter a situation devoid of such concerns. Perhaps, then, it is no accident that without the public orientation of lineage reckoning, the internal functional aspect of family and home life is rightly expressed by "mother's house" rather than by "father's house" (Meyers 1986, 219).

Meyers typifies the Song of Songs as a product of popular culture, "a compendium of love songs arising from the non-official and non-public arena of daily life" (Meyers 1986, 221). She avoids the term "women's culture" but does underline the fact that, in non-urban popular cultures, women rarely played a subservient role; on the

---

[44] For a keen analysis of this aspect of the current interpretation of the Song of Songs, see Bekkenkamp 1984. For recent examples of the Song of Songs read as a "male fantasy", see Landy 1983; Goulder 1986.

contrary: theirs was a prominent, even dominant one. Thanks to the Song of Songs we are shown a glimpse of this world in biblical times (although further specification of time and place is, of course, impossible to determine).

Double Voice

Obviously, irrefutable proof that the Song of Songs is originally, or perhaps even in its final form, a product of women's culture cannot be supplied by our discussion. Nevertheless, a number of important arguments has been advanced. Beyond that, it is has become clear once again that presenting the question about female authorship and female voices in the biblical texts opens new perspectives on it. I would now like to explore a little further what Rabin perceives as a conflict between men's world and women's world, since it seems appropriate to reopen the question at this point. In terms of Showalter's cultural model a "double voice" can and should be discerned in the Song of Songs. However gynocentric the world created in these songs is, the dominant world is still clearly present— whether in the form of watchmen, or brothers, or in the statements of the beloved (be they imaginary or actual). The woman-in-the-text does not permit herself to be silenced by it nonetheless. She undergoes the violent treatment of the watchmen without protest (Song 5.2-7) at her second search for her beloved, but in no way does she return home shamefaced or repentant. Determined to find her beloved, she calls for the assistance of the daughters of Jerusalem:

> I adjure you daughters of Jerusalem
> If you find my beloved
> What will you tell him
> That I am sick with love (SoS 5.8).

The "daughters" then ask the woman what is so extraordinary about her beloved. She answers their question by giving an extensive description of his appearance, after which they offer to go out together and search for him.[45]

In the Song of Songs 1.5-7 the female I persona resists the beauty ideal of the daughters of Jerusalem—thus also that of her beloved, who prefers to compare her with white flowers—and her guardian-

---

[45] I agree with Marcia Falk (1982, 71-79) that the Song of Songs 5.2-6.3 is a "composite poem" which is best read as a unified, continuous "story".

brothers' ideas concerning her chastity with the proud cry:

Black am I and fair[46]
daughters of Jerusalem
like the tents of Kedar
like the robes of Solomon
Do not look reprovingly at my blackness
because the sun has browned me.

My mother's sons snort against me
They made me the guardian of the vineyards
The one that is my own my vineyard I have not guarded.

The transition from "vineyards" in the literal sense to "vineyard" as a metaphor for female sexuality is typical of the Song of Songs. The "garden", and often the "vineyard", serve therein both as places where the lovers linger but often, and simultaneously, as a metaphor for the woman (see, for instance, Alter 1985, 185-203; Falk 1982, 88-106; Trible 1978, 144-165). The quoted passage demonstrates how the woman in the Song of Songs conforms somewhat to the dominant worldview. She accepts the traditional symbolism of the landscape for female sexuality as natural. But, concurrently, she gives her own interpretation of it: the vineyard which she had to guard so assiduously in keeping with the standards of her brothers, in other words her own "vineyard", she guarded not.

Similarly, in the Song of Songs 8.10 the "little sister" parodies and challenges her brothers' words, according to which she should be an impregnable fortress:

We have a little sister
She has no breasts
What shall we do with our sister
on the day when she is spoken for
If she be a wall
we shall build a battlement of silver upon her
If she be a door
we shall block her off with a beam of cedar.

I am a wall
My breasts are its towers
Thus I am in his eyes
as one who finds peace (SoS 8.8-10).

---

[46] Like Falk (1982) and Bekkenkamp (1984), I read *w* here as as straight forward conjunction, not as an adversativus.

The patriarchal care for and valuation of virginity, which is also to be heard in the words of the beloved,

A garden locked is my sister bride
an wave locked
a spring sealed (SoS 4.12),

is apparently not shared by the woman/women's voices in the Song of Songs (see also SoS 8.1-3). Significantly, these bold criticisms of androcentric morality frame the Song of Songs: the first passage (SoS 1.7) is placed near its beginning, while the second (SoS 8.8-10) almost concludes it. This is a reversal of the normal state of affairs, whereby women's culture is contained by and subsumed under the dominant (basically male) culture.

Finally, a marvellous example of the possibility of hearing a "double voice" in a passage from the Song of Songs which, at first sight, seems to give no reason for so doing is given by Brenner (1990). She shows that the Song of Songs 7.1-10/2-11 can easily be read as a parody on the *wasf* genre. In normal circumstances the songs of this genre describe the beloved's body from top to toe (see SoS 4.1-7; 5.10-16; 6.4-7). The reverse obtains here. Moreover, the language and the images appear, when compared to the other *wasfs*, to be much more daring (see for example verse 2/3), whereas the picture of the woman which the passage evokes is more desirable than charming. Is this song indeed, as Brenner earlier stated, a typical example of "rather hilarious male ribaldry" (Brenner 1985, 50)? The speakers in this text are unmistakably men. But just imagine, she says, that they are women who, for instance during the preparation for a wedding, sing this song in exclusive female company? The *wasf* in the Song of Songs 7 then constitutes not only a parody of the genre, but also a satire on the male view of women expressed therein. In that case the tables are turned: it is not so much the woman in-the-text who is the object of hilarity but, rather, the men who sing to her.

Brenner's reading is inspired by the fact that she has meanwhile recognized the possibility of reading the Song of Songs as a whole (or, at the very least, the greater part of it; see also Brenner 1989) as a women's song. Moreover, her interpretation links up with the tendency Rabin has perceived in the Song of Songs to poke fun at certain manifestations of male behaviour. Her suggestion to hear a "double voice" in the Song of Songs 7 is therefore fully defensible.

B. Songs of Harlots

In ancient Israel, even prostitutes had their own repertoire of songs. This can be inferred from Isaiah 23.16,

> Take a lyre go round about the city
> harlot long forgotten
> Play beautifully sing a lot
> so that you may be remembered again.

Goitein writes that two biblical passages give us an idea of what harlots' songs might have been like. These are the words of the "strange woman" to the young man in Proverbs 7.14-18 (discussed in 3.B above), and a quotation from Hosea 2. In the latter passage, where the relationship between YHWH and Israel is presented as a marital relationship, the I persona puts into the mouth of his "adulterous" and "whoring" wife, the following text:

> Let me go after my lovers
> the givers of my bread and my water
> my wool and my flax
> my oil and my drinks (Hos 2.7).

Goitein finds it remarkable that the prophets, in spite of their avid use of the harlot's image in their complaints against Israel's sins, are quite reticent about the number of words that they allow Israel, the metaphoric harlot. Against this he sets the Song of Songs, which is certainly and largely comprised of Israelite women's songs but which, according to him, has been committed to writing as an allegorized image of the relationship between God and Israel. In the last text Israel, in her capacity as YHWH's true lover, speaks extensively.

I would like to draw attention to some aspects not mentioned by Goitein concerning the texts which he characterizes as songs of harlots or prostitutes. (Since Goitein does not distinguish between the functional terms "prostitute", "harlot", and "whore", and since neither the Hebrew term *znh* nor colloquial usage differentiate them [see Brenner, chapter IV.2 below], we will assume that the Hebrew term somehow covers "prostitute" as well.) Prostitution is a matter of commercial "love". By definition, then, both texts cited reveal a financial or material motive for prostitution. The woman who prostitutes herself needs lovers in order to provide for herself

(Hos 2.7/4),[47] or in order to meet an incidental obligation (Prov 7.14). In both cases, the woman's need is not recognized as valid motivation for her song. Further, both texts show considerable similarity to the language of the Song of Songs. Proverbs 7.14-18 can justifiably be read as a pastische of phrases borrowed from the Song of Songs (Bekkenkamp 1986, 86-89), whereas Hosea 2.7/4 can be compared to the Song of Songs 5.1 (Van Selms 1964-65, 88). But the language of the Song of Songs is perverted in both. In Proverbs 7 and Hosea 2 the words of the woman prostituting herself are embedded in the monologues of the I personas who act as primary speaking voices thereof. The speech assigned to the woman in-the-text is called "scandalous" (Hos 2.7/4) or deceptive (Prov 7.10-13) in advance by those I personas (van Dijk-Hemmes 1987 and 1988). I have dealt with the tendentious manner in which the Song of Songs is "quoted" in Hosea 2 elsewhere (van Dijk-Hemmes 1989b, 1989c). For the moment it will suffice to conclude that prostitutes' repertoire in ancient Israel must have consisted largely of, or was closely related to, Israelite love songs, similar to the ones collected in the Song of Songs. One supposes that the erotic contents of the latter songs will have matched the contents of the former.

6. LAMENTS AND RITUALS OF LAMENT

A. Laments

Much like the ascription of love songs collected in the Song of Songs to Solomon (SoS 1.1), the laments preserved in the Hebrew Bible have mainly been attributed to male authors. And yet the practice of the lament genre was not in the hands of men only, and probably not even primarily so. In 2 Chronicles 35.25 male and female singers sing laments after the death of Josiah. From Zechariah 12.11-14 we can conclude together with De Vaux that the lament for the dead, as part of the mourning ceremony, was performed by men and women in separate groups (De Vaux 1961, I 116; see also Winter 1987, 50 n. 254). However, in a number of texts only women are mentioned in this connection. In David's lament for Saul and Jonathan "the daughters of Israel" are called to weep for Saul

---

[47] For an illuminating discussion of the marginal position of prostitutes in ancient Israel see Bird 1989a, 1989b.

(2 Sam 1.24); and in Ezekiel 32.16 there is talk of a lament that has to be sung by the "daughters of the people". A passage from Jeremiah 9 is especially informative:

> Consider your ways
> and call for the mourning women to come
> Send for the skilful (lit. "wise") women to come
> Let them make haste and raise a wailing over us
> so that our eyes run down with tears
> and our pupils drip with water
> For a voice, a wailing is heard from Zion
> > How are we destroyed
> > utterly shamed
> > For we have left the land
> > For they have cast down our dwellings
> Yea, hear O women the word of YHWH
> and let your ear receive the word of His mouth
> Teach your daughters a lament
> and let each woman teach her neighbour a dirge
> > Yea death has climbed up into our windows
> > It has entered our palaces
> > It cut off the small child from the street
> > and the young men from the squares.
> Speak—so says the word of YHWH -
> > The corpse of man must fall
> > like dung on the field
> > like a bundle of ears behind the reaper
> > and no one shall gather them (Jer 9.6-21/17-22).

It appears from this passage that the singing of laments was a trade which had to be studied and was often transmitted from mother to daughter. "Women who took up mourning as a vocation had to learn the formulae of their trade" (Brenner 1985, 37). During their appearances at funerals, and on similar occasions, the wailing women had to be able to draw on a reservoir of suitable texts on the one hand and, on the other hand, to possess the ability to suit these to the circumstances. Thus they gave the public the opportunity to express their emotions. It is to this function of emotional release which wailing women performed that an appeal is made in Jeremiah 9 (Goitein 1988, 25).

Brenner states that the song quoted in Jeremiah 9 about personified death, who "climbed into our windows", is an example of a formula, borrowed from a Ugaritic myth, which was part of the repertoire of wailing women. Interestingly, this song reads like an intertext and source of associations when compared with the passages about "women at the window": Sisera's mother (Judg 5.28); Jezebel (2 Kgs 9.30); and the I persona in Proverbs 7. In all three cases there is a presence of threatening death. The expression "through the window" can also be seen as a "vivid metaphor for the way in which death enters a building" (Lorenz, quoted in Christensen 1984, 402). Against this background the words which the mother of Sisera screams while waiting for her son,

> Why does his chariot tarry in coming
> Why does the clatter of his chariots linger (Judg 5.28),

can be recognized more easily as a lament formula, which must have sounded all too familiar to the ears of ancient Israel's women.

Lady Jerusalem in Lamentations

Goitein assumes that the Book of Lamentations, which is attributed to Jeremiah, contains reminiscences of the traditions of women's laments. He applies this notion particularly to chapters 1, 2 and 4, in which Jerusalem occupies a central role.

> She is addressed as if she were a mother or a virgin girl, or she speaks to herself. What is more, the atmosphere is feminine and women are spoken of a great deal—mothers with their babies, maidens, an abandoned woman and so forth. The environment is that of the inner city, not the field of battle (Goitein 1988, 26-27).

An important feature of the talk of or about Jerusalem in Lamentations 1, not explicitly reported by Goitein, is that this song not only contains the dominant cultural view of a menstruating woman, but that the actual experience of menstruation can also be heard in it (van der Toorn 1987, 48). Jerusalem, the city destroyed and plundered by the Babylonians, is avoided "as one who is unclean" (v. 8); "her uncleanness sticks to the hem of her garment" (v. 9). In verse 11 "Lady Jerusalem", who is compared to a widow, herself expresses her situation as follows:

> See YHWH and behold
> how worthless I have become
> Does it not concern you all (you) who pass by on the road
> Behold and see
> if there is any distress like my distress
> that is done to me
> wherewith YHWH has tormented me
> on the day his anger flared up

He sent fire from on high
into my bones and made it go down
He set a net for my feet
and made me turn back
He gave me over to desolation
all day long to indisposition (Lam 1.11b-13).

My Lord has trampled the winepress
of the young woman the daughter of Judah
Therefore I must weep
My eye my eye streams with water
for a comforter is far from me
who would refresh my soul
My sons have become desolate
So mighty is the foe (Lam 1.15b-16).

In addition to the isolation menstruation brought with it, this passage also depicts a woman mishandled and rejected by her husband. This picture links up with the marriage metaphor developed further in prophetic literature, in which YHWH is represented as the husband of adulterous Israel or Judah or Jerusalem. The various versions of this marriage metaphor (Hos 2; Jer 2-3; Ezek 16 and 23) are all presented and developed from the viewpoint of the (metaphorical) husband, the male I persona in the text. The (metaphorical) wife appears in these texts through H/his eyes (van Dijk-Hemmes 1988; see also 5.B above). In the passage from Lamentations 1 quoted above, the reverse is the case. It is the woman's viewpoint which is the focus of the discourse. Therefore, it is quite possible that Goitein is right in his assumption that "words like these were traditional on the lips of the professional lamenting 'wise women'" (Goitein 1988, 27); and that these words echo the lament of women whose individual situation was comparable to that of "Lady Jerusalem".

B. Rituals of Lament

So far we have discussed appearances of wailing women whereby the wailing is undertaken in the context of burials and, by extension, in the case of national disasters. In addition, we can find a number of indications regarding specific rituals of lamentation carried out by women. We read in Ezekiel 8.14 that the prophet saw women, sitting "at the entrance to the gate of the house of YHWH, to the north", who "wept for the Tammuz". Goitein links this passage with Jeremiah 7.16-20 and 44 (see also Ackerman 1989), in which the honouring of the "Queen of Heaven" is described and attacked on behalf of YHWH, but defended by the people and particularly by women (Jer 44.15-19). The "Queen of Heaven" refers to the Mesopotamian Goddess Ishtar (the Sumerian Inanna) who, upon the death of her beloved Tammuz (Dumuzi), the fertility God, went down to the Underworld and returned therefrom. Women played an important role in the popular religion of this Goddess, which flourished in the ancient Near East. It was customary for women to lament the death of Tammuz at the beginning of the autumn. From Ezekiel 8 we can glean that this ritual—depicted as a "great abomination"—was practised by women in Judah too, and that they occupied a space in the Temple which was set aside for this activity.

In contrast to Goitein van der Toorn does not relate Ezekiel 8.14 to the "Queen of Heaven" passage in Jeremiah, but to Judges 11.40:

> It became a custom in Israel
> that from year to year the daughters of Israel went out
> to retell of the daughter of Jephthah the Gileadite
> four days a year.

Van der Toorn does not regard it likely that the story in Judges 11, which he characterizes as a "cult legend" about the sacrificial death of Jephthah's daughter (see above on Songs of Victory, 2.A), forms the background to the ritual described in verse 40. "Are the secret women's festivities not placed in too innocent a light?" he asks himself. Subsequently, he names three points of contiguity between Ezekiel 8.14 and Judges 11.40:

> In both cases (1) it concerns a ritual lament of (2) a dead person, in the first place a god and in the second a man by (3) women (Van der Toorn 1987, 111).

In regard to Zechariah 12.11, where there is talk of lament for the god Hadadrimmon (who is analogous to Tammuz), van der Toorn suggests once more to view Judges 11.40 as a reference to the ritual lament for Tammuz.

The way van der Toorn (1987: 111) places question marks concerning the attempt of the author of Judges 11 "to answer the why about this annual women's ritual" seems somewhat tendentious. His suggestion to relate Ezekiel 8.14 to this text is not convincing.

The first analogy he draws between Ezekiel 8.14 and Judges 11.40 is not as precise as he would have us believe. In contrast to the women in Ezekiel, the daughters of Israel do not "mourn" (*bkh*) the daughter of Jephthah, but "retell" (*tnh*) her story. The distinction van der Toorn makes in his second point should be defined more closely in a gender-specific sense. The dead person is a *male god* in the first case (Ezek 8.14), while in the second (Judg 11.40) it is a *female person*. In view of these not unimportant differences, it seems plausible that in Judges 11.40 reference is made to quite a different women's ritual than in Ezekiel. The explanation of this ritual should first and foremost be sought for within the context it is placed in.[48]

In the story preceding Judges 11.40 we are confronted with a women's ritual, which lasts for two months and is described by the narrator as follows:

> She went away with her girlfriends
> and wept about (^{c}l) her *btwlym* on (^{c}l) the mountains
> (Judg 11.38b).

Here there is certainly talk of (ritual) lament, since weeping (*bkh*) is explicitly stated. The description links up with the words of the instigator of this ritual, Jephthah's daughter,

> She said to her father
> Let this be done for me
> Leave me alone for two months
> so that I may go away and go deep into (^{c}l) the mountains
> and weep over (^{c}l) my *btwlym*
> I and my girlfriends (Judg 11.37).

Bal (1988b and 1989), in an ingenious form critical analysis, plausibly suggests that this request of Jephthah's daughter refers to a *rite de passage*. It bears the characteristics of language used on the occasion of such rites. The striking use of the preposition ^{c}l, combined with the place the ritual is enacted in (the mountains), together with

---

[48] There is no call to accept Goitein's assumption that the historicity of the story in Judges 11, and of the announcement in v. 40 concerning the annual commemoration ceremony of "a daughter and a father who sacrificed themselves for the general good" (Goitein 1988, 23), should not be doubted. As far as the latter is concerned the father, Jephthah, is not referred to in v. 40 as an object of commemoration. Moreover, neither this verse nor the story that precedes it give any reason for equal valuation of the daughter's sacrificial disposition as against her father's.

the object of the ritual of lament, the *btwlym* of Jephthah's daughter, makes this ritual appear as a confrontation. The so far untranslated *btwlym* is usually rendered "virginity". According to Bal this translation originates from an uncritical adoption of the meaning which the narrator assignes to this term, when he says that Jephthah's daughter "had not known a man" (verse 39). The term *btwlym* is, however, by no means identical with "virginity". It designates the phase in a girl's life, when she becomes sexually ripe (see also Wenham 1972). The social implication of this physical change is that the girl is now marriageable and can thus be "given away". In other words the *btwlh*—the sexually ripe nubile young woman—is in a transitional stage between that of *n'rh*, a young girl whose social status is that of her father's possession, and *'lmh*, a young married woman whose social status is that of her husband's possession. It is this meaning of *btwlym*, this new phase of life which, socially speaking, is a transitional stage fraught with uncertainty, of which Jephthah's daughter is aware as she asks to be left to her own devices for two months. Distancing herself from her father, she wishes to go up into the mountains together with her friends, there "to lament in confrontation with her nubility" (Bal 1988b, 65). The words Jephthah's daughter speaks to her father can, Bal says, be seen by us as a "wandering rock", the remains of female ritual language embedded within a chiefly male discourse.

> The wandering rock is my picture of the remains of the cultural traditions of women which are preserved within the patriarchal culture (Bal 1989, 16).

Peggy Day compares Jephthah's daughter to Iphigenia, the heroine of Greek tragedy, and to the goddess Kore/Persephone. She too concludes that the ritual of Jephthah's daughter is a *rite de passage*. The characteristic "weeping" or "lament" in such rituals implies a recognition of the "death" of one phase of life which stimulates the shift onto its next stage (Day 1989, 60).

In view of the discussion so far, what is the nature of the relationship between (1) the *rite de passage* initiated by Jephthah's daughter, whereby she weeps with her friends about/in confrontation with the stage of life in which she is sexually mature and can thus be given away; and (2) the ritual in which the daughters of Israel sing her praises? It seems obvious that the "praise" constitutes a recollection of the *rite de passage*. Jephthah's daughter is recalled as being the originator of the ritual. In other words, the story of Jephthah's daughter can indeed be characterized as a cult legend—but in a sense other than van der Toorn's. It accounts for the origin of a ritual which marks the transition to a new stage a woman's life. The ritual's origin is introduced within the context of the sacrificial death of Jephthah's daughter. She demands this personal space and time before suffering the fate she herself regards as inevitable. After the ritual, she will not be given away to her future husband. The promise her father has made renders this impossible. She will be "given away" to the God to whom her father owes his success in battle as the price for his victory. The singing of the praise of Jephthah's daughter by the daughters of Israel is given a gender-political connotation by the coupling of women's *rite de passage* with men's war ritual. The verb *tnh*, which means "sing the praise" in the sense of "commemorate" (see also Judg 5.11), should not be understood as an equivalent of the verb "to mourn" but, rather, "to recount in order to keep (her) memory alive". In short, *tnh* here has the meaning of "to perform oral history".

> If the sons of Israel make history by fighting wars and going astray, the daughters of Israel recount the price that such a history requires. What has happened must not be forgotten (Bal 1988b, 67).

To surmise a connection between the lamentation ritual for Tammuz and the ritual described in Judges 11.40 is in no way necessary for a satisfactory explanation of the latter. Neither does such a connection do any justice to the differences between the two texts (Day 1989).

7. Vows and Prayers

By Way of a Prelude

The application of Goitein's method—tracking down biblical references to the literary traditions practised by women, and checking whether their remains have been preserved in the text—has yielded some additional interesting traces of women's texts. Of the four genres—vows, prayers, birth songs, and naming speeches—which will be discussed in the next two sections, Goitein recognizes the prayer genre, but does not discuss the other three.

A. Vows

So far we have twice come across references to vows made by women. The "strange woman" introduced in the exhortation of Proverbs 7 seduces the young man because she "must fulfill (my) vows" (Prov 7.14); and, Lemuel's mother addresses her son as the "son of my vows" (Prov 31.2). That these references point to a practice often cultivated by women in ancient Israel can be gleaned from Numbers 30. The regulation found there is an attempt to limit this popular custom somewhat. Fathers and husbands are given the right to annul vows made by their daughter or wife. This implies that in so doing they could not be held responsible for financial and other consequences thereof. In view of their economically dependent status, daughters and wives were often not in a position to handle the obligations they had taken on by vowing independently. We may gather from Proverbs 7 how women acquired the means for payment when they had made a vow without the knowledge of father or husband.

In Jeremiah 44 the cult of the "Queen of Heaven", largely practised by women, is presented as the fulfilment of vows made to this Goddess (verse 25). In this case, the women expressly state that their actions are backed by their husbands's approval.

> And when we burned incense to the Queen of Heaven
> and poured out libations for her
> Was it without the approval of our husbands
> that we made sacrificial cakes for Her bearing Her image
> and poured out libations to Her (Jer 44.19; cf. 7.18).

The story in 1 Samuel 1 contains an example of a vow formulated by a woman. Read as an intertext for Proverbs 30, it also indicates what the phrase "son of my vow(s)" signifies. The childless Hannah, who has travelled to the shrine of Shiloh with her husband Elkanah for YHWH's annual feast, addresses a prayer to YHWH. Her prayer assumes the shape of a vow.

> She was bitter of soul
> and she prayed to YHWH
> and wept yea wept
> She made a vow and said
>   YHWH of hosts
>   When you look look upon the misery of your servant
>   When you remember me
>   and do not forget your handmaid

> and give your handmaid the seed of men
> Then I will give him to YHWH all the days of his life
> A razor shall not touch his head (1 Sam 1.10-11).

The story in which this vow is embedded indicates that it is more than likely that a woman could initiate a vow without consulting her husband; and that he had to uphold it. The vow formula itself—promising a gift to YHWH *on condition that* the requested object be granted (TWAT V, 261-274)—gives a gripping picture of the way childlessness must have been experienced by women: as misery and humiliation (*ʿny*), as being not "remembered" but "forgotten" by the deity. The misery experienced is so great that the woman in question, rather than offer a sacrifice in exchange for the son requested by her so urgently, is prepared to give this required son once she got him back again to YHWH. Just like Samson's mother is instructed to do, Hannah promises that her son shall remain unshaven, thus dedicated to God. He will be a *nāzîr* (see Num 6). Hannah's vow can be compared with the vow made by Jephthah (Judg 11) but is nevertheless presented in stark contrast to the latter. The vow made by the father costs his daughter, a sacrifice to YHWH, her life. The mother's vow brings about a long and prestigious life for her son who, in his turn, is a sacrifice to YHWH too.

B. Prayers

For women in particular, vows and prayers functioned as an opening for communicating with the deity (Bird 1987, 408-409; van der Toorn 1987, 85-96; Winter 1983, 25-29). Goitein limits his discussion to the prayer genre. Apart from a reference to Genesis 25.22, in which Rebekah "went to consult YHWH" because of her difficult pregnancy, he deals at some length with the passage following Hannah's promise.

> Hannah spoke in her heart
> Only her lips moved
> but her voice was not heard (1 Sam 1.13a).

Hannah did not pray aloud, as customary, but in a whisper. This is considered by Goitein an important innovation.

> Whispered prayer is certainly not "literature" in the ordinary sense of the word. But it is one of the greatest conquests of the human spirit. It is meaningful indeed that it was a woman who created this innovation (Goitein 1988, 21).

In the light of Showalter's cultural model, we can indeed join Goitein in recognizing the innovation attributed to Hannah as "one of the greatest conquests of the human spirit", as a conquest of personal space in a bulwark of the dominant culture. But this also exemplifies Hannah's situation. As a representative of an exceptionally "muted" group of women, the barren Hannah literally puts herself in the position she finds herself in anyway: the position of the silent/silence. Thus she successfully retreats from the control of social and religious authorities—her husband and the priest. She can withdraw into herself, and this she does in order to appeal to YHWH in a prayer which they—the men—literally cannot hear and, therefore, cannot understand.

8. Birth Songs and Naming Speeches

A. Birth songs

This genre is not, as has already been mentioned, referred to by Goitein. Hannah's prayer/song in 1 Samuel 2.1-10 does not feature in his account. This is perhaps justified. Many scholars consider this text a later and somewhat misplaced addition: a "kraftvollen, männliche Psalm" (Hertzberg 1956, 19), or a "song of victory and triumph" (Willis 1973, 142) which does not sound appropriate when put into Hannah's mouth. And yet, Bekkenkamp and I hazard the conjecture that Hannah's song contains elements which are perhaps characteristic of a postnatal thanksgiving song (Bekkenkamp and van Dijk 1987; see also Doornebal 1984). Our arguments are as follows.

1) There are indications in the Bible that women practised a genre of birth songs. After Asher's birth Leah says "By *'šry*, the daughters will call me blessed" (Gen 30.13). The cry "By *'šry*", which is usually translated "to my joy", is according to Patai (1978, 23; 280) a mutilated version of the originally intended "By Asherah". The assistance of this Goddess was called for by women during childbirth (Reed 1949, 80-81; 87). Gray assumes that this applies to ancient Israel as well as the surrounding countries.

> (. . .) at the birth and even at the begetting of a child "skilfull women" were employed, probably to sing and improvise incantations, like the professional keeners whom Jeremiah (9.16ff.) terms hakamoth, "wise women" (Gray 1964, 152).

Leah's cry is probably a reminiscence of a promise made to Asherah during the birth, or a prayer/song of thanksgiving to this Goddess. One example of the post-birth blessing, to which Leah refers in her cry, is to be found in Ruth 4, where the neighbouring women say to Naomi,

> Blessed be YHWH
> who did not allow you to do without a redeemer today
> Let his name be shouted out in Israel
> May he let your vitality return
> and care for you in your old age
> For your daughter-in-law who loves you has given him birth
> she who is better to you than seven sons (Ruth 4.14-15).

The fact that Hannah, after she has weaned her son, travels to the shrine and renders a thanksgiving hymn there, probably indicates a much practised custom. Obviously, the deity whose help is called for before and during pregnancy and birth should be thanked when the process is successfully concluded (see Gen 29.35).

2) The second argument for the supposition that Hannah's song contains characteristics of post-birth thanksgiving derives from the fact that giving birth was (and is) often experienced by women as a struggle for life and against death. It is therefore not surprising that a song of thanksgiving sung on the successful conclusion of this "battle" has the character of a victory song. In an incantation to Marduk (Van der Toorn 1987, 83; Winter 1987, 383-384), giving birth is described in terms of a battlefield, whereby the woman in labour is compared to a war hero:

> As a hero who has striven, there she lies in her own blood.

In Isaiah 42.13 YHWH is represented as a victorious warrior who, on the way to his victory, compares himself to a woman in labour.

> From time immemorial I have been silent
> have kept quiet kept myself under control
> Like a woman in labour I will now scream
> snort and pant at once (Isa 42.14).

In Jeremiah 4 the daughter of Zion is represented as a woman giving birth. Her scream of anguish is like that of a soldier in the throes of death.

> For I hear a voice as of a woman in labour.
> anguish as of one who is giving birth to her first child

The voice of the daughter of Zion gasping for breath
stretching out her hands
Woe is me for my soul gives way to murderers (Jer 4.31).

It is hardly surprising, then, that women experience the successful outcome of their labour as victory. The expression of women's joy in the form of a thanksgiving/victory song has nothing to do with typical "masculinity" (*contra* Herzberg 1956, 19, who reads that into Hannah's song). The typification of Hannah's song as a "kraft-vollen männliche Psalm" is unjustified for another reason as well. In this text strong, aggressive masculinity is derided, just as there is derision in mockery songs. See, for example, verse 9c,

For not through strength does a man become a hero.

See also at the beginning of the song, where the I persona who recites it contrasts the opening of her mouth against her foes with their proud and impudent manner of speaking,

My heart exalts in YHWH
My horn rejoices in YHWH
My mouth opens wide against my enemies
for I rejoice in Your salvation

No one is as holy as YHWH
for there is none beside You
and there is no rock like our God

Do not speak too much
arrogantly arrogantly
Let nothing impudent come forth from your mouth
For YHWH is a God of knowledge
through Him deeds are calculated (1 Sam 2.1-3).

Within the narrative context the song is placed in, we may consider the "enemies" as the society in which barren women are despised. In 1 Samuel 1 this society is personified by the fertile woman Penin-nah. The contrast between the I persona who rejoices in the deliverance YHWH has brought her and her proudly speaking foes is continued in verses 4-5, which are antithetically structured. The reversal of the balance of power, here celebrated in song, culminates in the reversal of fortune meted out to barren and fertile women:

The bow of the heroes is broken
but stumblers surround themselves with power
Those who were satisfied with bread have to hire themselves out

but the hungry may rest for ever/become fat with spoils[49]
The barren has seven children
but she who has many sons wilts (1 Sam 2.4-5).

The passage which follows, where YHWH is presented as the subject to bring about this reversal of personal fortune, shows notable similarities with contemporary birth songs sung by women in the Near East, as Keel (by means of a reference to Granqvist 1950, 35) has shown:

> Hilma Granqvist, die lange als Ärztin im nahen Osten lebte, berichtet, wie Frauen, die ebem ihr erstes Kind geboren hatten, kleine Lieder improvisierten, die etwa folgendem Inhalt hatten:
> "Er bringt zum Leben / und er schickt in den Tod.
> Er macht reich / und er macht arm.
> Er gibt und er verweigert
> Alles kommt von Gott / Lob und Dank sei Gott" (Keel 1980, 198).

The experience of being delivered unto the sovereign power of God, which such a text imparts, is rooted in the experience of bringing forth new life through a life-and-death struggle. This experience may form the background to the comparable passage in Hannah's song:

> YHWH kills and brings life
> He makes people go down to the kingdom of the dead
> and He makes them rise
> YHWH makes poor and He makes rich
> He humiliates and He also elevates
> He makes the poor arise from the dust
> He raises the needy from the dung
> in order to make him sit among the nobles
> and he makes him inherit a seat of honour (1 Sam 2.6-8d).

To conclude. It is clearly possible to read Hannah's song as a women's song, particularly as a song of thanksgiving for giving birth. The fact that this text is assigned to a woman, and the context in which this happens, support this suggestion too. This does not imply that the *Sitz im Text* necessarily agrees with the *Sitz im Leben*. Perhaps Hannah's song has indeed originated in a quite different situation. That, however, has not prevented the author(s) of 1 Samuel from assigning the song to (the fictive) Hannah.

---

[49] The latter translation rests on the fairly general notion that in addition to the common *ḥdl*, "cease", a homonymic *ḥdl* II denotes "be satisfied" (TWAT II, 748-755).

The words with which the prayer/song of Hannah is introduced, "And Hannah prayed", instruct the reader to regard the voice speaking in this text as a woman's voice. When Hannah's song is labelled "masculine", this implies that the *voice of the woman-in-the-text* has been "muted" and transformed into a man's voice.[50] Such a transformation does no justice to the opportunity, offered by the textual context, of seeing Hannah's song—and the joy expressed in it concerning the personal salvation, the experience of trust in YHWH, and the belief that He can reverse the existing balance of power—as an expression of women's experience, expectations and hopes.

B. Naming speeches

The genre here considered is closely allied to the birth song genre discussed above. It could be regarded as a specific variant or sub-genre of the former. Giving a name to a newborn child is often accompanied in the Bible by a declaration of motivation, a so-called naming speech. These naming speeches are mostly constructed as follows: "She called his name X, because she said ... (explanation / motivation for the name)"; or: "She said ... (explanation / motivation), therefore she called his name X." Characteristically, "the speech always consists of a pun which creates a phonetic link between the name and its interpretation" (Pardes 1989, 167).

Puns based on sound play in name-giving are characteristic of oral tradition (Watson 1984, 245). In the Bible a woman or women name(s) a child 27 times; this is far in excess of the occasions on which men do the naming—14 times. Hence, once more, we can plausibly talk about a genre often employed by women.

Naming speeches act, as Ilana Pardes rightly states, as "an im-

---

[50] An interesting interpretation of the voice speaking in the Song of Hannah has been offered by Robert Polzin (1989, 30). According to him there are "at least three voices, each with its own perspectives and multivoiced accents, each cooperating with the other two to form, in Bakhtin's terms, a 'polyphonic composition' that is both harmonious and dissonant, transparent yet opaque, looking backward and forward, full of thematic variations on themes already met or soon to be encountered. The 'chorus' performing this song forms a trio of voices: 1) Hannah, the rejoicing mother; 2) a persona of the exultant king; and 3) the Deuteronomist, the 'author' of the song in its present setting at least. This final voice subtly but powerfully casts a melancholy tone over what is at first glance a psalm of personal and national thanksgiving."

portant means of characterization for women in the Bible'' (Pardes 1989, 165). The giving of a name often tells us more about the giver of the name than about the one who receives it (also Sternberg 1985, 330-331). Thus, the study of this genre allows us (once again) to catch a glimpse of women's worldview in ancient Israel through the views put into words in various naming speeches. It is probably superfluous to state explicitly once more that we, indeed, get a glimpse only. Biblical women who function as givers of names are literary personas, women-in-a-text and, as such, constructs created by their authors. This, however, does not alter the fact that the naming speeches attributed to them were very probably inspired by, possibly even directly derived from, the oral tradition appropriate to the occasion.

The situation **barren women** found themselves in has already been discussed. I would now like to draw attention to a number of naming speeches which have this situation for background. In Genesis 30 Rachel acts as a prototype for the "barren woman". She too, like Hannah in relation to Peninnah, experiences her fertile sister Leah as an adversary. In verse 1 she expresses her despair:

> She said to Jacob
> Give me sons or else I am dead.

Her first naming speeches, on the occasion of the birth of the sons her slave woman Bilha brings into the world, are as follows. She says about the first son,

> God has pleaded my cause (*dnny*)
> He has also listened to my voice
> and given me a son.
> Therefore she called his name Dan (*dn*) (Gen 30.6).

And about the second,

> Wrestlings (*nptwly*) of God I have wrestled with my sister
> Also I have prevailed
> And she called his name Naphtali (*nptly*) (Gen 30.8).

The birth of her first biological son is greeted by Rachel with the words,

> God has removed my disgrace ('*sp*)
> And she called his name: Joseph (*ywsp*) saying
> May YHWH add (*ysp*) to me another son (Gen 30.24).

The condition of barrenness is implicitly characterized in these naming speeches as an injustice and, explicitly, a disgrace and reason for rivalry among women. The name Joseph, according to the double pun used in the last passage, expresses both the removal of the disgrace of infertility and the desire for a another son.

The rivalry between the infertile and fertile woman is doubly emphasized in this story: the first woman is loved by her husband while the second is "hated". The naming speeches of Leah, the **unloved woman,** present a harrowing picture of her equally unenviable position, and her desire for the love and appreciation that giving birth to sons brings with it.

> Leah became pregnant and bore a son (*bn*)
> And she called his name Ruben (*r'wbn*)
> for she said
> > Truly YHWH has looked (*r'h*) on my misery (*bʿnyy*)
> > Truly my husband will now love me (Gen 29.32).

> She became pregnant again and bore a son
> And she said
> > Truly YHWH has heard (*šmʿ*) that I am hated (*śnw'h*)
> > and he has given me this one also
> She called his name Simeon (*šmʿwn*)
> She became pregnant again and bore a son
> And she said
> > Now this time my husband will be attached to me (*yllwh*)
> > for I have borne him three sons
> Therefore she called his name Levi (*lwy*) (Gen 29.33-34).

> And Leah became pregnant once more and bore a sixth son for
> > Jacob
> Leah said
> > God has bestowed me with a pleasant gift
> > This time my husband will extol me (*yzblny*)[51]
> > for I have borne him six sons
> And she called his name Zebulun (*zblwn*) (Gen 30.19-20).

The fact that Leah twice expects the number of sons she has borne to motivate a change in her husband's attitude toward her underlines once more the measure of appreciation a mother of many sons could hope for. The explanation for its lack in this story lies in the

---

[51] For this translation, see TWAT II, 533-534.

fact that Leah, in contrast with Rachel, was not "beautiful of sta-
ture" (or, "beautiful to look at", Gen 29.17).[52]

The story in Genesis 16 illustrates that **making a slave girl
available to the husband**, with a view to allowing her to act as sur-
rogate mother, was no easy task either for the woman in question
or for the slave girl (Bal and others 1984, 27-46; Trible 1984, 8-35).
We can probably glean that also from Leah's naming speech on the
occasion of the birth of her fifth son,

> God has given me my reward ($\acute{s}kry$)
> because I have given my slave girl to my husband
> And she called his name Issachar ($ysskr$) (Gen 30.18).

These examples demonstrate that naming speeches often contain the
characteristic feature of a **prayer of thanksgiving** after birth. This
applies, for instance, also to the naming of Samuel by Hannah.

> She called his name Samuel ($\acute{s}mw\ 'l$)
> For from YHWH I have asked for him ($\acute{s}\ 'ltyw$) (1 Sam 1.20).[53]

The thanksgiving element is explicitly stated in Leah's naming of
Judah.

> This time I will thank ($\ 'wdh$) YHWH
> Therefore I will call him Judah ($yhwdh$) (Gen 29.35).

Two of the naming speeches pronounced by Leah probably contain
reminiscences of prayers of thanksgiving to other gods. Both concern the sons her slave Zilpa has borne for her. The second, which
can be interpreted as an appeal to Ashera and from which the name
"Asher" is derived (Gen 30.13), was already presented in the previous section. The first is as follows.

> By Gad (often translated as "What luck/joy")
> And she called his name Gad (gd) (Gen 30.11).

A deity of this name is mentioned in Isaiah 65.11 too. This God was
worshipped in Canaan, among other things, as the God of good fortune (Patai 1978, 280).

In a number of cases the naming speeches are relevant to the

---

[52] For an analysis of this "typical" reason for rivalry among women see Bal
1987, 68-88; Brenner 1986.

[53] In fact, the motivation does not include a pun on the name of Samuel but on
Saul's (Deurloo/Eykman 1984, 12-13, and many others).

circumstances of the birth. The mother of Jabez relates the name of her son to the distress which accompanied her giving birth to him.

> His mother called his name Jabez (y^cbs) saying
> For I bore him in pain (^csb) (1 Chron 4.9).

Pharoah's daughter motivates the name Moses ($m\check{s}h$), which she gives to the Hebrew child adopted by her, by the words,

> For out of the water I have drawn him ($m\check{s}ythw$) (Exod 2.10).

In 1 Samuel 4.19-22 political occurrences function as explanation/motivation for the child's name. In this grippingly described scene, Eli's daughter-in-law is overtaken by contractions while simultaneously hearing that the Ark of God has been taken by the Philistines, and that her father-in-law and her husband are dead.

> When the time of her death had come
> the women who stood around her said to her
>   Fear not for you have borne a son
> She did not answer
> and she did not take notice
> She called the boy Ichabod ($'y$-$kbwd$) saying
>   Honour ($kbwd$) has departed from Israel
> - for the taking away of the Ark of God and for her father-in-law
>   and her husband -
> She said
>   Honour has departed from Israel
>   for the Ark of God has been taken away (1 Sam 4.20-22).

This scene is comparable to the one where Rachel gives birth to her second son (Gen 35.16-18). Like Eli's daughter-in-law, Rachel dies after her son's birth. The irony of her fate is that she does not die because of childlessness (Gen 30.1), but because of her second son's birth. Rachel expresses her despair in the name she gives him.

> While she had severe labour in delivering the child
> the midwife said to her
>   Fear not for you shall have this son too
> And as her life's breath departed for she died
> she called his name Ben-oni (son of my disaster).
> But his father called him Benjamin (son of the right hand)
> (Gen 35.17-18).

Since Jacob here assumes the right to correct the name given by his wife,[54] Benjamin is the only forefather of Israel who has his father to thank for his name. Jacob's intervention makes the suffering of the mother invisible (De Jong 1989, 75).

A comparable example of "correction" regarding the authorship of name-giving is to be found in Genesis 4 and 5. In Genesis 4, normally ascribed to J, it is Eve who gives Seth a name.

> She called his name Seth (*št*) for
> God has provided (*št*) me with other seed instead of Abel
> for Cain had murdered him (Gen 4.25).

In Genesis 5, assigned to P, it is Adam who gives Seth his name (5.3). It seems that a name-giving mother does not belong in the worldview held by the priestly writers. In their writings, attention focuses on the "procreations" of fathers; therefore, they are the ones to name their sons.[55]

The last naming speech to which I wish to draw attention is Eve's speech in Genesis 4.1. In her article mentioned earlier, Pardes (1989) discusses this issue in depth. Following Cassuto (1961, 201), she translates the naming text as follows,

> Together with YHWH I have created (*qnyty*) a man.

Pardes claims that by using the verb *qnh*, which elsewhere in the Bible may designate God's creative activity (see, for instance, Gen 14.22; Ps 139.13; Prov 8:22), Eve presents herself as co-creator with YHWH. We can hear in her declaration traces of myth, in which the Mother Goddess is presented as creator or co-creator of humans and the world.[56] Pardes then reads Eve's naming speech as a commentary on, and correction of, Adam's naming of Eve in Genesis 2.23.

---

[54] Winter (1987, 24) concludes, on the grounds of this text, that the father had the final say in regard to name giving.

[55] See Genesis 5.3; 16.15; 17.19; 21.3.

[56] Pardes points out that the title of Asherah, the Ugaritic Mother Goddess, is *qnyt 'lm*, 'the creatress/bearer of the gods'. She writes, "Skinner (1910, 102-103) points to a strikingly similar verse in the bilingual Babylonian creation myth: "Aruru [the mother goddess], together with him [Marduk] created the seed of mankind." Similarly in the Atra-hasis, as Kikiwada (1972, 33-37) points out, the creatress Mami (. . .) shapes a man out of clay with Enki's help. In both cases the word *itti*, meaning "with" or "together with" (analogous to the prepositional sense of the Hebrew *'et*) appears' (Pardes 1989, 169).

[I]t is a response to his almost dream-like reversal of the order of things, to his indirect claim to have created woman out of his body, to his celebration of the generative capacity of his flesh and bones. She responds in the medium he chose to use: naming speeches. It is not you who created woman out of man (with divine help), she seems to claim, but it is I who created you—*'ish*—together with YHWH! Second person is avoided, but the dialogic thrust is unmistakable. The rivalry between the sexes, not unlike the rivalry between Leah and Rachel, is represented at this point through a remarkable exchange (a match, almost) of naming speeches (Pardes 1989, 171-172).

If Pardes is right in her conclusion that the naming speeches of Adam and Eve can be read as a manifestation of the struggle between the sexes concerning the creative force, then more than traces of ancient myths can be heard in Eve's cry. A kind of female self-awareness resounds in it; and this must have been recognizable for the women of ancient Israel too.

All the namings by women here discussed, arranged according to the different situations/conditions in which they are spoken and on which they express a view, refer to sons. No explanation or motivation is supplied for the only biblical mention of the naming of a daughter.

> Then she (Leah) bore a daughter
> and she called her name Dinah (Gen 30.21).

Should we draw the conclusion from this sparse biblical information that mothers did not attach any importance to their daughters? It is probably more credible that, by and large, the authors/editors of the Bible were not much interested in the interrelations between mothers and daughters. Two possible exceptions for this authorial indifference are the Song of Songs and Ruth (and see Brenner, part II below, on Proverbs 31).

9. FINAL CONSIDERATIONS

Almost at the end of this quest for women's texts in the Hebrew Bible, and before making a number of concluding comments, I turn for the last time to Goitein. He concludes his case by emphatically pointing out once more that the women's songs discussed by him are not usually "free creation(s)", but that every song had a *Sitz im Leben*. It was sung by (a) special woman (women) on specific occasions. They/she made use of set formulas, rooted in tradition. Some songs, however,—within the Song of Songs, Lamentations, Proverbs, and Deborah's song—also reveal traces of "a refreshing personal talent" (Goitein 1988, 30).

Finally Goitein hazards the notion that traces of female narrative traditions are to be found in the Bible as well as female poetic traditions. There are no direct indications of this, but one example is perhaps the exhaustively drawn-out story of Abraham's agent and Rebekah (Gen 24). Features of content and form suggest a female origin for this narrative. The heroine of this story is a young girl who finds a good husband; "and it is good for young girls to know that good behavior is rewarded with a suitable match" (Goitein 1988, 30). Goitein states that the construction of the story, with its many repetitions, is "characteristic of female narrative structure", an observation he corroborates by his study of the narrative traditions of Jewish women in Yemen. He derives the explanation for this repetitious style from the customary, gender-bound division of labour.

> [W]omen were usually busy in group tasks which occupy the hands but left the mouth free. Long is the path of the women who draw water from the well at the foot of the village, and they must wait there in a long line until each one has filled her jug; hence the humorous depiction of the excessive talkativeness of the water-drawers who answer Saul's brief question, "Is the seer in the town?" (1 Sam 9.11-13). The women sit for long hours busy with weaving and spinning and other handicrafts, or performing tasks at the gate of the Tabernacle (Exod 38.8, 1 Sam 2.22), without themselves taking part in the cult. These long hours were seasoned not only with conversation, but also with stylized speech, story and song (Goitein 1988, 31).

The story about Rebekah and Abraham's agent would fit very well into one of the contexts sketched here. Moreover, it includes a song that belonged to a genre that, according to Goitein, was used mostly by women, farewell songs. He infers the existence of this genre from Genesis 31.27. Laban reproaches Jacob, for the latter's secret departure rendered it impossible to take leave in a suitable manner.

> Why did you flee in secret and have stolen from me
> and did you not tell me of it
> so that I might have accompanied you with shouts of joy and with
>   songs
> with the tambourine and the lyre.

The accompaniment of a departure (here of Jacob's and his family), was an important popular occurrence. On the occasion of such a *"shiluah"* (send-off; Goitein 1988, 27), the village community was accustomed to walk with the guest or relative leaving (in many cases for good) for some distance, and accompany the procession by music. The Rebekah story contains an example of a song sung at the departure of a daughter married off to a man from abroad.

> They blessed Rebekah and they said to her
>> Our sister
>> May you become a thousandfold multitude
>> May your seed take possession of the gate of its haters
> (Gen 24.60).

Goitein gathers that, in the main, women sang this and comparable farewell songs because of the musical instruments mentioned in Genesis 31.27. In my opinion, however, the formulation and context of this passage, like Genesis 24.60, appear to express a tradition practised by men and women together.

Goitein's plea to regard Genesis 24 as a women's creation is deficient in one important respect. During the discussion of the Song of Songs we saw that, in that text, the term "house of the mother" (SoS 3.4; 8.2) is used instead of the habitual "house of the father". Meyers (1986, 219) appeared to construct this as an indication that the Song of Songs was a product of popular culture or of women's culture. Significantly, in Rebekah's story the phrase "her mother's house" is found as well, although the term "father's house" features in it too. The latter, however, is used when one of the male personae acts as focalizer (see for example v. 7). What is regarded by Rebekah as the "her mother's house" (v. 28) is for Abraham's agent automatically "your father's house" (v. 33), or "the house of my lord's brothers" (v. 27). This difference in focalization betrays insight into and sensitivity to the difference in vision and interests of men, as opposed to those of women. That too could be an indication of the female origin of Rebekah's story.

The only other text in which the term "mother's house" appears is the story about Ruth (Ruth 1.8). Goitein attributes this narrative to an old prophetess or wise woman. But since he has limited himself to a discussion of those biblical genres for which clear indications are to be found that they are practised by women, Goitein decides not to clarify this matter further. In my discussion of Goitein's methodology (1.C) I have undertaken to return to the point. There I mention two criteria for attributing stories about women to female authors, or, as we have to add now, to female voices.

1) Does the text contain traces of a less androcentric intent?

2) Is there in it talk of a (re)definition of reality from a female perspective, so that the story contains defineable differences between the views of the male as against the female figures?

As for the first criterion, Brenner (1986) has pointed out that the story about Naomi and Ruth offers a marked correction to the stereotypic biblical image of women as rivals (Sarah-Hagar; Rachel-Leah; Hannah-Peninna). Naomi and Ruth reveal in an exemplary fashion how fruitful (in the literal sense too) the cooperation between women can become. The relationship between them is so close that it is described with the verb *dbq*, "cling together" (compare Gen 2.24!). The second criterion is applicapable too. At the beginning of the Book, in her extensive address to her daughters-in-law (Ruth 1.8-13), Naomi defines reality expressly from a woman's perspective. Her daughters-in-law have to return to their "mother's house", in order to subsequently find peace in their "husband's house". The bearing of sons does not occur in Naomi's speech in the interest of the "father's house", but rather as life insurance for women (see also Trible 1978, 166-199). And again, at the end of Ruth, a similar vision is tersely pronounced by the "neighbouring women". They redefine the reality wished for Boaz by the men of Bethlehem—the birth of great posterity (Ruth 4.11-12)—by proclaiming that a son has been born to *Naomi* (v. 17). The meaning the women assign to the birth of this son is formulated completely in terms of its significance for the grandmother. He is *her* "redeemer" who makes her vitality return, and who will look after her in her old age (vv. 14-15).

In addition to these arguments regarding content, formal arguments can be added for supporting Goitein's proposition to see Naomi and Ruth's story as a product of women's culture, and then as a creation of an old prophetess or wise woman. It has the characteristics of a folktale (Sasson 1979; 1987) which—in view of its "elevated prose style" (Campbell 1975, 19)—probably came into being, and has been transmitted within circles of professional narrators. Following Gunkel (1920, XXXI) and inspired by the studies of Parry (1971) and Lord (1960), Campbell suggests that in ancient Israel there existed a "guild" of professional storytellers. These were itinerant Levites whose task it was to educate the people, but also wise women. In the village square, or at the well, they would recite their stories to the assembled public at fixed times; and these stories were handed down within the "guild" from generation to generation. If this suggestion be accepted, then it is quite possible that the Ruth and Naomi story belonged to the repertory of a professional female storyteller, a woman old and wise like one of the heroines of her story, Naomi.

With regard to another characteristic of style, the *inclusios* that surround the various episodes in Ruth, Campbell risks the assumption that

> (...) the audience participated in crafting these delightful *inclusios* during the period of the oral transmission of the story (Campbell 1975, 14).

This statement draws attention to the fact that oral transmission always happens in an interplay between narrator and public. If this interplay in Ruth can be advanced hypothetically only, in the Song of Songs it is clearly visible in the dialogues between the I persona and the "daughters of Jerusalem". Orally transmitted songs or stories are thus, though in varying degrees, always the products of a collective process (see for instance Bal 1988a, 66-73).

The body of texts I have collected in Goitein's footsteps, is considerable. Moreover, the application of his methodology makes it possible to classify three additional oral traditions practised by women: vows, birth songs, and naming speeches. The body of material thus assembled largely consists of fragments, sometimes minute, which had been embedded within narratives. Only in two cases are whole biblical books (the Song of Songs and Ruth) identified as possible products of women's culture.

In many cases, Showalter's cultural model facilitates the highlighting of the interpretations Goitein and later interpreters have assigned to the texts and their history. The "double voice" concept enables us to discover the reverse side of the dominant story in various texts, to uncover the "muted" story in which reality is defined from women's viewpoint. In some cases the story muted is a bitter or cynical story (songs of mockery and lament; a number of naming speeches). Sometimes the songs are surprisingly challenging (love songs), or rebellious in relation to the dominant pattern of gender role (prophecy). In a single case a "double voice" was not or almost not recognizable. The motherly admonitions in Proverbs appeared merely to reproduce the dominant discourse; these texts reveal a picture of the extent to which women, in this instance from the higher strata of society, are able to internalize this discourse.

The concept of "women's culture" stimulated the discovery of connections between various oral traditions of women on the one hand whereas, on the other hand, it in no way minimized the great variety among women in regard to their social status, worldview, and interests. With the help of this concept a ritual, like that known as "the retelling of Jephthah's daughter" (Judg 11.40), is illuminated afresh.

The results of the present quest for biblical traces of women's texts can perhaps be best summarized by tracing the significations which the term "women's texts" has meanwhile gradually acquired. At the beginning of this quest the term designated "texts, written by women". Within the framework of the search undertaken such a definition appeared almost immediately too limited and, indeed, misleading. Asking whether women did contribute to the written traditions of the Bible is to be sure relevant, but it is far from clear which texts are actually implicated. In view of this situation and in view of the complex history of biblical tradition, "women's texts" then also acquired the meaning of "texts, transmitted orally by women, but (probably) written down by male authors". I agree with Goitein that a distinction must be made and defined as follows. "Women's texts" in the Hebrew Bible are not so much literal quotations from (reconstructed) women's oral traditions but, rather, "texts which have been so formulated by (probably) male authors, that they give a 'recognizable impression' (Goitein 1988, 5) of these oral women's traditions". All the Biblical passages discussed can be classified as "women's texts" in that sense with a certain degree of plausibility, but without certainty. Another legitimate question is, whether the last definition of "women's texts" still justifies the use of the term. What is the validity of designating texts which only "give an impression" of the singing or speaking of women "the product of female authors"?

As I worked, it became clear by degrees that it was not helpful to remain imprisoned by a concept of female authorship. The question as to whether a woman's voice can be heard in the texts became just as important as the problem of authorship, or even more so. The question can now, without exception, be answered positively. All the biblical passages discussed can be seen as "women's texts", in the sense that the voice of the primary speaker or narrator in them can be identified as a woman's voice, or could be interpreted (read) as such. The meaning of the term "women's texts" is thereby extended. It no longer indicates exclusively an (original) author's gender, but also points to characteristic features intrinsic to the relevant texts themselves.

This is the point when the terminology shifts: it is helpful to name the concept of "women's texts" thus defined as F voices emanating from the text. Texts and authors or readers are not gender-neutral. There always is either an M voice or an F voice speaking in them (or both). It is important to differentiate which of the two possibilities applies in a certain instance. Sometimes both possibilities are defensible. A number of mockery songs and the Song of Songs 7.1-10/2-11 are examples of this last possibility. These texts tell a different story, depending on whether they are read as M texts or F texts.

The hypothesis that a number of Biblical texts contain F voices which are indigeneous products of (and serve as representational and referential clues to) "women's culture" does not only illuminate the creativity of women in ancient Israel, but also focuses our attention on the voice-in-the-text. Thus, a chorus of women's voices becomes audible. Thus, a variety of women's views becomes visible by inference.

PART II
PROVERBS 1–9: AN F VOICE?

ATHALYA BRENNER

PROVERBS 1-9: AN F VOICE?

An extended example of a possible, hitherto unconsidered, F voice in a larger biblical text unit belongs to the biblical genre, or group of genres, entitled Wisdom Literature. The following analysis is a rereading of the Book of Proverbs, in particular Proverbs 1-9, from the perspective of an F reader listening for F textual voices and the cultural model(s) underlying them.[1]

The "Female Rebuker" Figure

Let me begin by referring back to Goitein (English 1988, Hebrew 1957). Goitein describes a literary (presumably of oral origin) "genre"—perhaps "literary convention" would be a more suitable term—whereby a female rebuker, or female scold, admonishes her husband or son. Although there are biblical examples of common mothers who admonish their sons and instruct them (Jacob and his mother, Gen 27; Micah and his mother, Judg 17;), it is the queen mother's teaching (Prov 31.1-9, perhaps also a hint in the joint fate of the queen mother and her son the king in Jer 22.26) which became the biblical representative of this recurrent life situation (Goitein 1988, 12). Goitein supports his classification citing the stock literary figure of the female rebuker in ancient Arabic poetry as a parallel: the preaching of virtue to a male, by his wife and particularly by his mother, was a common topic of ancient Arabic poetry; and the chief targets of that stylized rebuke were women and wine. To quote,

> The woman complains that the man is wasting his substance in wine and hospitality...; meanwhile his mother protests that her son has cleaved to his wife, "an outsider", and forsaken the one who naturally loves him, his mother. (1988, 3).

My project in this study is to reassess Goitein's notion of the Female Rebuker genre and reapply it to the Book of Proverbs, especially to

---

[1] I acknowledge my gratitude to Professor Claudia V. Camp, who read an earlier draft of this study and made generous and acute comments.

Proverbs 1-9. By so doing I shall build upon van Dijk-Hemmes's treatment of the same issues (I.3.A-B above) and develop it further. Van Dijk-Hemmes diagnoses women's voices and F personas-in-the-text; I would like to show that Proverbs 1-9 can actually be read not only as a repository of quoted F voices but, rather, as an F text.

The Frame of Proverbs: F Personas and Voices, M discourse?

Claudia Camp (1985) observes that the Book of Proverbs is framed by female literary figures. Personified Wisdom together with her antitheses, the "strange" woman (more of that translation of the Hebrew zārâh in a little while) and personified Folly, feature largely in chapters 1-9. And the Book is concluded by two poems assigned to women—Lemuel's mother's instruction, which is assigned to a woman's voice; and the ʾēšet ḥayil poem in chapter 31. Camp holds that the female literary configuration of Proverbs has theological as well as sociological significance. In her opinion this configuration, or envelopment, points to a transposition of the family, as symbolized by a centrality of the female, for kingship as the main institution of postexilic Israel. Nevertheless and somewhat surprisingly, most readers assume that the framing discourse of Proverbs (1-9) is an M discourse. Woman and personifications of woman—be they as indicative of woman's import and status as they may—are perceived as the object of discourse rather than its subject(s).

Recently Camp has modified her previous views. She now interprets female imagery in Proverbs, especially the "strange" woman imagery, in terms of the trickster figura (Camp 1988); the fresh perspective engenders a re-consideration of the "strange" woman theological significance anew (Camp 1991). Still, Camp remains convinced that M discourse is here the predominant and framing discourse.

While many aspects of Camp's analysis are radical and original, she conforms to the interpretive norm in respect of the gender authority inherent in Proverbs 1-9. Her interpretive position is not unmatched: many feminist critics join the traditional chorus. Virtually all commentators, non-feminist (for instance Crenshaw 1981; McKane 1970; Scott 1965; Toy 1899; Whybray 1965, 1966, 1972) as well as feminist, inasmuch as they recognize the problem of genre and gender for Proverbs 1-9 (and 31), perceive the voices in these passages as M voices. In Newsom's phrases, the discourse here exhibits characteristics of "an essentially patriarchal authority" (Newsom 1989, n. 4). More specifically, the relevant passages are widely classified as belonging to the "father's instruction to son" genre. This, ultimately, is Camp's view (see above) and also, for instance, Gale Yee, albeit with commendable circumspection:

> Assuming that the present overall framework of Proverbs 1-9 is the instruction a father gives to his son about how to become acquainted with Wisdom, definite speeches within this instructional framework are delivered by various personages as part of the heuristic method of the father. (1989, 55).

Carol Newsom characterizes the discourse of Proverbs 1-9 as an M discourse preoccupied with and reporting F discourse. Therefore, she maintains,

> All readers of this text, whatever their actual identities, are called upon to take up the subject position of son in relation to an authoritative father. . . The familiar scene, a father advising his son, is important. . .that *Hôkmôt* (personified wisdom) is an extension of the cultural voice that speaks through the father can be seen in the complementary authoritative position she occupies. (1989, 145-6).

Newsom notes that the overt M voice, although preoccupied with F discourse, reproduces the latter through its own filters. Consequently, the "strange" woman's rhetoric constitutes a verbalization of the quintessential *vagina dentata* threat; within this M discourse, the embedded F voice represents an emblematic Everywoman. Newsom sums up her reading position in regard to the undoubtedly phallocentric vision of Proverbs 1-9 and its patriarchal presumptions by comparing the text to a recent film, "Fatal Attraction", and by offering loopholes for resisting M (fatherly, patriarchal, authoritative) discourse and for deconstructing it in both fictive texts. For her, although

> . . .the mother's authority as well as the father's is invoked. . .In no way is she [the mother] seen as constituting an independent voice, however, but serves as a confirmer of what is presented as an essentially patriarchal authority (Newsom 1989, n. 5).

My response to these interpretive positions is: What if we adopt the readerly privilege of denying the "father's instruction to son" genre for Proverbs 1-9 and 31? Positing a "What if" question at this junction is by no means idiosyncratic. The question reflects dissatisfaction with the multiplicity of explanations advanced to date for

Proverbs 1-9, explanations whose common denominator is the assignment of some space to presumably "quoted", fictive F discourse within a frame of an M discourse and an M text.

This dissatisfaction can be summarized as follows. I am not convinced by Camp's conjecture—in my view, the most serious attempt to date—concerning the motivation for positioning F literary voices as the frame for Proverbs. Why should such an M editorial decision be made? I agree that an F frame for Proverbs does exist and must hark to some literary and/or sociological, perhaps even theological significance. But even if Camp's view of the growing supremacy of the family establishment during the Second Temple era is valid, it does not clarify personified Wisdom's supremacy and/or the centrality of her antithesis, the *'iššâh zārâh* ("strange" woman), within an M discourse whose situational context is learning, in which participation by women was presumably unusual. Does an increase in the import attached to the (extratextual) family and, consequently, womenfolk convincingly account for the literary figure of an F teacher (personified Wisdom) advertised by textual M teachers?

Theories about "Goddess imagery", preoccupations with exogamy and cult (Blenkinsopp 1989 in Camp 1991), or others, contribute to the understanding of this textual paradox no more than the "father's instruction" interpretations. Neither is this textual phenomenon adequately explained by referral to the threatening fascination the female of the species exercises over her male victims (Newsom): F voices are given so much space, hence power[2], that the text is in danger of achieving the reverse of what it claims to be doing—it might actually deconstruct any M reluctance to listen to it! While this paradoxical understanding might in itself constitute the beginning of a feasible reading strategy, such a reading of Proverbs 1-9 as self-subversive M discourse is not the only viable readerly option one might entertain.

Moreover, if the discourse in Proverbs is indeed an M discourse, why the placing of the *'ēšet ḥayil* poem at the end of the whole Proverbs anthology? And what about Lemuel's mother's instruction? Can we relate the editorial reason for the placing of this poem

---

[2] The textual position of female figures is clearly illuminated by applying narratological criteria to the text (Bal 1985, 1988b). Women-in-the-text occupy such central positions within the narration—even when the narrator's voice is ostensibly derogatory—by speech, action, and visibility that the end product is astounding.

almost at the end of the collection to the ascending (social) importance of the wife/mother alone, and that after numerous instances of M biased misogynistic remarks within the Book itself? And whose figment of imagination is Wisdom and her attendant literary figures? These queries are addressed to the text in as much as to its interpreters.

We have learnt from Goitein that a ''mother's instruction to son'' genre is indeed documented outside the literature of ancient Israel. As discussed by van Dijk-Hemmes above, there are a few clues for the life situation which informs this literary convention in biblical literature itself. Rebekah tells Jacob what to do to further his ambitions for inheritance (Gen 27). Athaliah's locus of later power is attributed to her position as adviser to her son Ahaziah (2 Chron 22.2-3). As Camp rightly states, women counselled their husbands as well as their sons, perhaps primarily the formers, using discretion and indirection, as a matter of course. Jezebel counselled her husband Ahab, for instance, in the matter of Naboth's vineyard (1 Kgs 21). On the strength of that Camp postulates an informal educational position for the wife and mother depicted in Prov 31. Why not consider, then, the possibility of a woman's discourse, specifically a mother's, for the whole of Proverbs 1-9 too?

Father's Instruction and Mother's Instruction in Proverbs 1-9

The only passage in Proverbs 1-9 where a father's instruction is specifically referred to is 4.1-4. The speaker employs the first person singular to appeals to the literary ''sons'', the fictive listeners, to hark to the ''father'' 's *mûsār*; and then reverts to the recurrent (in this collection) father/mother bound compound (v. 3; and cf 1.8, 6.20). Then again the father's teaching is evoked, using first person singular speech, (v. 4).

> Sons
> Hear a father's instruction
> and listen in order to acquire understanding
> For I give you sound learning
> and do not abandon my teaching
>> I was my father's son
>> Tender and my mother's only (child)
>> And he taught me and said to me
>>> Let my word support your heart
>>> Keep my commands so that you live.

The gender of the grammatical first person in the Hebrew is, of course, not marked: we supposedly rely on the word context for defining it as gramatically f. or else m.; failing that, we construct an extrinsic understanding based on interpretation. If we forgo such quick procedures, then the following picture emerges. The passage is constructed as three discursive circles, each enveloped by the boundaries of its predecessor, each dominated by a voice. As the lay-out and, especially, the indentation of my translation shows, there is no doubt as to the boundaries of each voice. The identities of the second and third voice—a textual ''son'' delivering his ''father'' 's teaching—are indisputable. But who is the narrator-in-the-text, the privileged I persona? Should we take a logical leap and decide that like father, like son, like initial speaker? Does the identity of the fictive target audience, the textual ''sons'', automatically imply the same gender for the ''teacher'' who addresses them?[3]

An alternative reading would look something like this. It is possibly a ''mother'' who is encouraging the ''sons'' to listen to their ''father'' (4.1). Then the ''father'' speaks briefly (v. 2ff.), reporting his own ''father'' 's teaching within the frame of the ''mother'' 's exhortation. The reported speech of the ''father's father'' is placed within a ''father'' 's speech urged by the ''mother'', thus actually within both speech acts! Read in this manner, the passage serves as a nice example for Camp's observation on Women's discrete indirection[4] and their ''muted'' voice (Van Dijk-Hemmes in Part I above, after Showalter and Ardener), masquerading as an M voice and hiding behind an M convention. Wait until father comes home, my son—he will tell you off, he will pull his authority to get you back to harness! Also, this is perhaps a revealing instance of women's ''double voice'': the convention of seemingly upholding M authority while, simultaneously, deconstructing this same authority, for nobody is fooled as to who is the behind-the-scene boss.

Far be it from me to claim that reading the narrator's voice in this passage as an overriding F voice which envelopes within it two M voices, is ''more correct'' than any other reading. I merely want to

---

[3] It is worth remembering that father and mother (in this determinate and bound order) are mentioned together 12 times in Proverbs in similar educational contexts, as against this single reported occurrence of father's instruction only!

[4] Although Camp herself, in a letter, politely views my reading here as a trifle forced.

upset an interpretive inference that has gained such ascendancy that it obscures an ambiguity in the text. By itself, such a counterreading is in its turn not decisive for the gendering of Proverbs 1-9 as an F text. Admittedly, further supportive evidence is required for subverting the common notion that a narrational M discourse provides the frame for the inner M discourses here (and in Prov 1-9 as a whole).

A renewed examination of Proverbs 1-9 demonstrates that there is a certain gender distribution for words such as *mûsār, miṣwâh,* and *tôrâh.* There is no *tôrâh* attributed to the "father", which is somewhat surprising. There is *tôrâh* attributed to the "mother" (1.8, 6.20) and, in addition, a woman has *tôrāt ḥesed* in 31.26. *mûsār* and its source verb *ysr* are, on the other hand, not gender specific in their application: they are the father's (1.8), but also the mother's (31.1, Lemuel's mother) and personified Wisdom's (1.25,30, 8.10). It is therefore neither necessary nor justified to postulate that the "mother"'s authority in Proverbs 1-9 is by definition secondary; by adhering to the notion of a framing, borrowing and "quoting" M discourse, we transform the voice of the mother-in-thr-text into a second hand, distant echo. The word order of the bound compound "father and mother" does indeed betray an androcentric hierarchy and patriarchal ethos. The common textual object of education is the son rather than the daughter (and we shall come back to this point later). Nevertheless, a mother's discourse is as viable as a father's for these passages; and there is no need to view that maternal voice as a mother's discourse reported by a father's discourse.[5] To conclude: It seems to me that a "real" F voice, independent in stance if not in message (see below), can be discerned in 4.1-4 as well as other passages, to which we shall turn now.

---

[5] I am not talking merely about the cooperation between father and mother dictated by family affairs, especially family crises. Neither is the somewhat strange case of the "rebellious", incapable-of-learning son (Deut 21.18-21) conducive to the present discussion. The same applies to the shared instructive action in Zechariah 13.3, where both fathers and mothers diagnose their son's prophesying as false (I am indebted to Carol Meyers for drawing my attention to the last reference). I am trying to define an independent maternal voice and to separate it from the secondary position it has acquired in Proverbs interpretation.

The "Female Onlooker" Figure

Proverbs 7 presents an all too attractive picture of the seductive ʾiššâh zārâh, a woman of impressive rhetoric and sexual designs on unsuspecting "sons". The speaker, presumably the instructor/ teacher, pretends to look through the window onto the scene of seduction—a woman, a male youth, persuasion reported. For virtually all commentators the onlooker is a male teacher. Van Dijk-Hemmes demonstrates (I.3.B above) how this figure, read without the usual preconceptions, can be construed as a female figure or, more specifically, a maternal figure. Read thus, Proverbs 7 belongs to the rebuking genre; and the F voice in it reproduces M discourse to perfection. I subscribe to this reading, and would like to add a few observations to van Dijk-Hemmes's case.

The literary figure of the woman at the window is substantiated by archaeological finds: the Samaria ivories are a case in point. The convergence of literary description and artefact signifies a plausibility, even a probability (cf. Brooten 1985 for the methodological value of archaeology for feminist research), that the woman gazing out of a latticed window is a transartistic stock figure. It therefore seems perverse to ascribe this literary figure to a male "teacher" posing as "father" simply because there is a tacit agreement that an M voice is in operation in this passage. A woman's figure at the window, a representation of the decent woman who (contra personified Wisdom and her reflections, the woman Folly and the ʾiššâh zārâh) looks at what goes on in the street, but does not step outside her domain, makes a viable picture. One suspects that a male teacher, less bound by societal conventions, would have rushed outside to get a closer look. The textual woman stays inside (like the ʾēšet ḥayil at the end of Proverbs), but this does not prevent her from observing, from making comments, and from passing those comments on to a male audience.

Once the figure of a woman, a mother, is conjectured, various features of the first Proverbs collection can be explicated by this hypothesis. We shall here confine our remarks to just a few of them, namely: the discourses on the ʾiššâh zārâh; the personification of wisdom as woman; and women's teaching.

The Other Woman

Newsom (1989) observes that the world of female eroticism in Proverbs 1-9 is symbolized by the ʾiššâh zārâh and largely conveyed through her reported rhetorical ability. Sexual intercourse becomes discourse. Once more the question presents itself: is the reading of these passages as M warnings reproducing F discourse the only, and exclusively so, viable reading option?

Love talk and love poetry in the Bible are often attributed to F voices—so notably in the Song of Songs, where F voices are much more dominant than the M voices, much more outspoken. So also in Egyptian love poetry (Fox 1985), so also in Tamil love poetry and in other analogues. It looks like an established literary and sociological fact: Even within patriarchal frameworks, F discourse on love is not coerced into silence and is seldom, if ever, muted. F love poetry is not merelely tolerated but actually allowed to equal, even surpass, M love discourse. This phenomenon is curious, perhaps inexplicable; still, it is a widely distributed cultural phenomenon. It is not exceptional, then, that women enjoy the privilege of discussing sex and love freely within the biblical texts cited. In fact, this is one of the human discourse areas that are not closed to them, perhaps because love belongs primarily to the domestic and personal domain.

The voice of Lemuel's mother, a voice which instructs the "son" to shun women (and drink) at the end of the Book, matches the voice of the figure at the window (chapter 7). Both voices sound maternal. Both know the danger other women embody for their "sons" intimately. Both voices contain more than a hint of jealous possessiveness in them; they sound like voices which use F maternal authority, the F authority par excellence, to assert control over M sexual behaviour.

Woman as Other

And now to the figure of the *zārâh*. I would like to add some notes to the interpretation of this literary figure, well attended in biblical criticism, notes pertinent to the case of "mother" 's instruction I advocate.

I want to state that, from the outset, I object to traditional as well as current practices of translating *zārâh* as "foreign" or "strange". It seems to me that even "wise and strange" (Camp 1988) is not adequate.[6] My objection stems, first and foremost, from lexical and

---

[6] Camp herself, in a recent essay (1991), has retreated from previous positions and now reads the "woman" as "other"; and see below.

semantic data, but also from thematic and content considerations. There is no overt indication in Proverbs that the (type of) woman described is, specifically, either a foreigner or else instrinsically strange (difficult to understand, funny, ridiculous). These translations are inferred by analogy to other biblical passages but are neither upheld nor voided by the Proverbs texts themselves.

Two points are of linguistic import. First, other collocations of noun phrases with *zār* (and various formations derived from it) as noun modifier have it:

with "incense", Exodus 30.9;
with "God", Psalms 44.21, 81.10;
with "fire", Leviticus 10.1, Numbers 3.4, 26.61;
with "water", Jeremiah 18.14;
with "sons", Hosea 5.7;
and with "man", *ʾîš*, Leviticus 22.12, Deuteronomy 25.5.

To go by the word and situational contexts of these occurrences, in all of the collocations *zār* denotes the quality of "an Other", or an outsider, something or somebody who—from the narrator's or textual speaker's perspective—stands outside the right order of things. The *zār* is An Other with an upper case. None of these denote simply a "strange" or "foreign" phenomenon. It is conceivable that an ethnic and/or social foreigner would also be so designated but, primarily, *zār* denotes otherness in general. A good example for this primary sense is the sentence,

> Let an Other praise you
> rather than your own mouth (Prov 27.2).

Secondly, although the term which sometimes parallels *zārâh* in Proverbs, *nokriyâh* (2.16, 5.20, 6.24, 7.5), indeed signifies "foreign" in numerous instances,[7] This in itself does not automatically invest *zārâh* with a parallel, exclusively "ethnic" or social signification: few scholars will argue nowadays that parallel stichs must imply near or full synonymity. Full consideration ought to be accorded to the fact, for instance, that *zārâh* always is the first component of the pair; *nokriyâh* always appears in the second stich.[8] On the face of it, this

---

[7] See further for the possible significance and the approximation of the two terms in Camp 1991.

[8] So also in Proverbs 27.2, 13 and in all other passages in Proverbs where the two lexemes occur in parallelism.

stylistic feature may constitute a "parallelism of greater precision" (Clines 1987). However, subsequent glances will reveal that this is hardly the case. In all the instances cited the parallel and second stich containing *nokriyâh* looks like poetic expansions of a basic notion residing in the first stich, expansions motivated by a formal bonding together of a conventional word pair (in that rigid order) rather than by a specification of *zārâh*. The placing of the two lexemes in parallel units, then, is not conducive to the understanding of *zārâh* as "foreigner" in Proverbs 1-9, even though in other biblical texts foreign ethnicity or social origin is indeed denoted by *nokriyâh*.

Interestingly, narrative texts which attack exogamy, and specifically intermarriage with ethnically foreign women, never use the lexical term *zārâh* to denote those women. The pointedly ideological loci of 1 Kings 11 (a supposedly Deuteronomistic diatribe against King Solomon's exogamic habits), Ezra 10 and Nehemiah 13 (against the exogamic epidemic in the Restoration community), specify the women concerned exclusively as *nokriyôt*, never as *zārôt*. This linguistic difference should conclusively preclude the identification of the *ʾiššâh zārâh* in Proverbs with the ethnically foreign women of the alleged historical circumstances of the mid-fifth century BCE community. If we assume that *nokriyâh* in narrative discourse somehow becomes *zārâh* in the poetic discourse of Proverbs, we should explain that terminological shift. Failing that, and the more the pity, the anchoring of a historical locus of the Proverbs 1-9 in the Restoration community's concerns remains speculative. In other words, the attribution of the predominant warnings against the *ʾiššâh zārâh* to (M) worries over paternity, land tenure, and cultural autonomy are not convincing. A more general—albeit less historically locatable—concern with F Otherness seems to be in evidence here.

Moreover, there are instances in which *nokriy/âh* itself may have an edge, may signify something like "someone recognized as having outsider's status" (Mckane 1970, 285-6, after Snijders).[9]

Furthermore, an examination of the content shows that the *zārâh*

---

[9] This or a similar semantic usage probably facilitates the wordplay in Ruth 2.10, where the two occurrences of the root *nkr* in different formations should be translated as (Ruth saying to Boaz),

Why have I found grace in your eyes so that you *recognize* (from the hif. formation of *nkr*) me and I am but a *foreigner* (*nokriyâh*).

woman is not always one and the same literary figure (contra Yee 1989), and not always a married one; in other words, we have "women" rather than "a woman" modified by *zārâh* in Proverbs 1-9, types rather than one single type. This is illustrated by the fact that the linkage between that "woman" and adultery is, at least in some of the relevant passages if not in all of them, secondary and somewhat forced (whereas in others adultery is part and parcel of the "woman"'s circumstances). In 2.17, for instance, the woman has already left her husband: her liminal status (Camp 1988) rather than adultery seems to motivate her depiction as a threat to the normative social system. In chapter 5 the exhortation against adultery comes at verse 15, almost an afterthought linked by association to the erotic encounter with the unattached liminal *zārâh* woman evoked in the previous verses. And 6.26, presumably the link between another *ʾiššâh zārâh* situation and adultery, is corrupt beyond comprehension.

A certain amount of ambiguity is retained even in Proverbs 7. "The man" has departed on a long journey, thus says the liminal woman in verse 18. A male relative and custodian, no doubt; however, the word *ʾîš* with the first person singular genetive suffix would have been a much more convincing Hebrew usage for "my husband"—not to mention the even more specific *bāʿălî*.[10] The millennia-old practice of not questioning the ambiguity of the Hebrew term should not obscure the opening such an ambiguity provides for alternative readings. Is the *zārâh* in chapter 7 married or, perhaps, just under the wing of a male relative (as customary for women in all life stages) and exploiting his absence? *hāʾîš*, "the man", is less than specific.

Since the connections between the *ʾiššâh zārâh* passages and adultery are not unproblematic, I think that the voices warning their literary "son/s" against liminal women, women who are somehow positioned outside the accepted social order, may be read as voices speaking against fornication as much as against adultery. The message seems to be as follows. Sex and life and marriage go together; sex between unmarried partners is to be avoided, even and perhaps especially when the woman involved is free (permanently or tem-

---

[10] Van Dijk-Hemmes joins the universally accepted opinion that a "husband" is denoted by the non-specific "the man", although she recognizes the ambiguity of the Hebrew noun phrase; cf. I, p. 60, n. 34 above.

porarily) from family ties and male control. In this case woman as Other is perceived, by other (maternal) voices, as a danger to life for sociological rather than psychological reasons (which would have been appropriate for an M viewpoint).

I am aware that even when my reading is deemed viable it can nevertheless be argued that the textual voice is an M voice, presented as typically guarding paternity and its ensuing morality. Could it not, however, be the reflected dominant voice of a culture as it is introjected by F participants of that same culture (see van Dijk-Hemmes above)? It has often been observed (especially since Hegel and Nietzsche) that in the dialectics of class relations—of master and slave, oppressor and oppressed, aggressor and victim—the weaker partner tends to absorb the values and ideology of the stronger partner. Moreover, subordinates tend to adopt the ethos of their social superiors even when that same ethos is detrimental to their own self interest, and to uphold it more rigorously than the master beneficiaries themselves do.[11] The road from acceptance to rationalization of a situation, then to complicity and ideologization and moralization, then ultimately to enforcement, is travelled all too easily. Such a social journey, motivated by self-defense and the wish to survive, seems to underlie an F voice in the Proverbs texts. It appears that we read here not just complicity with androcentric values, not simply voiced conformity, but also overzealousness in protecting those values. Sex taboos—if the master-slave dialectics is accorded some weight—are rendered more comprehensive by the F voice, to the exclusion of any form of socially unregulated sexual liason. The object of the attack is not only married, but also unattached persons of the speaker's own gender.[12]

The consequences of the adoption and expansion of this M ideology for the female gender, whose spokesperson is the textual F voice, are serious. Within the literary F voice, F self interest is silenced through identification with M interest; control over female sexuality

---

[11] For another example of this process see below in the discussion of "prophetic" pornography, Part IV.

[12] Claudia Camp asks in a letter whether I think that women are more likely to view another "woman" as An Other than men do. I agree that the question is crucial for the identification of the dominant voice in Proverbs 1-9 as an F voice. In my view, the exaggerated enlargement of scope, so that warnings are pronounced against all "other" women, forbidden as well as eligible, signifies female—and specifically maternal—interest rather than male interest.

is recommended at least implicitly; maternal possessiveness merges with the internalized M voice for the purpose of preserving an existing world order and worldview. The price, here as in other passages in Proverbs, is the subscription of an identifiable F voice to misogyny and self-inflicted gender depreciation and gender disparagement.[13]

The F Wisdom Figure

The hypothesis of a "mother's instruction to her son" can be utilized to explain some of the features of personified Wisdom too. The Wisdom hyperbole certainly exhibits traces of Goddess imagery (see chs.8 and 9), albeit little more than traces. One of these traces is the multiplicity of images applied to her figure: she is bride, erotic consort, mother, daughter, and teacher.

Wisdom's depiction in terms of a lover and bride, the erotic transformed into discourse, corresponds to the predominance of F voices in biblical love poetry. The erotic language applied to her description is highly noticable: note, for instance, 4.5-9. Also, the verb *qnh*, often used in the Hebrew bible as the technical term for "acquire a wife", appears in numerous instances of personified Wisdom passages, especially where "she" is referred to in the third person. Does this imaging identify the textual voice as an M voice discussing M concerns through an image of female sexual attractiveness? Hardly. The imaging identifies the *target audience*, the "son", as a male potentially interested in such a sexually attractive picture of the woman Wisdom; it does not identify the speaker as M or, for that matter, F. A maternal voice, well aware of her maturing "son"'s concerns, is as plausible a choice as any other.

Curiously, however, when Wisdom is given her own voice-in-the-

---

[13] While discussing the subject of gendering literary voices and texts, Joseph Blenkinsopp made the following acute observations. If it is claimed that an F voice has totally internalized the culturally and socially dominant M voice, or when it is made to have done so by an editorial framework, how can one tell the difference between the two "voices"? To all intents and purposes such a process would have obliterated any distinguishable gender positions, assuming that such positions had originally existed!

It would appear that, in order to account for these observations, two parameters have to be emphasized. One is the "muted" or "double" voice that can be discerned in possible F texts (see van Dijk-Hemmes after Showalter and Ardener in Part I above). The other is the amplification of a norm beyond its reasonable and rational exigency, as indicated here.

text, it is maternal and commercial rather than erotic; she defines herself in terms not dissimilar to those describing the Worthy woman of Proverbs 31 (so in 1.20-33, 8.1-21).

In the second part of chapter 8 Wisdom is God's possession, consort (note the verb *qnh* again) and then child—both normal positions of dependence for a socially adjusted female. Then, in chapter 9, "she" and her counterpart Folly are transformed into a mother figure (contra Camp)—home and nourishment are offered to the literary "son" by good and bad "mother" alike. The fantasy of the two sides of motherhood may indeed be an infant son's fantasy, so Melanie Klein teaches us; but the voice which delivers this fantasy is decidedly F, expressing F knowledge and F maternal temptation exercised by mothers in their relations with their sons, more than ever when the relationship is threatened, when the sons are about to go out and enter the wide world of the father and other women, leaving mother cloistered (sitting at the window?) behind and trying to pull the "son" back by the umbilical cord one more time.

Chapter 31—A Mother's Instruction to Son, and to Daughter

My proposed reading of Proverbs 1-9 and the F voices which inform, or are submerged within, it is concluded by referring once more to chapter 31, the other side of the F frame of the whole Proverbs collection (Camp 1985).

Biblical information about the involvement of women in matters of state—be those women a young king's mother or "wise women" posing as literary "mothers" (2 Sam 14, 20; see van Dijk-Hemmes above)—points to the existence of a literary subgenre, the "mother's instruction to a young king". The speech delivered by Lemuel's mother is perhaps an indication that the literary convention survived after the social institutions of *gĕbîrâh*, king's mother, and "wise woman" became extinct. At any rate, at the end of Proverbs we are reminded of the mother's instruction to son genre operative in the first part of the Book. And a neat inclusio plus it is, since the "son" here is a royal rather than ordinary "son". And so is his mother. A role model for commoners like you and me, readers called on to identify with the textual royal "son" (Newsom 1989)?

Finally, what about the daughters? Where do they come in? My hypothesis is that the *ʾēšet ḥayil* poem (Prov 31.10-22) is the single biblical instance of a "mother's instruction to daughter" genre, the opposite and complementary number of the "mother's instruction to son" convention of chapters 1-9 and the first part of chapter 31.

A single instance, we said. However, there is another possible allusion to a mother's instruction to daughter in an equivocal phrase in the Song of Songs 8.2. There an F voice says, ambiguously, to her male lover,

> "I would lead you
> bring you to my mother's house
> You will teach/she (my mother) will teach me
> (*tĕlammĕdēnî*. . .)

Is the F speaker's mother, or the male lover who is wished to come into the mother's house as the F speaker's brother, the subject of the verb *lmd* piel, "to teach"? The verse's structure is far from clear. Its problematics is reflected already in the ancient translations. Modern translations and commentaries are divided in this respect. The NEB has "you (the lover) will teach me"; The KJV, on the other hand, has the "mother" as the subject of the verb. Pope supplies a discussion (1977, 658-9) but finally opts for the removal by emendation of this grammatically ambiguous form on metric and other grounds. Landy celebrates the ambiguity, hence retains it while inclining toward accepting the "mother" as the subject (1983, 114-6, 118-119). At any rate, even if we retain the "mother's teaching" in the Song of Songs 8.2, it is accidental; it should not be over-interpreted as relating beyond a life situation to a literary *genre*.

When we talk about a didactic genre, we imply formalized (if not necessarily institutionalized) teaching. There is no doubt that women did informally educate their children, male and female alike, within the family. There is also every reason to believe that patriarchy, although the preeminent social order, was not the only social option in biblical times. Evidence of matrilineal and matrilocal customs abounds: in the latter circumstances, a mother's instructive role would have been enhanced, especially when its life setting is that of a *bēt ʾēm*, a mother's house (Meyers 1991b). Nevertheless, I hesitate whether to accept the notion that there existed formal academies for young ladies of good breeding in ancient Israel (Crook 1954), for the same reasons that militate against the existence of formal academies for young boys of good breeding. The existence of this social institution or its absence from Hebrew life is not decisive, however, for the definition of the F and M instruction genres in Hebrew letters. And as McKane observes, the literary source for the school-teacher's authority—if schoolteacher's voices of either gender indeed represent it—is modelled upon parental authority, not vice versa (McKane 1970, 303).

Many threads converge here, where a daughter's textual figure can be discerned as being taught what a decent and proper daughter should undertake. She should become an industrious wife and mother. The image is that of a woman overworked in the service of her husband and sons (sic!), undoubtedly a reflection of prevailing social norms. And yet, she possesses *hokmâh* and *tôrâh* (v.26) too, possibly a reference to the wisdom she has transmitted to her sons in chapters 1-9; and those same "sons" are the ones who do/will praise her here (v. 28). A mother can thus empower her textual "daughter" in a way unimaginable by the (M) world outside the realm of women's culture.

The language which describes the Worthy Woman echoes the language employed for describing the female Wisdom figure. The former is in fact Wisdom the bountiful, the kingpin of (family) existence. She is the personification of a role model, hopefully to be emulated by other females (Camp 1985). Her voice might indeed be muted within the public culture she shares, a predominantly male culture. This is partly explained by her sitting at home while her menfolk pass their time in public places (at the gates). She lives to advance male interests and male well-being. In so doing, however, she ultimately subverts the male order by becoming its focal point and essential requisite. Or so the F voice imagines, or so it hopes. Appearances aside, it seems to say, in ancient Israel as in many other cultures, ancient and latterday, men have the authority. Nevertheless, women can gain power while formally appearing to defer to M authority (Meyers 1989). The final victory and perhaps revenge—so whispers the secondary muted voice—is the woman's, for she is the actual controller of the family.

Even the values operating in love poetry, like the importance of female physical beauty, are of no consequence here. Whether males find "her" physically and sexually attractive or not (v. 30), "she" is the ultimate winner. The price for this implicit victory is explicit complicity with the system, the perpetuation of its values, the introjection of its ideology. Thus is male dominance preserved while being overcome.[14] A double voice, a dual existence (Showalter

---

[14] It is worth noting that in Jewish lore this poem is recited on various

1986)—so a woman seems to be saying to her daughter by obliquely referring to her own experience.

Finally, the ʾēšet ḥayil poem is an acrostic. A woman teaching her daughter the alphabet and social adjustment at the same time? Most systems of education combine the instruction of technical skills with the teaching and internalization of social skills and mores. And that brings us back to the notions of women's literacy and literary activity in biblical times. And the problematics of the F voice, its presumed oral origins, and its transformation into record and text.

---

prescribed occassions—such as before a wedding, or on the Sabbath eve—by a husband to his bride or wife. If the reading suggested here is accepted, this Jewish custom constitutes an example of how women's texts may be appropriated by the dominant M voice of a culture and are then reframed and reorientated.

PART III
M TEXT AUTHORITY IN BIBLICAL LOVE LYRICS

ATHALYA BRENNER

M TEXT AUTHORITY IN BIBLICAL LOVE LYRICS: THE CASE OF QOHELETH 3.1-9 AND ITS TEXTUAL RELATIVES

Qoheleth 3.1-9:—A Framed Male Love Lyric?

"For everything there is a season, and a time for every matter under heaven. . .What gain has the worker from his toil?". (Qoh 3.1, 9; RSV). These two statements frame[1] a poem which lists human actions and reactions in contrasted pairs.[2] My project is to counter-read the poem itself (the frame notwithstanding) as a male poem of desire rather than a poem on chronology, that is, some kind of human time; and to refer to the issue of defining textuality as gender-motivated, perhaps even gender-specific, in biblical literature and in biblical scholarship. I shall commence from a consideration of some of the problems involved in defining certain portions of biblical love lyrics as gender-specific, of F or M provenance. My admittedly gender-motivated readership will certainly problematize issues and texts which, without recourse to gender perspectives, might appear unworthy of emphasis.

My premises are those of a reasonably informed F reader raised and taught within an androcentric, Western, Jewish, and academic framework. I shall read Qoheleth 3.2-8 inevitably under the influence of those factors.[3] To recap: Within my readerly framework, asking about the author's (or compiler's, or editor's) gender, is more a question of "what" than of "who" (naming). Contem-

---

[1] Most commentators divide the chapter differently: for them, the section continues up to verse 13 (H.L. Ginsberg 1961, 73) or 15 (Gordis 1968, 228; Barton 1909[1970], 97; Scott 1965, 203; Fox 1989, 190ff.; Whybray 1989, 36, 46; Whybray 1991). On the other hand, Zimmermann (1973, 9) regards verse 9 as the section's conclusion, and C.D. Ginsburg's treatment (1861[1970], 303) implies the same opinion. There is no compelling reason, however, to accept majority opinion here, since the demarcation line most often drawn (v. 15) is far from convincing. Why not go backwards, then, to 1.2, which voices the same sentiment of 3.9? Or forward to 3.17c, which echoes 3.1?

[2] The notion of (divinely) preordained and cyclic events in human life, arranged in contrastedf pairs, appears also in Ben Sira 33.14-15.

[3] Cf. the Introduction.

porary research has come to realize that gender issues are, in an explicit or else subversive manner, part of the ideocontents of a text (and its reading). If I look for gender-motivated authority, or authorship, it is in that sense: the sense of tracing gender-determined attitudes as illuminating for the procedure of reading. The actual sex of the author is, in the case of anonymous literature even more so than in the case of named literature, no less and no more relevant than her/his identification or date. The point to be discussed is the gender *positions* inherent in a text, to the extent that its authority can be gendered. Having gendered the poem under discussion, I shall then collate it with and contrast it to some of its literary kin within the admittedly limited corpus of biblical erotic poetry.

Ultimately, feminist reading and writing alike are grounded in the interest of producing a community of feminist readers and writers, and in the hope that eventually this community will expand to include everyone; reading M texts, however, might prove painful to F and particularly feminist readers (Schweickart 1986, 50ff.). Reading as a woman whose interests may be defined biologically, linguistically, psychologically, culturally, and historically (see van Dijk-Hemmes's adoption of Showalter's model above, I.1), I now ask once more, What is the gender imprint of Qoheleth 3.2-8 (and its frame, vv. 1 and 9); and, What is it comparable to in biblical literature?

Qoheleth 3.1-9: A Poem within a Frame

The poem[4] (vv. 2-8) which is framed on both sides by 3.1 and 3.9 is generally interpreted by commentators in the light of the framing

---

[4] Whybray (1991) argues for viewing the poem as a *list* of numerical sayings which evolved gradually (hence the variations), instead of poem. Poetic repetition and a tight structure (which are perhaps grounded in oral mnemotechnics) may indeed appear as similar to, even identical with, stylized lists. While the identification of the passage as a list does not damage my ensuing arguments, I retain its definition as a "poem" not only for the sake of convenience but also because the rigid structure is broken in *significant* junctures. Hence, departures of style cannot be related to a (conjectured) compositional process only. For further considerations of Whybray's approach see below.

Prof. Whybray first delivered his paper, "'A Time to be Born and a Time to Die'? Some observations on Ecclesiastes 3.2-8'', for the (British) Society of Old Testament Study in January 1990. He then rewrote it under the same title for: *Bulletin of the Near Eastern Culture Center* (MECCJ), volume V: *Near Eastern Studies Dedicated to H.I.M. Prince Takahito Mikasa on the Occasion of His Seventy-Fifth Birthday*, Tokyo: 1991. Prof. Whybray kindly allowed me to read the typescript of his essay. Since I could not obtain the published version and, therefore, responded to the typescript, I tried to give as full an account of Whybray's views whenever relevant but refrained from citing page numbers.

statements, and/or more generally after the ideology of Qoheleth as a whole. Broadly, opinions fall into two contrary positions.

The more common view is pessimistic: Qoheleth, whoever or whatever he may be, expounds the futility of human endeavour. Everything in this world, in the cosmos (ch. 1) and in human life (our passage), is preordained and cyclic. Human effort is neither required nor effective. The cycle of paired contrasts the poem reflects proceeds apace with or without human interference. Human beings are but pawns of their destiny. Thus despair and futility, in the existential if not also necessarily moral sense, are what humans are left with—in keeping with many other passages in this Book (1.2ff.; 2.11; 3.15a; and more).

The second, and minority, view is optimistic or at the very least neutral. Life changes all the time. Today's catastrophes may turn into a blessing tomorrow. One cannot, perhaps, fully control one's own destiny, but—and this is the authentic nature of things—situations are bound to change for better inasmuch as they change for worse. Hence, although no real choice is implied, patience and hope are. This view is in keeping with another strand in Qoheleth: since human existence is insubstantial (*hebel*), the only hope is to enjoy or hope to enjoy when an oppurtunity for pleasure arises (2.24-25; 3.12,22; and more). The proponents of this view, needless to say, will find it more convenient to separate verse 9 from the poem itself, since that verse contradicts this neutral, or realistic, or optimistic approach.[5]

Both views are anchored in the conflicting sentiments expressed elsewhere in the Book and throughout it in a kind of see-saw movement. Hence, either interpretation of the poem is possible so long as it is considered in the light of the Book as a whole. In order to avoid a stalemate, I propose to review the poem itself by considering it independently of its immediate context, because the poem appears to be stylistically and semantically independent of the statements which frame it. But, in order to distinguish the poem from its sur-

---

[5] The commentary for our passage, given in verses 10-15, indeed lends itself to both interpretations. Cf., for instance, Whybray 1989 for the second option. For another classification of interpretations for the passage see Gordis 1968, 228-9.

roundings, the language of the frame (vv. 1, 9) has to be discussed first.

The Language of the Frame

Verses 1 and 9 are written in prose (the partial parallelism of v. 1 notwithstanding). Their style is at stark variance with that of the poem,[6] and so is their vocabulary. Out of *twelve* lexical items and the linguistic phenomena they consist of, *seven* are either relatively late or else idiosyncratically used. The late lexical items are: *zěmān*, "time, season";[7] *hāʿôśēh*, "(he who) toils";[8] *ḥēpeṣ*, "matter";[9] *baʾăšer*, "in what".[10] Three other lexical items, as used, are peculiar to Qoheleth: *yitrôn*, "profit, advantage"; *ʿāmēl*, "toiling";[11] *taḥat haššāmayim*, "under the heavens".[12] Another item—*lakkol*, "for everything, anything, anyone"—is chronologically dubious.[13] In short, about two thirds of of the lexical/grammatical stock of

---

[6] This arrangement of prose enveloping poetry at both ends resembles the arrangement of the Book of Job, albeit on a much smaller scale. There too the prose sections frame a poem, the themes of which they subvert. In the case of Job, however, it seems that the prose frame is the quoted or borrowed material, while the poem is the indigeneous literary matter. In my reading of Qoheleth 3.1-9 the situation is reversed: the poem is a "borrowed" element, whereas the frame is the author's original contribution.

[7] *zěmān* is late (Neh 2.6, Esther 9.27,31), probably a borrowing from the Aramaic. See also Whybray 1991.

[8] So also 2.2. No object is implied. When preceded by the definite article, this formation features as a semantic equivalent of *ʾîš*, "man", as in Mishnaic Hebrew. Cf. Bendavid 1971, vol. II, 666ff.

[9] In the sense of "matter, thing" rather than "delight", *ḥēpeṣ* is late and also Mishnaic. Cf. BDB, 343. As Whybray notes, it occurs in Qoheleth in the same sense four times.

[10] To distinguish from *baʾăšer*, "because of" and "where", which are less definable chronologically. All instances of the present sense, "in what/which", occur in postexilic texts (also Isa 47.12, 56.4, 65.12, 66.4).

[11] As an adjectival form it appears only in Qoheleth (also 2.18, 22; 4.8; 9.9). Cf. BDB, 766.

[12] Similar expressions, such as "from under the heavens'" (Gen, Exod, Deut) or "under all the heavens" (Gen, Deut) have a wider distribution. "Under the heavens", though, is peculiar to Qoheleth—so also in 1.13, 2.3. Perhaps this is a calque from the Aramaic: cf. Jeremiah 10.11, Daniel 7.27. See also Whybray 1991.

[13] *lakkol* occurs only in texts whose exilic or postexilic status is beyond doubt (Jer 13.7, 10; Ps 145.9; Ezr 8.34; 1 Chron 7.6, 29.12) and elsewhere in Qoheleth (3.19; 9.2,3; 10.3). However, similar constructs—*hakkol, bakkol*—have a wider distribution. Hence, *lakkol* itself cannot be considered unequovically late.

verses 1 and 9 are either late or else specifically Qoheleth's. This state of affairs is in marked contrast to the linguistic picture obtaining in the poem.

The Language of the Poem: Verses 2-8

Out of *twenty six* verb bases featuring in the poem,[14] *twenty one* are not period-specific, that is, they feature in both classical and postexilic Hebrew (as well as, in most cases, Mishnaic Hebrew).

The remaining five formations are difficult to date: they are probably of late provenance since they mostly occur in late texts but, for various reasons, their late status is far from certain. They are: ^{c}qr qal, "uproot";[15] *rqd* qal, "dance";[16] *kns* qal, "gather";[17] *rḥq* qal, "distance oneself";[18] and *ḥšh* hif., "be silent".[19] Whybray adds *tpr*, "sew" to the list of dubious forms (1991, n. 6).

To summarize. The language of the poem is different from that of the introduction and conclusion enclosing it. The difference cannot be accounted for as, simply, a difference between poetry and prose. The poem seems to be linguistically and stylistically earlier and more conventional in its linguistic usage, much less idiosyncratic than its frame. The language of verses 1 and 9, with which we have compared the poem, is entirely characteristic of Qoheleth as a whole, whereas the poem's is not. Therefore, it is reasonable to conclude that the poem is quoted out of another context. The poem, then, is embedded; and embedding, by definition, affects the indigeneous sense of the source text.

---

[14] The verbs are, in order of their first occurrence: *yld*, "give birth"; *mwt*, "die"; *nṭ*ᶜ (twice), "plant"; ^{c}qr, "uproot"; *hrg*, "kill"; *rpʾ*, "heal"; *prṣ*, "demolish"; *bnh*, "build"; *bkh*, "cry"; *śḥq*, "laugh"; *spd*, "mourn"; *rqd*, "dance"; *šlk* hif. (twice), "cast, throw"; *kns*, "gather"; *ḥbq* (qal and pi.), "embrace"; *rḥq*, "distance oneself"; *bqš* pi., "search"; *ʾbd* pi., "lose"; *šmr*, "keep"; *qrᶜ*, "tear"; *tpr*, "sew"; *ḥšh* hif., "be silent"; *dbr* pi., "speak"; *ʾhb*, "love"; *śnʾ*, "hate". Unless otherwise stated, the verbs appear in the qal formation.

[15] So also Zephaniah 2.4. But see the pi. formation and the adjective *ᶜāqār, "sterile"—BDB, 785. Whybray (1991, n. 6) concludes that there is therefore no reason to classify it as late.

[16] Also Psalms 114.4,6. However, a pi. formation occurs in 2 Samuel 6 and a hif. in Isaiah 13.21.

[17] BDB, 488: "mostly late". As Whybray says (1991, n. 6), the root is "characteristic of late Hebrew rather than specifically of Qoheleth"; but see below.

[18] Mostly late, although other verbal and nominal forms of the root have a wider distribution.

[19] BDB, 364: "Chiefly poetical and late".

The practice of embedding and framing is not unique to this Qoheleth passage. There are other, admittedly less extensive, instances of texts which are quoted and framed in the Book, a subject to which we shall return later. As noted above, a similar procedure is used in the Book of Job too (Brenner 1989).

The Poem out of Context: Structure and Sense

Searching for the "original" literary setting/meaning of a quoted poem is a legitimate quest. It has intrinsic interest and, besides, may well affect the way we understand the poem's adaptation to the frame. The original meaning, be it known to the author and his readers or not, necessarily becomes a component of any new meaning imposed by the frame. It remains to be seen to what extent a detailed analysis of the poem will uncover an intrinsic sense which has nothing or little to do with the frame.

The poem's structure is fairly rigid and its style epigrammatic. Each stich begins with the phrase "a time", $\varsigma \bar{e}t$.[20] This lexeme is mostly succeeded by the preposition $l\breve{e}$, "to".[21] Then comes a construct infinitive (apart from in the second half of v. 8). The contrasted parallelism dictates an identical structure in the second half of the line. The parallel stich is introduced by the appropriate conjunction $w\breve{e}$. Every two stichoi form a formal and thematic stanza (signified as a verse in many printed editions).

Three stanzas follow this pattern (vv. 2—4).[22] Then, a departure from the fairly tight structure is introduced. Verse 5 has the same basic pattern of its predecessors, albeit with a difference—in three of its four stichs (5a, 5b, 5d) a complement succeeds the infinitive form (a nominal object in the first two, a verbal complement in the

---

[20] For a discussion of $\varsigma \bar{e}t$ see Whybray 1991. He maintains that $\varsigma \bar{e}t$ does not have a fixed meaning throughout the "list", as he calls the poem: sometimes it signifies an appropriate time, at others an oppurtune time, at others an occasional time. In other words, Whybray postulates lack of consistency for the "times" itemized; and uses that to uphold his theory of the passage's gradual evolvement. I wholly agree, but my reasons are different. I shall presently refer to an order of coherence which Whybray dismisses as hardly relevant.

[21] Excluding the second half of verses 4 and 5b, and the second half of verse 8.

[22] $n\bar{a}t\hat{u}\varsigma a$ in 2d is almost certainly a secondary, perhaps tendentious, gloss. The phrase $la\varsigma \bar{a}qor\ nat\hat{u}\varsigma a$, "uproot the planted", contains a redundancy; the complement, apart from not being necessary to the sense, repeats the root $nt\varsigma$ of the previous stich. We shall come back to this point later.

last stich). Given the poem's tight rhythmical and metrical structure so far, this deviation is quite conspicuous, even if the semantic deviation can be explained away as the outcome of gradual textual amplification.[23]

Thereafter the shorter pattern of verses 2-4 is resumed in verses 6-8, albeit with one additional departure. In the very last line (8c-d) the parallelism between the two pairs is inverted, so that the infinitives "to love" and "to hate" in the first stich are matched by the inverted nouns "war" and "peace" (not "peace" and "war", as expected) in the concluding phrase.

When we get to the poem's end we realize that the poem contains the conventional number of seven units,[24] and is distinctly if somewhat loosely chiastic.[25] Accordingly—and contra Loader—attention is, must be drawn to the middle and central stanza—verse 5, whose content significance is underlined by its departure from the otherwise fairly consistent stylistic/structural pattern.

The final line too, quite evidently, carries a sting in its tail, for after thirteen matched pairs, the final inversion cannot but be highly suggestive. In short, even if we maintain that a chiastic structure (at least of sorts) obtains throughout the poem (with Loader and contra Whybray), the key to understanding the poem resides less in the understanding of particular positive/negative contrasts and their inversions (Whybray, contra Loader). Rather, the significance of the central stanza (v. 5)—together with the final inversion of verse 8c-d, and the latter's interrelation with the opening (v. 2) and the central stanzas—should be marked as indicative for the poem's indigeneous purpose.

Verse 5: The Central Stanza

The poem's structure indeed obliges us to expect that verse 5 will contain the key to, or express the essence of, the meaning of the

---

[23] A theory of gradual expansion (Whybray 1991), during which explanatory glosses were added to the basic, rigidly stylized text seems feasible. Accounting for the specific loci, and nature, of the supposed amplifications remains, however, unexplained by the theory. Chance expansions should not be ruled out, of course; but neither should meaningful ones. In any event, since we are dealing with a *text*, an end product, those amplifications require especial consideration as they are *in situ*.

[24] Or, rather, $7 \times 2 = 14$; a sonnet structure? Cf. Loader 1969.

[25] Loader 1969, 1979, 1986; and cf. Whybray's critique (1991) of Loader's tendency to allot values that are too precise to the poem's chiasms and oppositions.

poem. However, whether deliberately or due to our modern (mis)understanding, both the contextual and connotative senses of verse 5 seem less than obvious.

The wording of the first stich, a time for "casting stones" and "gathering stones", is vague figuratively as well as metaphorically. What does the "casting" and "gathering" of stones, in whatever sense, mean in the poem's context? Some commentators insist that a literal sense is quite acceptable: there are times for casting stones—such as when a field is being cleared, or in war; and there are others for gathering them—when clearing ground, or for building (so for instance most recently Fox 1989, 192-3 and Whybray 1991). Personally I find this quasi-literal interpretation unconvincing: the other verbs in the series, be their connotations and/or denotations "desirable" or "undesirable" (Loader), positive or negative,[26] do not receive complements (apart from the last verb in v. 2). As a result, their stichs are much shorter than the three longer ones in verse 5.

Other verbs in the poem have a much clearer—if less specific— denotation than the idea of casting/gathering stones: one does not question the possible denotation of "plant" or "uproot", for instance (2c-d). In the case of verse 5a-b, though, defining a denotation is not enough. If one opts for the literal interpretation, connotations and further explanations demonstrate that literality here is not

---

[26] The contrasted pairs of the poem, each containing a "positive" and deconstructive (if not always "negative"; see Whybray 1990) constituent of the same human experience, are arranged in a loose chiastic order of + /- alternating with -/ + . Thus,

    v. 2: + /-;
    vv. 3 and 4; -/ + ;
    v. 5 (like v. 2): + /-;
    v. 6: + /-;
    v. 7: + /-;
    v. 8: + /- // -/ + .

Within each of the verses (strophes) an identical order is twice duplicated. The only exception is verse 8, which starts as + /- ("to love/hate") and ends on an inverted -/ + note ("war/peace"). The inversion of the inner parallelism in the seventh strophe closes the poem on a positive note, and also retains a chiastic arrangement with the beginning (v. 2a, "give birth/die"). Although I agree with Whybray's critique of Loader's too mechanical evaluation of the chiastic structure, I think that the chiasm's force cannot be ignored altogether. For my purpose, I find it instructive that the central strophe, verse 5, loosely displays the same structure as verses 2 and 8a (before the inversion)—another indication of these verses's centrality.

as tranparent as it should be, by definition. In short, formal and semantic considerations cancel the acceptance of a "simple" reading for the "stones" and the activities linked with them.

Another approach is to turn to the next line. Could it be that an internal clue resides the contrasting pair in the second half of verse 5: there is a time for "embracing" and for "refraining from embracing"? Now, in almost all the other strophes the two contrasting pairs are complementary (only in the case of v. 7 is this not obvious). On the primary reading level at least, verse 2 deals with the life-cycle, verse 3 with creation and destruction, verse 4 with joy and sorrow, verse 6 with acquisition and loss and verse 8 with conflict and harmony.[27] Verses 2 and 8 (quality of life) are interlinked, in addition to the internal duplication within them of the strophe's topic. Since verse 5 is at the exact centre of the poem, one can begin interpreting the problematic 5a-b by expecting the verse's sense structure to be similar to that of verses 2 and 8. In other words, do the two lines of verse 5 (5a-b and 5c-d) relate to each other like the two lines of verses 2 and 8 do?

The second half of verse 5 (5c-d) has the contrast "embracing" as against "refrain from embracing". Hence, interpretations of the parallel 5a-b as architectural activity[28] or the stoning of adulterous wives[29] are entirely inappropriate as single, exclusive interpretations. There is no reason to object to reading a polyvalent metaphor in this verse.[30] Nonetheless, such a reading should ultimately assign proper weight to the second pair of verbs, "embracing" and "refraining from embracing".

Verse 5a-b: The "Sexual" Interpretation

The sexual connotation of "casting" and "gathering" stones was proposed for this verse already in ancient times. The Jewish sages asserted that one "casts stones" when one's wife is "pure" (ritually clean), and should abstain from doing so when she is "unclean"

---

[27] The first part of verse 7 deals with tearing and sewing, the second with the seemingly unrelated subject of communication and non-communication.

[28] So the Aramaic Targum, Ibn Ezra, Ginsburg (1861), Barton (1908), and many others.

[29] So also, not surprisingly, Zimmermann 1973, 9-10.

[30] For the concept of polyvalent, or multilevel, metaphors in Qoheleth see Fox 1989 for Qoheleth 12.

(within the menstruation period of uncleanliness; So, with minute differences in the phrasing, in Qoheleth Rabbah and Yalqut Shimeoni for the passage). In the ancient sources cited the "casting" and "gathering" of stones is read as an oblique (metaphorical) reference to performing/abstaining from the sexual act and, it is worth noting, the reading is done from an obviously male perspective.

What gave rise to the "sexual" interpretation in the Jewish sources? At first glance it seems so far fetched as to be inconceivable—unless it is anchored in solid information which, unfortunately, is not readily available to modern readers. Levy (1912), who advances this interpretation, supplies some parallels but, as Whybray notes (1991, n. 15), remains unconvincing. Gordis who, by and large, accepts an "erotic significance" for the metaphor (1968, 230), relies on the same Jewish sources and cites biblical passages which link "stones" with matters sexual and reproductive (Ex 1.16, Jer 22.27, the obscure Matt 3.9), but does not successfully explain the connotative meaning of the metaphor—if a metaphor it is.[31] In short, how can the "sexual" interpretation be substantiated by the context or by other biblical intertexts?

Let us deal with the immediate context first, that is, with the second half of verse 5. Whybray and Fox (see above) point out that *ḥbq* qal and pi., "embrace", does not always designate erotic or sexual behaviour. This is indeed so, especially in the Wisdom literature idiom *ḥbq* + "hands", "to be idle" (Qoh 4.5; Prov 6.10, 24.33). Two other occurrences are figurative, hence not instructive for the present passage (Job 24.8, Lam 4.5). The remaining—and majority—eight occurrences all designate physical intimacy: four with family kin (Gen 29.13, 33.4, 48.10; 2 Kgs 4.16) and four with a lover of either sex (Prov 4.8, 5.20; SoS 2.6, 8.3). In view of this inventory, an "intimacy" denotation at least should be accredited to *ḥbq*; and it is a toss whether the specialized erotic signification is not as primary, in the sense that it perhaps was as often or even more widely used, as the general (intimate but non-motivated by erotics) "embrace". "Take into one's arms as an overt sign of affection" is certainly the referent shared by both groups of occurrences. Verse

---

[31] Zimmermann, whose thesis of Qoheleth's inner life stems from an analysis of Qoheleth's sexual circumstances, prefers to relate the metaphor here to "stoning", although this does not account for the subsequent "gathering" of the stones.

5a-b, as argued above, would be best understood when linked up parallelistically with 5c-d.

Stones, Sexuality, and Gender Relations

Where else in the Hebrew Bible do "stones" have a semantic link with sexuality and reproduction? A metonymic link of sense obtains in the use of "millstones" and "grinding" as an allusion to the sexual act and gender roles within it. Thus says Job in his final confession,

> If my heart has been tempted by a woman
> and I have waited at my brother's door
> Let my wife grind for another
> and others will kneel over her (Job 31.9-10).

> The NEB has another translation for verse 10,
> May my wife be another man's slave
> and may other men enjoy her.

This is a remarkably free translation, which operates on the "grinding is a woman's work" convention (so also BDB *ad loc.*) and, at the same time, obscures the image by delimitation instead of clarifying it. The link between the grinding with millstones and sexuality is derived not only from social convention but also, perhaps primarily, from the image of two millstones, one on top of the other. The woman is the user of the millstone as well as, by contiguity, its metaphorical referent.

This extralinguistic image, when transformed into the realm of language, may become a particularized metaphor. The upper grinding stone—*rekeb*, "riding" stone—becomes the "male" stone. When a woman throws[32] an upper millstone from the town's wall and kills Abimelek (Judg 9.53, 2 Sam 11.21), he quickly perceives the significance of her action. The woman has become the upper millstone, she is now male; by force of symmetry, Abimelek is now in danger of becoming female. The only antidote for this outrageous reversal of gender role is for him, a dying man, to ask his armour-bearer to kill him (Judg 9.54).[33] Sexual mockery interwined with

---

[32] The verb used is *šlk* hif., as in Qoheleth 3.5.

[33] As Bal writes (1987, 10-35), the same gender role ideology underlines the textually difficult recollection of the Abimelek's episode in Joab's instruction to the messenger he sends to King David (in 2 Sam 11.21).

social mockery is easily discenible here. For this and the next passage cf. van Dijk-Hemmes on mockery songs, Part I above.

In Isaiah 47.1-3a we read,

> Go down and sit in the dust
> O virgin daughter of Babylon
> Sit on the ground
> down from your throne
> For you shall no more be called soft and delicate
> Take millstones and grind flour
> Uncover your tresses
> Reveal your train
> Bare your thigh...
> Let your nakedness be revealed and your shame exposed...

Here too sexual (and social) mockery serves as a foil for something else, this time for political ridicule. Once more, the metaphor acquires "sexual" force through the imagery of the woman using a millstone, being a millstone (as well as, in this case, through the allusions to Babylon, the metaphorical woman, who is described stripping off her clothes and exposing her nakedness).

We learn from post biblical Hebrew that the upper stone's spouse is the šekeb, "lying down" lower stone (B. bab bath 2a, Tos bab bath 3a). By analogy, this lower stone will be associated particularly with women (see the image in Job 31.10). And yet, the associative differentiation of "millstones" into gendered parts does not exclude the application of the whole to "women" in post biblical Hebrew sources (and see below).

To return to the Hebrew Bible, another link between stones, reproduction and women can be established through Exodus 1.16. The Egyptian king says to the midwives,

> When you assist the Hebrew women in giving birth, look at the stones.[34] If it is a son, kill him; if a daughter, let her live.

Even though the "stones" in Exodus 1.16 are, literally, "two stones", as the pointing prescribes, no "millstones" are specifically designated. Like in the case of the potter's "two stones", that is, the potter's wheel (Jeremiah 18.3), the "stones" seem obscure but are defined by the context. Here they imply a construction made of

---

[34] Literally, "two stones". Most English translations have "(birth)stool" here, from the context.

stones and identified as birth aids. Like Qoheleth 3.5, the Exodus passage has "stones", not "millstones". Nonetheless, the "stones"' affinities with "women" are obvious. Since the context of Qoheleth 3.5a-b is far from clear, only hinted at by the parallel 5c-d, the possibility—illustrated by the biblical intertexts cited—that "women" are metaphorized into stones in Qoheleth 3.5a-b should be entertained.

Women, then, use (mill)stones for reproduction, are (mill)stones —especially the lower stone, since the upper (mill)stone is considered male. Furthermore, in post-biblical Hebrew a woman, specifically a wife, is likened to millstones round her husband's neck (B. kidd 29b): in the light of the passages just read, she is so defined not because of the weighty need to support her only; there is a joke involved in the metaphor. And the act of marrying, taking a wife, is denoted in post biblical Hebrew by the technical term kns[35]—a term which appears in our verse together with "stones".

So far links between "stones" and female sexuality have been observed. Another alternative is to explore associations of "stones" and male sexuality. In this regard, the euphemistic and metaphorical reference to testicles by "stones" is well known. This euphemistic usage seems to underlie the Rabbis' explication of 3.5a-b in Qoheleth Rabbah, cited above.

Where do these allusions lead us? The following possibilities now emerge. The "stone" metaphor is complex, indeed can be invested with polyvalent levels of meaning.[36]

Initially, the throwing of stones (5a) might be a beneficial or peacefully motivated act. Nevertheless, it would probably conjure up violent associations for most beholders and readers. The image evokes battle scenes (see below) as well as the biblical practice of stoning—of sinning individuals, especially of an adulterous woman—more than it recalls the clearing of a field, for instance. The verb $\check{s}lk$ hif. conditions this response, since it is much stronger in connotation than its synonym, zrq qal. Gathering stones (5b)—for building, for stoning, for waging war?—remains opaque for the moment.

---

[35] So for instance B. keth 3b; the subject of the verb is always M, while its object is alwyas F. Cf. Jastrow, 649.

[36] For the procedure and method of reading a passage (Qoh 12.1-8) polyvalently see Fox 1989, 281ff.

If, on the metaphorical level which is mutually inclusive in relation to the "literal" level "stones", like millstones, might represent
women, a few questions emerge. What happens to women within
the "life" described in the poem? Are they women cast away?
Women being taken as wives, as spouses, as (mill)stones? When all
these possibilities are viewed together, a certain mood is established.

On the next level, perhaps a figurative one now, the idea of casting and afterwards gathering what has been cast, coupled with violence of action and the gender/sex allusions of the other two levels
of meaning, may also recall the sexual act on the male's side and
from a male's viewpoint (see Qoheleth Rabbah and the associations
with male sexuality). The same mood is enhanced by verse 5c-d: "to
embrace", as previously pointed out, is not always "sexual" but
does signify intimacy. It therefore appears that a "sexual" interpretation for the whole of verse 5 is indeed plausible, albeit not transparent. As stated above, the fact that birth and death (v.2a), love
and hate (v. 8a) frame a poem for which verse 5 serves as a centre
enhances the plausibility of this suggestion.

In the light of the preceding digression, verse 5 advances the following message. There is a (correct? proper? set? oppurtune?) time
for indulging in the sexual act, or for getting rid of a woman; as for
refraining from sex or, conversely, for taking a woman for a wife;
just so, there is a time to embrace and a time to abstain from embracing.

The Poem in the Light of Verse 5

If this interpretation is entertained, and since verse 5 is central (in
both senses) to the poem, we are obliged to reconsider the meaning
of the whole poem in its light. We have already observed that the
poem's careful structure suggests an overall meaning rather than
simply a sequence of contrasts. I now suggest once more to convert
unified structure into unified message, and to look for that message
inside the poem rather than *outside* it—that is, in the frame (vv. 1
and 9).

The sequence does not, as is often assumed, offer a kind of sum-
mary of the human life cycle. This might be the case if v. 2a were
the key hemistich, but the poem is not structured so as to allow such
a reading. The activities itemized in the poem, verse 2a-b apart, can
only refer to frequently-repeated actions which recur during the

whole of life. Verse 2a-b should be seen only as a prelude to these actions, which constitute the interchangeable bi-polarity of human events and experience. Is it surprising that central to these actions are sexual and gender relations, sometimes suitable to an occasion and at others not so?

In what way, however, are sexual/gender relations so central that the entire poem is constructed around them? Does it merely imply that these are the most important things in life? Or does the emphatic structural place accorded to them suggest that the whole poem is to be read—at least on one reading level, at least as a *double êntendre*—as alluding to gender relations and sexual activity, to their causes and consequences? What is proposed here is a reading of the poem which regards its highly compressed and laconic language as a riddle, the additional toungue-in-cheek meaning of whose parts falls into place once the code is recognised. The result is a metonymic reading in which each pair of activities can be assigned a meaning related to the sexual/erotic behaviour of humans, over and beyond its more obvious semantic and metaphorical value.[37]

The opening contrast, birth/dying (v. 2a-b), seems to refer, unlike all the others, to unique experiences of human life—for each, there is *one* time only. As suggested earlier, it is possible that this contrast stands apart somewhat from the others in expressing the general view that all things are transient. However, although most commentators so translate, it is questionable whether *lldt* signifies "to be born" rather than "to give birth".[38] If the normative signification is retained, the contrast is between the giving of life and its loss; and that is not an exact logical contrast. Birth, however, is the outcome of a sexual act, and the sense of the whole verse may be the conjoining of love and death (as in SoS 8.6, as in imaginary and mythic life cycles) by means of equating love with giving birth. This reading

---

[37] The implication of my suggestion is that, rather than reject other readings, we gain an additional level of meaning.

[38] Although regular Hebrew usage clearly refers *yld* qal to an F subject (H.L. Ginsberg, 73), *lldt* here is habitually rendered "be born" or even "beget" (with a universal, or else an explicit or implied M, subject). The irregular passive denotation, while supplying a better parallel to the second pole ("to die"), does not make linguistic sense even if it is analogous to Arabic usage (Zimmermann, 142). Positing "to be born" here is clearly an interpretive move influenced by the poem's frame, and by the interpreter's gender ideology. Furthermore, if the poem is directed primarily at an F audience (see below), the regular "to give birth" makes a better sense.

also prepares us for the love = life metonymy, which the remainder of the poem preserves.

The verbs "to plant" and "pluck, uproot, pull out" (2c-d) reinforce fairly exactly the first pair; the planting of seed is a natural metaphor for the sexual act (from an M perspective), while pulling out or plucking will play on both sex and death associations. In addition, a derivative of the root ʿqr also signifies "barren". Consequently, the riddle metaphor is sustained or, at the very least, hinted at. When recognized, this supplies a plausible reason why the gloss nāṭûʿa was introduced—precisely in order to remove what was seen as an ambiguity, to suppress a metaphorical (sexual) meaning in favour of a more "literal" one. The trouble is that the addition disfigures not only rhythm and metre but also mood and sense.

The clue, then, is already furnished by verse 2. Some of the remaining stichs lend themselves to this riddle metonymy, others less or not at all. The apparent lack of consistency, I feel, does not detract from the argument. Total consistency would have undermined the riddle quality of the poem by making it too transparent.

Thus in verse 3a-b, killing cannot be undone by healing, unless the killing and healing refer metaphorically to dealing with emotions rather than, or in addition to, physical entities. In 3c prṣ may be translated as "breach"; and the metaphor of breaching a symbolic "wall" does not need to be searched too far afield. Let us read the "brothers'" words in the Song of Songs 8.8-9,

> We have a little sister
> and she has no breasts
> What shall we do for (to) her
> when she is asked for in marriage
> If she is a wall
> we will build on it a silver parapet
> If she is a door
> we shall shut it with cedar planks.[39]

The metaphor of breaching the wall-as-virginity, to be guarded and locked up against violation, hardly needs further elaboration.

Admittedly, sexual riddle associations are not easily demonstrable in verses 4, 6, and 7. Nonetheless, the actions designated by the verbs in them and the emotions underlying those actions can apply

---

[39] Cf. van Dijk-Hemmes's translation of this passage and her discussion of it in I.A.5 above.

as fittingly to matters of love and interpersonal relations as to matters of life and death; perhaps here too the metonymy of eros/life as against thanatos, established already in verse 2, is being reaffirmed in an oblique manner. Let us remember that the verbs listed deal with extreme human emotions and their consequences. There are crying/laughing and lamenting/dancing in verse 4. Searching/losing[40] occurs in verse 6a-b; the remainder of verse 6, which refers to keeping/casting away, looks like a shorter variant of verse 5 (see below). Although tearing bears a modern allusion to the tearing of the hymen, its opposite number, sewing, does not confirm this for our text (v. 7a-b). The latter pair cannot be construed as a reference to a habit of mourning either, since a torn mourning garment should not be repaired afterwards. Here too we can make do with the general notion of cyclic contrasts, or opt for their serving, on the riddle level, as reference to human emotions and their behavioural consequences: at times relations are broken, at others sustained or repaired. Finally, an interchangeable rhythm of keeping silent/talking (v. 7c-d) occurs in any human discourse, including the heterosexual one.

Thus, although overt references are not always available, even verses 4, 6 and 7 can be read as bearing a metonymic link to the riddle subject matter, erotic love and gender relations. Admittedly, such references as gleaned from verses other than verses 2a-b and 5 are not as strongly associative as those obtained from the latter and from verse 8a-b, in which love and hate are cited directly. This, however, does not detract from the argument: it is fitting that the poem's theme will shine the strongest at its formal centre, while the rest of the structure supports it more obliquely, with the theme becoming more transparent again at the beginning (v. 2) and the end (v. 8).

To sum up this reading so far. The poem emerges as a love poem whose theme is the fluidity of love and sexual desire. Like everything else in life, love and sex are not constant but dynamic, in the sense that at times they inevitably change and mutate into their opposites. Nevertheless, they are subject—again, like everything else within the human order—to a continuous point-counterpoint movement. Within this bipolar changeability there exists a redeeming option for

---

[40] Cf. the motif of an F lover's quest for the male lover in the Song of Songs—for instance, 3.1-4, 5.6-8, 6.1.

consolation (or despair?): the time for them always returns, inasmuch as it passes.

Recently the psychologist Robert J. Sternberg has published a series of intriguing essays in which he articulates theories of loving and liking (for instance Sternberg 1986, 1987). He has constructed a geometric model for defining "love". The model is a triangle whose three vertices are: sex/passion; intimacy; and decision/commitment. Needless to say, the actual shapes of individual persons' triangles vary greatly, although the basic constants remain in all.

I find it interesting that, in Qoheleth 3.2-8, there are three overt vertices in which the love/erotic theme is the most pronounced (vv. 2, 5, and 8). While two of these vertices (vv. 2 and 8) cannot be precisely defined in keeping with Sternberg's terms of reference, the third one (v. 5) can. The fact that this verse, whose subject is (in my reading) sexual relations, is centrally placed in the middle, or apex of the poem, is probably indicative of its thematic significance for the whole. One can hazard the guess that, for whoever composed the poem, the triangle of love (and the model of sex roles and gender relations it entails) is chiefly motivated by sex rather than by any other vertex.

Qoheleth 3.2-8: An M Poem of Desire

When I read a text, be it biblical or otherwise, I try to read it first and foremost and (un)naturally as a woman reader.[41] I cannot help but notice that the central metaphor which connotes the sexual act and/or gender relations in this poem—the "casting" and "gathering" of stones—is an aggressive metaphor. Its primary semantic, hence psychological, milieu is that of fighting and war.[42] The theme of war/peace is indeed introduced at the end of the catalogue of the bipolarized pairs (v. 8c-d), in parallelism with "a time to love and a time to hate" (v. 8a-b). Placed as they are, war and peace too can be decoded, on the "riddle" level at least, as a metaphor for sexual relations. The covert theme resurfaces explicitly in the very

---

[41] Cf. the Introduction; and also van Dijk-Hemmes above, Part I; and 1989b.

[42] In all the other passages in which the phrase "casting stones" (šlk hif. + ʾeben or ʾăbānîm) occurs, the military-aggressive association is unmistakable. So in Joshua 10.11, Judges 9.53, 2 Kings 3.25, Zechariah 5.8; and with another verb, "to shoot", in 2 Chronichles 26.15. For the military use of stones as weapon in the Near East throughout antiquity see Yadin 1963.

last couplet and, significantly, closes the proceedings. And I remember that other violent denotations in the poem—"uproot" (v. 2d), "kill" and "demolish, breach" (v. 3), "tear"—(v. 7) could be decoded on the sexual and gender relation (connotative) level too.

My instinct as an F reader therefore whispers that, most plausibly, an M voice is the voice the text assumes throughout the poem. The ejaculatory and thrusting nature connoted by key expressions is perceived as especially blatant when heard or read by a woman—which is not to say that M readers cannot or do not respond to it in a similar fashion.[43] The violence, and the war/peace metaphors, make an M viewpoint much more plausible for the sexual (extralinguistic) vision which underlines the passage than an F or "universal/neutral" viewpoint. The military metaphor here is as unmistakably M as the military imagery of the Song of Songs 4:4, a love lyric which describes a female lover through an M voice using military terminology (Meyers 1986, 213-4).

So far for the voice delivering the poetic discourse. But who, what, is the target audience the poem is aimed at? This is much more difficult to define than the source of the literary communication (the M voice). Is the poem intended for male consumption, an M voice communicating M experience and world vision to an M audience? Is it designed for the entertainment/teaching of male consumers, reflecting as it does on the mystery of M sexual/gender behaviour? Or, on the contrary, is it directed at women in general or one particular woman, an M discourse in an F ear? Is it, within the boundaries of poetic convention, directed at the poetic self? Or, finally, does it have no specific audience in mind other than a random, possibly heterosexual, audience, you and I, any listener or reader regardless of their gender?

Unfortunately, it is impossible to pinpoint an original target-recipient for the poem. I conclude this part of the discussion by returning to the speaking voice; and remind myself yet again that the identification of the poetic voice as stereotypically M should be

---

[43] While discussing this passage with graduate students at a seminar in Utrecht (September 1989), a male student said that, from his M perspective, the text seems an M text not because of the violence inherent in some key images but, rather, because of the image of planting and uprooting (v. 2c-d). Since that stich parallels the one introducing life and death, he said, his associations immediately ran to the male "planting" of the seed of life and, thereafter, "uprooting" himself physically by withdrawing.

related to the tone of the poem. And the tone is indeed the voice of clipped authority which can be neither argued with nor denied (which makes it suitable for framing by ''Qoheleth'' for his purposes, be they what they may according to the different interpretaions advanced). Ultimately, this is how things are—bipolarized. Ultimately, the repetitive ʿet, ''time'' and the fairly rigid structure are overpowering. Therefore, is it not fair to say that acceptance is recommended for the universal principle of point-counterpoint mutation? The trouble for me, an F reader, is that the recommendation is delivered from a vantage speaking spot of mastery in life's strife and struggle. May we assume that the speaker considers himself victorious in the war between the sexes, thus can afford to call for (quasi-philisophical?) acceptance of (post-coital) change? I detect sexism here, and that makes me feel less than comfortable. I feel like resisting it. And the only way to do so is to point out the conventional M character of the poetic voice.

When I first offered this reading of Qoheleth 3.2-8 as an M poem of desire for publication, I received decidedly negative responses from M readers (of both sexes) and enthusiastically affirmative ones from F readers. The M responses were characterized by vehemence and anger at my partisan (gender) reading attitudes. One of the recurrent counter-attitudes was this. Is it not true, some of the more sophisticated M responses argued, that *all* biblical literature is assumed M unless proven otherwise? And if so, what is so illuminating in the present exegesis?

I observed the anger, and the resistance (which matches my own vis-à-vis the text itself). My reaction is, well, there is a difference between accepting a cliche and exposing the perspective informing the text for what it is worth—an androcentric view read and interpreted as a *universally* applicable (for F readers too) truism. A view advanced can be read as either androcentric, or else universal (neutral from the gender perspective, as if this were viable); it cannot be both simultaneously. A reading choice has to be made, and this has consequences.

It is interesting to note in this regard that the Aramaic Targum assumes an overt M voice for the whole poem from its very beginning—actually, from the frame onwards. *lakkol*, ''everything, everybody'' (v. 1) is rendered *lĕkol gĕbar*, ''for every man (male)''. *lāledet* (v. 2) is rendered *lĕmēlad bĕnîn*, ''to beget sons'' (text as in Levine 1973). Even within the midrashic-homiletic framework of the Targum, there is no reason for these renderings apart from an automatic, intuitive diagnosis of the poem as an M text.[44] This is, of course, an overtly M rendering of an apparent M text. I, an F reader, find the exegesis undelining this rendering less offensive— more honest—than a supposedly innocuous (but tellingly indignant) contention that the text is an M text of universal (transgender) validity.

Before going on to examine some other instances of M love lyrics in the Hebrew Bible I would like to address three additional problems concerning Qoheleth 3.1-9:

a. Whybray's suggestion that the poem, 3.2-8, has evolved gradually.

b. Another possible example for Qoheleth's borrowing from the tradition of biblical love lyrics.

c. The practice of quoting in Qoheleth.

3.2-8: A Single Act of Composition or the Product of a Gradual Process?

Whybray (1991) suggests that 3.2-8 is the end result of a gradual process of composition and reduction. Such a view, he maintains, accounts for the various significations of the repetitive *ʿēt* and for minor departures from the otherwise rigid stylistic pattern,[45] as well as for the longer formats of verses 2d and 5. He concludes that the poem's arrangement in seven stanzas is deliberately designed to invoke totality; and that verses 1 and 2a-b (a general introduction, and a general comment on life and death) should be ascribed to Qoheleth himself, while verses 9-15 are obviously an appended comment.

Whybray's view seems attractive, since it relates seriously to the departures from the rigid style and the ring construction of the whole poem. I find it surprising, however, that Whybray does not attribute those same stichs which he himself points out as irregular—notably the longer verses 2c-d and 5—to Qoheleth, or to whoever framed the poem in order to comment upon it. While the idea of intervening with a beginning of an existing poem does have logic to support it,

---

[44] Surprisingly, the Targum does not adopt the "erotic" reading of verse 5a-b, even though it is suggested by the Jewish sources the Targum usually harks back to.

[45] The absence of *lĕ* before the two infinitives of 4c-d; the inverted order and nominal phrases of 8c-d.

Whybray's speculations about Who-did-what to the text seem to me unconvincing.

Furthermore, Whybray ascribes the sevenfold structure and its implied totality to an (anonymous) redactor, because in his view the idea of totality is absent from the "list" (his view) itself. But the same type of arrangement into a seven-item catalogue obtains also in the *ṭôb*..., " (It is) good..." list of Qoheleth 7.1-14 (see Gordis 1968, 229). There is no compelling reason to attribute the sevenfold arrangement of that passage to a redactor/editor, inasmuch as there is no reason to attribute it to 3.2-8. And there is no question of totality or its lack in the thematics (to distinguish from the format) of either text. Ultimately, it seems equally satisfactory, or unsatisfactory, to allow both texts to Qoheleth, or to whoever operated under that pseudonym as author of the Book (and our passage).

To come back to the longer stichs. It would appear plausible that if "a process of growth" is contemplated, those precisely would have been its loci. Modifications are most easily introduced into a discourse by minimal additions—a repetition of a verbal sequence is the simplest form for so doing. As mentioned above, I think that this is precisely what happened in verses 2d and 5, with longer stichs as a result. But, more important still, those same additions (if this is what they are), or deviations from style, strengthen the sexual/erotic interpretation of the poem by drawing attention to the riddle and its code. There is no reason to deny "Qoheleth" an understanding which produced such modifications by expanding the hidden level of the poem's theme. "He", as well as any other author or redactor, could be responsible for it. One remembers in this connection that, by and large, women are treated throughout the Book of Qoheleth from an M perspective—often if not always in a misogynistic fashion but always as an object and reflected image of, and target for, M needs.

To sum up. If we recognize a principle of gradual growth for Qoheleth 3.2-8, and its embedded status within its present context, possibilities other than the ones Whybray points out become equally plausible; and other forms of tampering with the poem's text can be contemplated by appealing to this same general principle.

Another Instance of Borrowing from Conventions of Love Poetry in Qoheleth?

I feel that demonstrating that another passage in Qoheleth exhibits knowledge of, and affinities with, biblical love poetry will promote my case.

Qoheleth 12.1-7 deals with the decay of the human body in old age and with dying. The text contains figurative and metaphorical descriptions of physical deterioration (according to some commentators) or an hyperbole of a decaying estate (according to others; but see Fox 1989, 281-310 for objections and another view). Here too there obtain some stylized repetitions, although in the form of a refrain. Finally, at any rate, death arrives with the third repetition of the phrase *ʿad ʾăšer lōʾ*, "until (it) does not", which introduces the ultimate conclusion of the process (v. 6). The apparent incoherence of the imagery leads interpreters to disagree on the literary genre of the passage: is it an elaborate allegory, or a parable (Ogden 1987, 197ff.)? As Ogden (pp. 197-8) and Fox maintain, no interpretation can consistently account for *all* the constituents of the imagery.

There is no reason why the passage cannot be regarded as an example of a double metaphor. In other words, two levels of metaphorical signification (body decay and, for example, estate decay) can be connoted concurrently. While reading, though, I have to make a choice. I have to decide what I want to concentrate on, and which of the two metaphorical "levels" might be more meaningful for my reading purpose.[46] I therefore prefer to sidestep the notion of a decaying estate—without denying it—and concentrate on interpreting the passage as an extended albeit not strictly consistent evocation of physical decay and approaching death, through a rather chilling description of what happens to various organs of the old/dying human body. I am aware of the fact that, while so doing, I am corrupted by the traditionally received critical practice started by Jewish sources (Fox). Such perhaps is the power of traditional exegesis: try as I may, whenever I read this passage I see, smell, touch, hear, almost taste the sickly substances of human physical decay.

The description does not follow a rigid order. Verse 1 can be read as a general introduction to the theme of old age. Verse 2 may be read as a depiction of old age in terms of darkness and lack of rain.

---

[46] Any other procedure will actually subvert reading polyvalency while, superficially, maintaining it.

Verse 3 is a bit more specific. It may be construed as referring (in metaphorical language) to the inefficiency of an old person's shaky hands ("the guardians of the house"), the incapacity of the remaining teeth, and the blindness of the eyes. Verse 4 may be untangled as referring to old persons' inability to sleep beyond the early hours of morning (when birds start to sing) and their early awakening, and to their proverbial deafness. Verse 5 can be read as depicting old persons' fear of stumbling and their physical insecurity of limbs, fears which often focus on high places and obstacles. Then comes the loss of sexual appetite or competence. While the rest of the world goes on multiplying, an aging or dying individual may go to his/her Maker (vv. 6-7). To sum up: the deterioration in functionality of an old person's hands, teeth, eyes, ears, legs, and sexual organs is cited as examples for what happens to humans just before their (un)natural (preordained) death. Or as a metaphor for other decay phenomena, or both.

A catalogue of bodily parts, typically in a descending or ascending order, is characteristic of the tradition of love poetry. It is conveniently referred to in biblical scholarship as *wasf*. We have at least three examples of this textual manifestation in the Song of Songs (4:1-7 = 6.3-6; 5:10-16; and 7:1-7; cf. Falk 1982, 80-87). Is Qoheleth 12:1-7, despite Fox's objections, related to the *wasf* genre?

The Book of Qoheleth proper begins at 1.2 and ends at 12.8, for those two verses are repetitious and form an inclusio. Apart from the Superscript (1.1) and the pious Afterword (12.9-14), and despite the inner inconsistencies and repetitions, there is no reason to doubt the Book's literary integrity. It is a unified composition whose "inconsistencies" can be accounted for by literary rather than historical arguments. Consequently, one author is deemed responsible for all of it. It follows that one and the same person formulated 3.1-9 and 12.1-7. That person, then, utilized the *wasf* tradition for chapter 12 by taking it outside its native milieu (praise of the loved one's appearance). Similarly, he (for there is, in my opinion, hardly a question of that person being a she) uses another instance of love poetry (3.2-8) outside its original context. I think that the possibility that "Qoheleth", a literary and/or historical figure who was well-versed in erotic poetry, wrote or set both passages derives an additional measure of strength from the recognition of both as literary offshoots of the Hebrew tradition of love lyrics.

Quoting and framing: Back to Verses 1 and 9

Gordis convincingly demonstrates how the author of Qoheleth utilized quotations—sometimes for substantiating his own opinions, but mostly in order to subvert those same quotations through a comment appended to them (cf., for instance, 2.13-14a to 2.14b-16). The identification of the central function this literary device fulfills for Qoheleth explains discrepancies between seemingly conventional and apparently personal views and constitutes a step toward refuting the convenient argument—that the Book's internal contradictions were effected by the activity of numerous compilers/ authors (Gordis 1968, 95-108). Whybray (1981) has taken the quoting principle further; and he also argues convincingly for the quoted status of Qoheleth 3.2-8 and its link with its frame (1991, especially notes 11, 12).

The analysis of 3.1-9 submitted here entails an acknowledgement that quoting, for Qoheleth, implies modification. What seems to be special about this ''quoted'' passage (3.2-8) is that a radical change (see Whybray) is effected not just by means of its framing, that is, contextualizing. An extended quote is lifted out of context and— within the present context—serves to heighten a point foreign to its original *setting* (whatever that might have been). A poem is quoted, probably verbatim (but see above). The original poem might have been about life and love and desire, from giving birth to death. The voice speaking within it sounds like an M voice. The theme, at least the covert/encoded/metaphorical theme, is the cyclic movement of [male] desire and the resultant nature of gender relations. As such, the theme links up with a central Qoheleth theme—the preordained, cyclic nature of cosmic events and human life (although it does not refer to another, related Qoheleth theme—the futility of human endeavour). The subversion or misuse of the original poem is achieved by:

a. Quoting it out of its presumed situational and verbal context;

b. embedding it in a new context;

c. enclosing it within a frame which gently but decidedly falsifies its primary theme. The introduction (v. 1) conforms to the poem's content and theme, but omits to indicate what the specific subject matter of the poem is; and the conclusion (v. 9) does not follow from the poem itself, but from sentiments advanced elsewhere in the Book (1.3, ch. 2, and more);

d. finally, minimally tampering with the poem's text (if we view stylistic and structural departures as secondary, see above).

Proverbs 30.18-19, 20

I would now like to turn to other texts of biblical love poetry whose voice may be defined as an M voice. My first candidate is Proverbs 30.18-19 and the comment appended to it in verse 20.

> Three things are incomprehensible for me
> and four I do not know
>> The way of a vulture in the sky
>> The way of a serpent on a rock
>> The way of a ship in mid-seas
>> And the way of a man in a young woman.
>
> Such is the way of an adulterous woman
> She eats and wipes her mouth and says
>> I have done nothing wrong.

At first glance, the structural similarity of this passage to Qoheleth 3.1-9 is perhaps not striking. It does, however, become apparent on successive readings. The points of contiguity between the two texts are: a frame which envelops the inner core at both ends; a structural "seven" of sorts; rigid and economic style; and the presentation of the theme in terms of a riddle.

The number "seven" is utilized in both passages for the overall pattern, although it is not a real "seven" unit structure but a "three" + a climactic "one" masquerading as a false 3 + 4 pattern in Proverbs (v. 18).[47]

Rigidity of style, peppered with some departures, obtains in the core section of both texts. There is a repetition of word, sound, and grammatical pattern in the main body of the Proverbs passage (v. 19). The key word *drk*, "way" in the construct state is followed by a nominal ("vulture", "serpent", "ship", and "man" respectively). A preposition (three times *bĕ*, "in"; once, concerning the ser-

---

[47] Zakovitch 1977; on the numerical saying category, applicable to both texts, cf. Whybray 1991, with literature in n. 7-9. Whybray stoutly denies the appropriateness of a numerical saying status for Qoheleth 3.2-8, inasmuch as he points out the inappropriateness of the frame's introduction, Qoheleth 3.1, to the poem itself. It is helpful to note that, as a title, Proverbs 30.18 is formulaic but nonetheless hardly a suitable preamble for verse 19 either.

pent, "on"") is then complemented by a nominal which functions either as a grammatical object or an adverb of location (in the "sky", on the "rock", in the "sea", in a "young woman").

Here too there is a riddle, although it is more transparent than the riddle of the Qoheleth passage. The crux of the latter—the "stones" metaphor which obliquely albeit forcefully refers to heterosexual relations from an M perspective—occupies the fourth stanza, the same fourth place as the climax of the "three-and-four(th)" riddle of Proverbs 30.19.

In Proverbs 30.18-20 the rigidly constructed catalogue is embedded within two comments too. Verse 18 is a numerical style introduction; verse 20 is a scathing misogynistic comment only loosely connected to the numerical riddle, hence sometimes viewed as a gloss.[48]

I would like to suggest that the underlying structural similarity of Proverbs 30.18-20 and Qoheleth 3.1-9 is indicative of thematic similarity. Here the textual voice sounds like an M voice too. The "wonderous" thing extolled is neither a woman's way "with" a man, nor a man's way "with" a woman, nor the sexual mutuality of men and women, nor that of women and men. Rather, it is male desire and the male side of sexual transactions: "the way of a man *in* (literally) a young (*sic!* Hebrew ʿ*almah*, "a young nubile maid") woman". My response as an F reader to this conjured picture of behaviour/control—the vulture penetrates the sky and halves it, the serpent slides over the rocks (indeed a deviation; but thus the serpent manages the rocks, so to speak), the ship pierces the waters, a man... A series of violent images: disturbance of surface, division, penetration, piercing. Majestic images, animalistic and mechanical. A totality of air, land, and sea: an image of all-encompassing control. The riddle's only redeeming grace, in my view, is the implicit knowledge that all the (extra-linguistic) referents of these images disappear without a trace and therefore, by analogy, so does the sexual control (including, ultimately, gender control) they metaphorize. This recognition modifies the androcentric perspective somewhat.

My point is not, like some critics will have it, that my reading

---

[48] In view of the parallel structure in Qoheleth 3.1-9, and other occurrences of stylistically repetitive poems in Proverbs 30, with or without introductory and/or reflective comments (see Whybray 1991), I suggest viewing v. 20 as a relevant M comment on stereotypic F conduct rather than a gloss.

rejects other readings (of the directional, or locational, or motional significations) of the riddle. Of course other readings are still viable. Neither do I object to the view that celebration of sex and gender relations informs the riddle. I do want to resist, though, the universalization of an apparent M expression of human experience here encapsuled, and its presentation as a transgender sentiment.

Like in my reading of Qoheleth 3.2-8, it seems to me that here too male mastery within the mystery of heterosexual relations is the phenomenon celebrated. This becomes even more pronounced when we understand *derek*, usually translated "way", as denoting the homonymic *derek*, "control" simultaneously with its more frequent sense.[49]

In short, the two passages share too many features (voice, structure, tone, subject matter, theme, style) for their affinity to be ignored. Proverbs 30.18-20 poses a question through the voice of an I persona: Who can understand the mystery of male way/control over a woman? Taken together with Qoheleth 3.2-8, a partial answer can be supplied: love and desire are wonderful yet incomprehensible. Like other human emotions and phenomena, they appear in cyclic motion. They come and go in order to reappear and disappear again, as is their (preordained?) nature. All this is true for M desire and M experience. F desire and experience are unaccounted for in both texts.

Samson's Riddles

Mieke Bal shows (Bal 1987, 41-48) how Samson's stories in Judges 14-16 are actually concerned with sex, sexuality, and male socialization through a process of maturation. Rather than repeat her admirable analysis, I would just like to relate to a few features of Samson's discourses which bear resemblance to the two M texts read above—Qoheleth 3.1-9 and Proverbs 30.18-20.

Unlike the two previous passages, the explicit situational context in Judges 14 is that of courting, marriage, desire. Samson's question to his wedding "companions", however, is obliquely encoded. Explicitly the riddle deals with eating and sweetness which are, implicitly, obvious symbols for sexual activities. Overtly, though, it

---

[49] So also in Ugaritic: *drkt* is "mastery, control". See also the possible double meaning and word play on *drk* in Numbers 24.17, 1 Kings 18.27.

relates to a feat of physical strength previously produced by Samson. The form of Samson's discourse (v. 14) is poetic, terse, repetitive. It is a riddle (like in Proverbs) which requires decoding on a level of signification other than the explicit level (somewhat like Qoheleth). The fact that the required answer,

> What is sweeter than honey
> What is stronger than a lion? (v. 18a),

is once more a question, demonstrates that the real answer lies elsewhere. The real answer does not hark back in simple or complex manner (Bal) to Samson's private feat of strength. The answer to the riddle is: Sex is sweeter than honey; sex is stronger than a lion. This answer is not stated because it belongs elsewhere: not to this particular narrative context but, rather, to the discourse of love and desire.

Within its presumably original context, the companions' answer is therefore a question whose answer is obvious. It is also an inclusive question. But is it a neutral question genderwise? if we read it as relating to the sweetness and vigor experienced by members of both genders, then it is genderless. If, on the other hand, our reading stereotypifies the "sweetness" as an F attribute, and the vigor as its M complementary counterpart, then the answer becomes gendered.

What happens when a poem, a saying, is lifted out of its original milieu and embedded in a particular context? Like in Qoheleth 3, the poem might acquire new motivation through it new placement. The verbal context serves as commentary and, consequently, as an ideoframe. Bal implies that the emphasis on the honey sweetness of F love is common to this instance and to the Song of Songs, where honey is a recurrent symbol of female sexuality (and see below). The emphasis on physical strength as a love metaphor, Samson's secret mastery (which is lost once it becomes public), is again a hallmark of an M approach. Hence, intertexts as well as the immediate context in which the question-answer is embedded point, once more, to its identification as a manifestation of an M voice.

It has long been recognized that Samson's retort to the companions' unmasking of his riddle is in itself a riddle with sexual connotations. Verse 18b reads,

> Had you not ploughed with my heifer/cart
> You would have not deciphered my riddle.

His heifer, his love. Samson's woman and her feelings for her lover are never disclosed: she is scared of her own people, they threaten her and she cooperates with them. But does she love Samson? No riddles disclose for us her perspective, so as to supplement the F side of this love story.

And yet, Samson does not learn. At the episode's end he is ready for another encounter with the F principle, his submission to which (Bal) will cost him his life. An F reader is quick to recognize that the defence of M positions of "strength", threat and control indulged in by all male parties in the narrative (Samson, the "companions", the woman's father, the Philistines) and exemplified by the sexual riddle game, are fatally injurious for all concerned.

Other Instances of M Love Poetry: Some Notes

For the purpose of the present study, I have defined M poetry as poems whose implicit speaking voice is male/masculine. This by no means constitutes a prejudice in regard to the actual authors' identities although, as most readers would agree, the imprints underlining most biblical voices are predominantly M. In the name of greater specificity, though,, I can think of some other biblical texts which may qualify as M poetry of love and desire. These are some passages of the Song of Songs, which the text implicitly attributes to a male voice, and some so-called prophetic texts.

In the Song of Songs, the most typically gender motivated poem seems to be 7.1-7 (concluded by an obviously M comment, 7.8-9), an M voice poem which displays a stereotyped approach to male sexuality. The mood of this passage is different from that of Qoheleth 3:2-8. It is much lighter and more humorous. Yet, the basic premise is similar in both cases. M desire comes over as aggressive, either overtly (the central war metaphor of Qoh 3) or covertly (the offensive sexual humour of SoS 7). An alternative reading of Songs of Songs 7—as an M voice imitated by an F voice—enhances our understanding of the former's literary qualities (Brenner 1990).

To be sure, other M voice passages of the Song of Songs, such as 2.14 or 4.1-14, display other and varied tones and moods. They do not belong to the present series of, shall we say, macho-style poetry. And the recognition that an M voice is implicit in them does not constitute a bias as to the actual authorship of the passage.

Another instance is that of Hosea 2. Van Dijk-Hemmes (1989b) convincingly argues that M love and desire displayed in this chapter (and in Hosea 1 and 3; see also Setel 1985 and Part IV below) constitute an aggressive inversion of parallel, albeit gentler, female sentiments expounded in the Song of Songs. M hallmarks are once more in evidence: the mastery, objectification of female sexuality, desire to control the F love object, abuse, superiority. One finally feels like saying that, as such, love is a much overrated motivation for socially sanctioned M behaviour.

Other "prophetic" texts contain descriptions of M desire disguised as the (divine) husband and (mortal) wife metaphor. The nature of some of these erotically-inspired texts will be discussed in Part IV below.

In Conclusion

Qoheleth 3.1-9, Proverbs 30.18-20, Judges 14, Song of Songs 7.1-7, and Hosea 2 have been viewed as instances of a certain type of love poetry. These poems were found to express male erotic love from an M viewpoint and by an M voice. The textual position they advocate is one of superiority. Their tone is masterful. Their imagery reflects male social concerns and psychological preoccupations. Although the facets of M love and desire explored in each instance may vary, their affinities are pronounced. They form a series and, perhaps, even merit the heading of a poetic genre or subgenre.

PART IV
DIVINE LOVE AND PROPHETIC PORNOGRAPHY

FOKKELIEN VAN DIJK-HEMMES

THE METAPHORIZATION OF WOMAN IN PROPHETIC SPEECH: AN ANALYSIS OF EZEKIEL 23[1]

The process of metaphorization of woman to a sign for something else enacts a form of disembodiment of the female subject. The imaging of woman as something else betrays habits of definition within a frame of reference that is dominated by the interests and the perceptions of the "first" sex.[2]

The Marriage Metaphor in Hosea

From a chronological point of view, the Book of Hosea is the first prophetic writing in which the relation between God and Israel is represented by the imagery of marriage. The Book belongs, or at least refers, to the eighth century BCE. The marriage metaphor created in Hosea 1-3 "develops the sacred marriage of Canaanite ritual into a figure for religious apostasy" (Marks 1987, 214) and, subsequently, replaces this "adulterous" type of marriage by an everlasting covenant in which H/he betrothes her to H/himself forever (Hos 2.21/18). According to numerous (M) interpreters, the Hosean marriage metaphor should be read as a parable of divine grace and forgiveness. I have argued elsewhere that such a prescribed reading can, and should, be challenged by an F reading of the text (Van Dijk-Hemmes 1989b). By way of an introduction to the discussion of Ezekiel 23, I shall first summarize my views on Hosea 1-3.

The main part of the Hosean marriage metaphor consists of an extensive monologue spoken by the metaphorical I persona, the "deceived husband" (ch. 2). The construction of this persona occurs in Hosea 1. In 1.2 Hosea, the prophet is commanded to take a "wife of harlotry" and "children of harlotry" because the land

---

[1] An earlier version of this essay was delivered at the IOSOT Congress in Leuven, August 1989. I wish to thank Prof. Mieke Bal, Prof. Athalya Brenner and Prof. Sarah Japhet for their helpful critical comments.
[2] This quotation is from the Introduction to the Utrecht Interfacultary Women's Studies Research Program, "Women between Control and Transition".

commits "great harlotry" by "whoring away" from YHWH. The implication of this metaphor is that YHWH acknowledges Himself as the husband of the Land of Israel; and while Hosea is transformed into a metaphor for YHWH Gomer, his wife, is designated a metaphor for the Land of Israel. The children (two sons and one daughter) who are born afterwards are, in their turn, immediately transformed into metaphors representing different aspects of the people's characteristics and fate.

In the first part of the monologue (Hos 2) the I persona, YHWH/Hosea, attacks his metaphorical wife in an extremely aggressive manner. He accuses her of going after her lovers ("Baals"), and threatens her several times to strip her naked. After this speech act—which exposes so much sexual violence—H/he then starts, from verse 16/14 onwards, to sing a "love" song to her, "Therefore, behold, I will allure her..." For the metaphorical wife, however, this transition means that she, after having been victimized by her "husband", now becomes H/his totally passive bride whose only task is to respond to H/his initiatives. A comparison between Hosea 2 and similar passages from the Song of Songs[3] reveals what difference it makes when the woman-in-the-text is presented not as the focalizer but, on the contrary, as the object of H/his focalization. A woman who, like the woman in the Song of Songs, expresses her desire for her lover is, in the Hosean context— where she is presented through H/his eyes and where her words are "quoted" by H/him—transformed into a harlot who shamelessly goes after her lovers (in the plural!).

The Hosean marriage metaphor culminates in a call for justice. This call appears to be "packaged" in a specifically male, misogynistic metaphorical language. The metaphor's plea, addressed to the people, to return to YHWH has a subtext. It is also, and simultaneously, an example of propaganda, addressed to men, extolling an ideal patriarchal marriage in which the woman has to submit to her husband and remain faithful to him in order to prevent the birth of "alien children" (Hos 5.7). The effect of the metaphor's message is greatly enhanced by the prophet's alleged personal involvement in it.

---

[3] As van Selms (1964-65) has shown, Hosea 2 contains phrases and motifs which must have been borrowed from love songs, the like of which were later on collected in the Song of Songs.

Features and Functions of Pornography

The marriage metaphor in the Book of Jeremiah will be discussed by Brenner in the following chapter. I now turn to Ezekiel. In the latter prophetic Book we find two examples of the marriage metaphor, in chapters 16 and 23. In the first chapter Jerusalem is metaphorized into YHWH's misbehaving wife, while Samaria is presented merely as her sister. In the second, however, metaphorical Samaria's status too is promoted to that of YHWH's consort. The one adulterous wife is thus doubled.

The point of departure for my analysis of Ezekiel 23, to which I shall confine myself here, are two statements from Carol A. Newsom's perceptive article "A Maker of Metaphors: Ezekiel's Oracles Against Tyre" (1987, 189).

1) "It is now generally understood that far from being merely decorative, metaphors have real cognitive content. If one tries to paraphrase a metaphor, what is lost is more than just a certain effect. What is lost is part of the meaning itself, the insight which the metaphor alone can give."

2) "Metaphor derives much of its convincing power from the fact that it does not allow its hearers to be passive but requires them to participate in the construction of the metaphorical meaning."[4]

For the purpose of my analysis I derive the following questions from these two statements:

1) What is the specific insight which the metaphor used in Ezekiel 23 can give us? In other words, what makes it necessary to present a re-enactment of Israel's history, within this specific metaphorical language, through imagery in which Israel's behaviour is represented in terms of the conduct attributed to YHWH's two adulterous wives?

2) How does the metaphorical language used in Ezekiel 23 require or entice its target audience and modern readers to participate in the construction of its metaphorical meaning?

I want to start my analysis with the second question, which focuses attention upon the interaction between the text and the audience or reader. This question involves the issue of efficiency. How do the

---

[4] For an extensive treatment of the concepts behind and the working of metaphors see, for instance, Lakoff and Turner 1989.

literary strategies deployed in the text affect the reader? How do they organize or mobilize his or her view? I refer to the audience or reader in a gendered manner not only because feminist literary theory has convincingly shown how relevant such an approach is (Culler 1983, 43-64; Showalter 1986), but also because, in this case, the text itself requires us to do so. Ezekiel 23 ends with an explicit warning for women not to behave like the metaphorical harlots Oholah and Oholibah (v. 48). Thus the extended metaphor which is presented to us in this chapter speaks not only *of* women, but also—albeit indirectly—specifically *to* women. What exactly is the message which this text conveys to women? And does it require women to participate in the construction of its metaphorical meaning in a different way from men?

As an F reader, I want to answer these questions and analyze the literary strategies deployed in the text by making use of a model which is offered by T. Drorah Setel in her article, ''Prophets and Pornography: Female Sexual Imagery in Hosea'' (1985). According to Setel there is a significant congruence between biblical and especially prophetic texts on the one hand, and modern pornographic depictions of female sexuality on the other hand. In both cases objectified female sexuality is used as a symbol of evil. This implies that contemporary feminist theory on the nature of female objectification can and should be applied to the examination of prophetic texts which deal with the same subject.

In summarizing the theoretical material on pornography Setel distinguishes four categories of analysis: *features*, *function*, *definition* and *causes*. Here, however, I shall confine myself to two categories only: features and function.

Setel characterizes the distinguishing *features* of pornography as follows.

1) Female sexuality is depicted as negative relative to a positive or neutral male standard.

2) Women are degraded and publicly humiliated.

3) Female sexuality is portrayed as an object of male possession and control. This includes the depiction of women as analogous to nature in general and the land in particular and, especially, in regard to imagery of conquest and domination.

The *function* of pornography can, according to Setel, be summarized as the preservation of male domination through a denial, or misnaming, of female experience. If this is accepted then I can say that the denial or misnaming of female experience should also be considered a distinguishing feature of pornography.

To what extent do we find this latter feature as well as those mentioned by Setel in Ezekiel 23? The text is presented to us as a speech (*dbr*) delivered by YHWH to Ezekiel, the (male) prophet who lives in exile in Babylon and who figures as the I persona in the text: "The word of YHWH came *to me*" (Ezek 23.1). This means that the intended target audience is required to hear the text via Ezekiel's (fictive) ears. YHWH's speech starts like a story, and Ezekiel is addressed by Him as "Son of humanity" (*bn 'dm*).

> Son of humanity
> Two women
> daughters of one mother were there (v. 2).

The close relationship between the two sisters is emphasized by the chiastic structure of the verse: *štym nšm, bnt 'm 'ht*. No mention is made of the sisters' father. The story then continues with a description of the two sisters' conduct. The first part of this description is again constructed chiastically.

> They played the harlot in Egypt
> In their youth they played the harlot
> There their breasts were squeezed
> There the teats of their maidenhood were pressed (v. 3).

The words "in Egypt", closely related to "in their youth", prevent the actual/potential audience from listening to the story further as more or less interested outsiders. They are engaged, they are invited to involve themselves in it. The story about the two sisters who play the harlot, i.e. her-story, seems to present the audience's own history. In the following verse, the suspicion that the two sisters are metaphors and that, consequently, the audience itself, as part of the people of Israel, is transformed into these two metaphorical women, is confirmed.

> Their names
> Oholah the big one
> and Oholibah her sister
> They became mine
> and they bore sons and daughters
> Their names
> Samaria-Oholah
> and Jerusalem-Oholibah (v. 4).

The implicitly formulated information concerning the two sisters/ cities' marriage to YHWH is enveloped by the twofold announcement of their names. Oholah, which is traditionally understood to mean "(she who has) her own tent (i.e. sanctuary)", metaphorizes the capital of Northern Israel Samaria while Oholibah, "My tent (is) in her", metaphorizes Jerusalem.[5] YHWH's portrayal of Himself as prepared to accept for wives two women "who already in their youth denied their virginity" (Andrew 1985, 115) must have been designed to shock the audience. After having been required to look at themselves as depraved since the very beginning of their history, they now have to shamefully acknowledge that YHWH was nevertheless willing to take the risk of a marriage-like relationship with them.

Although this might have been expected as the intended audience's response and although this in fact *is* the readerly response of most modern commentators to the beginning of our metaphorical story, one "detail" in the text has in fact been overlooked. The activities of the two sisters—activities which are signified by *znh*, "play the harlot"—are specified in the following part of verse 3 not as action but as receptivity. "They" were acted upon.

> There their breasts were squeezed
> There the teats of their maidenhood were pressed.

Or, literally:

> There they [grammatically masc., see also v. 8] pressed the teats of their [the women's] maidenhood.

As an F reader I have some difficulties in naming such a being-acted-upon situation as "playing the harlot", so I suggest that here we may have an example of what Setel calls "misnaming of female

---

[5] See, however, Zimmerli (1969, 542), "Die beiden Frauennamen dürften bei Ez ganz einfach den leicht archaischen Klang beduinischer namengebung wachrufen und sagen wollen, dass die beide Mädchen mit den gleichklingenden Namen (Ewald verweist hierfür auf die Ali-Söhne Hasan und Husein) in Agypten nicht zu den eingeborenen, sondern zu den von der Wüste herkommenden, in Zelten wohnenden, Herden weidenden (Gen 4 20) Leuten gehören. Ganz so wie bei der Erwähnung der kanaanäisch-amoritisch-hetitischen Herkunft Jerusalems (Ez 16 3) stossen wir dann auch hier auf ein element guter geschichtlicher Tradition." Nevertheless, Zimmerli does not exclude the possibility that the girls' names might also contain an allusion to the meanings which have traditionally been attributed to them.

experience''. It would have been more adequate to describe the events during the sisters' youth in the following manner: ''They were sexually molested in Egypt, in their youth they were sexually abused''. This way, justice would have been done to the fate of these metaphorical women, and the audience would not have been seduced into viewing women or girls as responsible for and even guilty of their own violation. In short, there would have been no question of ''blaming the victim''.

Does this mean that the people whom the metaphorical women represent should actually see themselves as a victim as well? This appears not to be the intention of the text. In Ezekiel 20, where we find a non-metaphorical evaluation of Israel's history, we read that Israel is accused of having been rebellious against YHWH and of worshipping idols already during its sojourn in Egypt (v. 8). This accusation, with no reference to Israel's oppression, should be viewed as YHWH's crushing response to Judah's rebellion against Babylon, undertaken in the hope of obtaining help from an Egyptian alliance during the last few years before the destruction of Jerusalem. So from chapter 20 onwards, in contrast to the foregoing chapters as well as the common prophetic view on Israel's history, Israel is indeed presented as apostate from the *very beginning* of its history. According to the illogical, arbitrary way in which Ezekiel 23.3 conveys this message, Israel's sin in Egypt actually consisted of its being oppressed. Such a statement's lack of logic can apparently be made acceptable by the transformation of a people into metaphorical women. The sexual molestation inflicted upon these women serves, therefore, as a metaphor for the people's slavery in Egypt. Within an androcentric framework women can easily be seen as guilty of their own abuse. Hence, the imagery of women is indispensible for conveying a message which is a contradiction in terms: the people are guilty of their own past enslaving inasmuch as women are, by definition, guilty of their own sexual misfortunes. Referring to the first question derived from Newson's statements (above, p. 169), we can state that it is this specific (and illogical) M insight which the metaphor of Ezekiel 23 can give us.

Ohola's and Oholibah's Perversion

The misnaming of female experience is continued further in the metaphorical story which depicts first Oholah's and then, in much greater length and detail, Oholibah's alleged behaviour. Oholah's lusting after her Assyrian lovers by which, according to an over-zealous interpreter, she exposes her "hankering after the flamboyance of foreign military masculinity" (Andrew 1985, 115) is explained by her having enjoyed the sexual violence inflicted upon her in her youth.

> Her harlotry from (her days in) Egypt she did not abandon
> For they lay upon/raped[6] her in her youth
> And these men pressed the teats of her maidenhood
> And they poured out their harlotry upon her (v. 8).

The audience, which has already been required to perceive the metaphorical maiden's sexual abuse as harlotry, is now seduced into viewing this abuse as something Oholah had enjoyed so much that she could not do without it for the rest of her life! Her "harlotry", however, is depicted here even more clearly as violence which is acted upon her.

The story of Oholibah too culminates in the remembrance of her youth in Egypt which is attributed to her own consciousness. Her behaviour is depicted as much more corrupt than her sister's. She not only "lusted after" the Assyrians (v. 12), "but she carried her harlotry further" (v. 14). After having seen "men portrayed upon the wall, the images of the Chaldeans" (v. 14), she sends messengers for them, "brazenly attracted by mere appearances" (Andrew 1985, 115). They, the Babylonians, "came to her into the bed of love" (v. 17), but when she has been defiled and polluted by them, "she turned from them in disgust" (v. 17). And despite the fact that her behaviour in its turn leads to YHWH's turning in disgust away from her "as I had turned from her sister" (v. 18),

> She increased her harlotry
> remembering the days of her youth
> when she played the harlot in the land of Egypt
> She lusted after the paramours there
> whose organs are like the organ of asses
> and whose ejaculation is like the ejaculation of stallions (vv. 19-20).

And then, for the first time, Oholibah is directly addressed by YHWH:

---

[6] For this meaning of *škb 't*, see also Genesis 34.2 and 2 Samuel 13.14.

> You longed for the lewdness of your youth
> when those from Egypt pressed your teats
> for your young breasts (v. 21).

The enjoyment of her own abuse, which had been attributed to Oholah, is surpassed by the perverse sexual appetite attributed to Oholibah. The latter's lusting after stallion-like males[7] is said to derive from "the lewdness of your youth". The depiction of Oholibah's desire in terms of the size of (animal-like) male members seems not just an example of mere misnaming of female experience, but an actual distortion of it. Instead of reflecting female desire, this depiction betrays male obsession.

In both Ohola's and Oholibah's cases, the remembrance of the sisters' youth in Egypt marks a transition from the accusation to the announcement of their punishment. The intention is probably to strengthen the audience's resolve that both metaphorical women, so perverse since their very maidenhood, indeed deserve the utterly degrading and devastating treatment to which they are to be exposed. Modern M readerly responses demonstrate how successful this literary strategy is. According to those, the sisters' torturing is appropriate and "brings out the ironic justice of being punished by their own lovers" (Andrew 1985, 115).[8] Thanks to the model offered by Setel, this mode of participating in the construction of the text's metaphorical meaning is no longer necessary. Setel's model enables us to recognize other distinguishing features of pornography in the description of the sisters' treatment too. Both women are degraded and publicly humiliated in order to stress that their sexuality is and ought to be an object of male possession and control.

M and F Readerly Responses

Coming back to the question of whether the text speaks differently to men and to women, we can now state the following. YHWH's speech to Ezekiel transforms the people of Israel and thus the target audience, males and—at least indirectly—also females, into His

---

[7] In contrast to Jeremiah's marriage metaphor, where the woman is metaphorisized into animals (see Brenner in the next section), here the detested male ennemies are presented as animal-like beings.

[8] See also Zimmerli 1969; Eichrodt 1966; Maarsingh 1988, and numerous others.

metaphorical wives. Both genders are thus required to identify with the metaphorized women—especially with Oholibah, since Oholah figures chiefly as a warning signal for her "sister". Through Oholibah the audience is directly spoken to by YHWH several times in an utterly degrading manner. The audience is forced into seeing the shameless stupidity of their religious and political behaviour and the absolute hopelesness of their situation: Jerusalem will definitely be abandoned to destruction. The impact of that insight, which implies the utmost humiliation, apparently can only be communicated by such gender-specific metaphorical language.

The androcentric-pornographic character of this metaphorical language must indeed be experienced as extremely humiliating by an M audience forced to imagine itself as being exposed to violating enemies. Nevertheless, it is exactly this androcentric-pornographic character which at the same time offers the M audience a possibility of escape: the escape of identification with the wronged and revengeful husband; or, more modestly, identification with the righteous men who, near the end of the text, are summoned to pass judgment upon the adulterous women (v. 45). Thus, the text also functions as a specific warning to women which is indeed contained in its penultimate verse.[9]

According to Zimmerli (1969, 553-555) and many other commentators, the last verses are later additions appended to chapter 23. If this is correct, the additions can be viewed as ancient M readerly responses to the metaphorical story of Oholah and Oholibah. (See also the M comment attached to Prov. 30.18-19, Brenner in pp. 158-160 above.) These readerly responses realize and, at the same time, testify to the possibility of escape that the text offers to its M readers.

No such possibility of escape is left to F readers. In respect to them, the metaphorization of woman in Ezekiel 23 performs first and foremost a violent speech act which is even more offensive than the Hosean version: it simultaneously shapes and distorts women's (sexual) experience.

---

[9] There is a continual back-and-forth movement within the text from the metaphorization of women as cities toward the metaphorization of women per se, and vice versa. Hence, any appeal to women (v. 48) should be understood as an appeal to the cities as well.

ATHALYA BRENNER

ON "JEREMIAH" AND THE POETICS OF (PROPHETIC?) PORNOGRAPHY

When we discuss "prophetic" writings we usually assume, tacitly if not overtly, that a prophet resides in them. The language employed in the text is actually perceived as a kind of metalanguage, as if it forgrounds the prophet-in-the-text as an extratextual "person": the prophet "hears", he "says", he "suffers". Perhaps we need to avoid falling into that trap of complicity with the text. Perhaps written documents superscribed by the phrases "prophecy" or "The word of YHWH" are too easily privileged in interpretation as not only historically and textually valid but also superior—and so are the messages read into them. I shall therefore begin by explaining the components of my title.

"Jeremiah", for me, conveniently designates the poetic sections in the Hebrew Bible ascribed to a real or fictive man named Jeremiah, and here I intend to discuss especially the first chapters thereof. Was the man cited real, "historical", or imaginary? Did he actually utter or compose the passages attributed to him which are to be discussed soon? Did he perceive himself, did his audience perceive him, as a "prophet"—which the God-in-the-text did, as reported in 1.5; which the collectors of "his" Book certainly did at a later time; as we almost automatically assume? Should *we*, contemporary readers, regard "his" words as *prophecy*, a term whose referents in the Hebrew Bible are far from self-evident? Or should we regard them as literature, poetry and sometimes prose? I here refer to the controversy recently stirred up by R. Carroll and G. Auld (1990). Since I find their conclusions convincing, I prefer to regard the texts attributed to the real/literary Jeremiah as poetry (for the sake of clarity; prose and narrative it may be too in places) rather than prophecy. And it seems worth noting that one of the advantages of such an approach is that it facilitates the crossing of a barrier. Poetic-textual authority is easier to undermine than so-called prophetic authority.[1]

---

[1] For details of the "Prophecy or Poetry"? debate see Auld, G.A., Carroll, R.P., and Overholt, T.W. in *Journal for the Study of the Old Testament* 48(1990), 3-54.

The Husband-Wife Metaphor: A Propaganda Vehicle

The Jeremiah passages relevant to our topic are mainly: chapter 2; 3.1-3, 13; and 5.7-8. In these passages, like in the Books of Hosea and Ezekiel, Israel and Judah (or Samaria and Jerusalem) are metaphorized into a faithless wife and a *zônâh*. YHWH, the metaphor's male counterpart, is depicted as a faithful husband who is aggrieved and deeply affected by his "female"'s behaviour. The descriptions of the "wife"'s sinful escapades and deserved punishment are vivid, detailed, outspoken. As van Dijk-Hemmes demonstrates in her essay on Hosea (1989b), such metaphorized language may pervert the language of love. In her analysis of Ezekiel 23 she traces some of the pornographic properties which underlie and underline such a presentation of politico-religious concerns. My observations here constitute an attempt to extend her line of analysis. It will be noticed that a certain amount of overlap obtains between our two discussions. Because of the affinity of the texts themselves, and because of the similar perspectives van Dijk-Hemmes and I read from, a certain overlap is unavoidable.

Since the poet wants something from his target audience, namely loyalty and the strengthening of loose bonds between them and his (presumably also their) God, it seems fair to assume that the husband-wife metaphor is used for propaganda. Its employment seems to draw on the following premises, considerations and expectations.

a. The metaphorization of human, as exemplified by female, sexual behaviour is attractive enough to secure the audience's attention and sustained interest.

b. For the metaphor to be effective, it should be recognized by the target audience not merely as a stock life situation but also, by an easily performed leap of logic, as universally valid.

c. Female sexual behaviour is thus recognizable as potentially deviant even when unprovoked by a legitimate male partner: "she", in the life situations evoked and within the textual metaphor, is guilty from the outset.

d. The metaphor will therefore involve the target audience and will elicit a strong emotional response.

e. The audience will be trapped into identification with the speaker even despite itself and thus into understanding the speaker's message.

f. It is hoped that the response will be the one desired by the speaker, so that illicit (in his view) religious and political alliances in Judah and Jerusalem will cease through the agency of conscious guilt and shame.

In everyday speech many of us use love- and sex-talk for communicating religious experience. And the other way round: we use god-talk for communicating sexual experience. This language practice is so common as to render the biblical passages unproblematic for both female and male readers. Furthermore, even when it is agreed that texts in Hosea and Ezekiel contain pornographic elements, this in itself does not automatically apply to the reading of the same metaphor in the Jeremiah texts. Therefore, the question to be asked now is, Should we problematize the Jeremiah texts in which the husband/wife metaphor features and regard them as pornography or rather, more simply, settle for viewing them as "just" sexual imagery?

General Definitions of Pornography and Biblical Pornography

Most dictionary definitions of pornography run something like this. Pornography is the "Explicit description or exhibition of sexual activity in literature, films, etc., intended to stimulate erotic rather than aesthetic feelings". It is also "literature etc. containing this" (The Concise Oxford Dictionary, 1979).

This paradigmatic definition (and its like), often unquestioningly applied in colloquial usage, is far from satisfactory. To begin with, it refers to "feelings" but not specifically to the element of erotic pornography, in its turn, stimulates. Moreover, its "objectivity" excludes some relevant factors.

Pornography, like rape, is a particular syndrome of a widespread social malaise. Pornography, whether we are aware of it or not, is not just about sex and desire. It is a fantasy of power, domination, violence, and gender relations. In other words, in pornography sexuality serves as a metaphor which reflects and reinforces social "reality" or individual and social fantasy. Therefore, a definition or discussion of pornography cannot be deemed satisfactory unless it clearly qualifies the role models assigned to males in contradistinction to females (and to children in contradistinction to adults; and in matters of class, colour or ethnic origins) within pornographic (re)presentations. The definition should also relate to the degree and nature of each gender's response to the (re)presentation, and the cooperation in fantasy and "real" life which allows the fantasy (whose fantasy?). Stating that Desire is a primary human motive is a truism as well as a cliche. Defining pornography "objectively" as a stimulant to Desire, without taking socio-psychological factors into account, is at best misleading.

Persuasion through stigmatization, shaming as a means for bonding, and the exploitation of love for manipulation is practised by all of us within the family and outside it—in our relationships with our subordinates (like children), superiors (like parents), and peers. The manipulation of stigmatization and shaming, intended to persuade the addressees of their guilt and inferiority, is a powerful propaganda tool. The stigmatization of sexual behaviour and its abusive presentation is an elementary trick and commonly targetted on weak social groups, men and women alike. Nevertheless, since women are weaker as a social group, their stigmatization through pornographic presentation is more widespread than that of males (Janeway 1989). This holds true for the Bible as well as for other sources, ancient[2] and modern alike.

The Jeremiah passages are illuminating examples of the principles cited by Janeway. Male sexuality is indeed attacked here too. But, although one passage does stigmatize the sexual behaviour of the male addressees in terms of male adultery and male animalistic desire (Jer 5.7-8), other passages are devoted exclusively to stigmatization in terms of female sexual behaviour.

Carroll writes,

> Since Hosea, religious pornography has become a standard form of abusing opponents. Once the metaphors of marriage are transferred to describing the relationship between Yahweh and Israel, then all the abuse that might be heaped on a faithless wife will become part of the arsenal of religious denunciations. This transference will explain the degree of emotion generated in such statements...

---

[2] Semonides' poem about women, perhaps "The first satire on women in European Literature", is roughly contemporaneous—it is dated to the end of the 7th century BCE—with the Jeremiah-in-the-text. In this Greek work, whose tone is certainly misogynistic, the (male) author depicts one of the ten womanly types he lists as an ass, and specifies: "...when she comes to the act of love, she accepts any partner." (The reference is to p. 44 of the English edition, Lloyd-Jones 1975.) Since the Greek poem can be read as an intertext or subtext of the biblical husband/wife metaphor, we shall later return to it.

Carroll then cautions against viewing the relevant texts, as some feminists have done, as misogynistic (1986, 134).

Should we agree with Carroll that the Jeremiah and other "prophetic" passages, although pornographic, are not implicitly directed against women? Whose fantasy are they? Whom do they serve, and how do they do it? Van Dijk-Hemmes's answer (after Setel), which is adopted here, is: "There is a significant congruence between biblical and especially prophetic texts on the one hand and modern pornographic depictions on the other hand" (van Dijk-Hemmes above, p. 170). Hence, the relevant biblical texts can be problematized as follows. If contemporary pornographic literature is found to contain anti-female bias, the same should apply to pornographic biblical literature. This might at first sound too radical. In order to defend the statement's applicability in general, and to Jeremiah 2—5 in particular, I shall have to continue as follows.

a. Define my conceptual assumptions concerning pornography more closely still.

b. Discuss in more detail passages which conform to the definitions.

c. Compare passages of "prophetic" pornography with a corresponding modern literary piece. For that purpose I have chosen to deal with a book some of you might have heard about, the *Story of O*.

Feminist Definitions of Pornography and Jeremian Pornography

Contemporary feminist theories define pornography by distinguishing four categories: *features, function, definitions*, and *causes* (Setel, p. 87). Van Dijk-Hemmes has examined the application of the first two categories—features and function—to Ezekiel 23. Here we shall proceed to examine all four categories by sorting and applying them to the Jeremiah passages (and afterwards to the *Story of O*). For the sake of clarity short summaries of the first two categories will be repeated, although they have already been cited above (pp. 170-171).

The *features* of pornography are: female sexuality is depicted as negative in relation to a positive/neutral male sexuality; women are publicly humiliated; women, like nature and the land, are subjected to male possession and control. One might add that in modern pornography minors of both genders—another weak social group—receive a similar treatment: they are there to fulfil the

Other's desire. Social minorities are also similarly stigmatized.

Let us examine Jeremiah 2.23-25. Jerusalem, or the nation, or the community, is addressed as a female, YHWH's legitimate spouse. The fact that the words for "town" and "land" are grammatically of the feminine gender in Hebrew (Carroll 1986, 133) is not much of an explanantion for the abuse that follows; nor does the grammatical usage supply adequate reasoning for the rise of the "YHWH, the loving husband/the community, an errant wife" metaphor in general. Thus is the community addressed,

> How can you say
>   I am not defiled
>   I have not followed the Ba^cals
> See your way in the valley, know what you have done
> (You are) a young camel deviating from her path
> (You are) a wild ass accustomed to the wilderness
> sniffing the wind in her lust
> Who can repel her desire
> All who seek her need not get tired
> For they shall find her in season...
> And you have said
>   No
>   I love strangers and will follow them.

There is no doubt that the passage exhibits the three features of pornography delineated above. In the metaphor, female sexuality is irregular, abnormal. It is animalistic, "natural", earthy. The immediate association is that of bestiality; and in biblical morality bestiality, it is easy to recall, is punishable by death for both partners. The metaphorized female creature is motivated by lust rather than by love or the accepted conventions of human normative social behaviour. In other words, female sexuality is objectified in this passage. By contradistinction male sexuality, represented by God's behaviour, is praiseworthy both socially and morally: it conforms to the acceptable conventions of human sexuality.

It follows, then, that the "woman" is publicly degraded because she degrades herself by her behaviour. The previous verses (2.20-21) explicitly qualify "her" as the legal possession of her male/God; hence, her sexual conduct violates his rights.[3]

The animalization of the metaphorized woman-in-the-text is

---

[3] The same three features recur in Chapter 3.

perhaps the most striking feature of Jeremiah 2. It is an innovation, an original contribution to biblical pornographic lore. It does not feature in Hosea. It is absent from the enthusiastic and detailed pornographic descriptions of the same "woman" in Ezekiel 16. It is not to be found in Ezekiel 23.[4] The naturalization of nation, town, city is achieved in Ezekiel through their metaphorization into land and earth on the one hand, and women on the other hand. The two strands of the metaphor are linked, as van Dijk-Hemmes and Setel show, by their shared reference to the (extra-textual) female principle applicable to both: women are associated with the land. Thus metaphorizing the land into a "woman", and vice versa, is common practice in pornographic as well as other texts. The naturalization of woman by animalization is much more powerful. It constitutes an extra step in the ongoing construction of the husband/wife metaphor. For this animalization cannot be waived aside as relatively innocent or gender-neutral. While the metaphoric force and inherent value judgement are indicated by verbal context as well as the actual choice of animal referent,[5] the metaphorization of humans into animals is often either explicitly pejorative or else carries a sting.[6] In short, the link established between woman and land in other instances of the metaphor facilitates its progress—or shall we say deterioration?—into this next, "animalistic" stage.

Does this new elaboration of the metaphor heighten its pornographic qualities? I think that it does. The dehumanization of the woman-in-the-metaphor is expected to reflect the condemned inhuman behaviour of its extra-metaphorical referent, the addressed

---

[4] Although in Ezekiel 23.20 the metaphorical "males" are stigmatized by comparing their members and sexual behaviour to that of animals; see also Jeremiah 5.8 and van Dijk-Hemmes above, pp. 174-175.

[5] The metaphorization of an eponymous group into a lion cub—Judah in Genesis 49.9, Dan in Deuteronomy 33.22—certainly connotes positive associations of power and vigour. On the other hand, the metaphorization of a group or person into a dog (1 Sam 17.43, 24.15; 2 Sam 3.8, 9.8, 16.9; 2 Kgs 8.13; Isa 56.10; Ps 59.7,15) is clearly pejorative. In Psalms 22.17 the speaker's enemies are imaged first as "dogs" and then as "lion"; the former, together with the rest of the word context, sets the tone for the emotive content invested in "lion" in this instance.

[6] There are too many examples of this principle to be listed here. One, however, seems especially pertinent. When the women of Samaria are reproached and accused of greed and avarice, they are addressed by the epithet "Cows of the Bashan" (Amos 4.1). Bible commentaries for this passage supply valuable, supposedly non-tendentious, information concerning the extralinguistic referentiality of this metaphor.

community. This objective cannot be achieved through semantic or literary contiguity alone. A necessary interim stage is to reach out of language and examine the metaphor's validity from the extraneous vantage point of emotion and desire. A recognition that women are (like) animals will make the metaphor work. This recognition does not have to be conscious: if unconscious, when stemming from a fantasy of desire, its impact is significant enough; but when fantasy couples with awareness the impact is indeed explosive.

Is this new development an expression of misogyny? If we feel that the "voice" disapproves of woman-as-wild-animal in the text as well as outside it; if we surmise that the target audience in the text will disapprove of such women outside the text; if we are aware of the pornographic fantasy appealed to—then the conclusion is inescapable. Yes, misogyny does feature in the dehumanizing animalization of female sexuality, even when this is done in jest, as "just a metaphor".[7]

The *function* of pornography is the maintenance of male domination through the denial of female experience. This is done, among other things, by representing female objectification as universal human experience rather than male experience of femaleness. Women are expected to identify with this perspective. Also, the distinctions between prostitution, harlotry and whoring are blurred (Setel 1985, 87-88).

Thus the woman, the community, Judah and Jerusalem and also

---

[7] Or "just a satire". Lloyd-Jones insists at length and by utilizing various arguments that Semonides' poem is not misogynistic (1975, 22-33). He writes, "The whole point of Semonides' poem is that certain types of women do resemble certain animals; perhaps the same is true of certain types of men, but that is not relevant." (p. 29). Since Semonides lists ten categories of women, seven of which are typified as animals and derided in an unambiguous fashion, this sincere apology cannot be taken seriously.

The woman-as-animal metaphoric types in Semonides' poem are: sow, vixen, bitch, ass, ferret, mare, and monkey. Out of these, only the "mare" is praised for some of her qualities (translation on p. 48). Two other types are "naturalized" as well: these are the earth woman and the sea woman. These two hardly fare better in the poet's judgement than their other "natural" sisters. The tenth type—an obedient wife—is again metaphorized into an animal, a bee. In contradistinction to the others, she is industrious and a good wife and mother. However, she is denied sexuality for pleasure and the corrupting company of her gender (52).

Although Semonides' poem is by and large not pornographic, the view of woman expressed in it (and in its Greek antecedents, like Hesiod's) is androcentric in the extreme. In this respect, as well as in the utilization of female animalization, it resembles the speaking voice in Jeremiah 2.

Israel, is never asked to defend herself. Her voice is not heard. She is an adulteress who deserves to be divorced (Jer 3.1, 8). The message to the target audience is clear. If you, the speakers, endorse the truth of metaphorized female behaviour as described—and this can be done only by an acknowledgement that the picture drawn is "real"; if you, as males, want to preserve male social domination inasmuch as the male voice within the metaphor does; if you, as females, accept the fantasy's view of your gender as your very own; if you, as a community, want to forsake pornography in favour of love and loyalty—then you must accept the validity of the poet's (male) perspective for his God and for yourselves.

The metaphorized "woman" is called zônâh. What exactly is she accused of? Is she a prostitute, who sells her sexuality? A harlot, whose sexuality is uncontrollable? A whore, controlled by a male patron? The Hebrew verb znh—used liberally here (2.20; 3.2,6,8) as well as in Hosea and Ezekiel—is non-specific, hence variously translated. The distinction between the three (English) designations is conspicuously absent from the Hebrew text. To complicate matters of terminology and interpretation further, the non-specificity of znh and its derivatives is problematized by the usage of the additional term qĕdēšâh. This term's verbatim signification is "(a) hallowed female", but it is often rendered "cultic prostitute" and sometimes interchanged with zônâh within the same verbal context (like in the Tamar and Judah story , Genesis 38).[8] The semantic confusion in the biblical text passes on to biblical interpretation. Perhaps we should wait for the results of Phyllis Bird's research into this issue (a preliminary report in Bird 1989a, 1989b). Meanwhile, and in-spite of the obscurity of the terms used, we are all required to adopt God's and the poet's indignation at what we are supposed to accept as easily recognizable, stereotypic female sexual behaviour.

Feminist *definitions* of pornography vary. However, most of them agree that pornography deals with the objectification and degrading of "woman" in a manner that makes the abuse of females acceptable or even commendable; that it restricts female sexual choice to

---

[8] Van Dijk-Hemmes (1989c) explains the interchange thus: Judah perceives Tamar as a zônâh, whereas the Canaanites perceive her (and her like) as a qĕdēšâh. This reading is possible but not exclusive. It is the narrator, not Judah, who tells us that Judah saw a zônâh in Tamar 's covered figure. Besides, if the reading is adopted, it implies that the narrator could effect the interchange precisely because the listeners/readers perceived the two terms as analogous.

an actual state of slavery; and that it stresses the nature and meaning of male power (Setel 1985, 88). Reading Jeremiah 3 in this light, a new picture emerges. The depiction of the "wife" in chapter 2 has now blossomed into a picture of two errant "wives" in the next chpater. One thing leads to another of the same kind. The same process occurs in the Book of Ezekiel: the metaphorization of one community in terms of "woman" (chapter 16) evolves into the presentation of two communities as "woman"—the same type of "woman" doubled. And this can go on, since it is facilitated by drawing on a male stereotype of female sexual behaviour— graphically described to engage attention, desire and emotion— which is extremely strong. It has now become even more apparent that God/the male has been treated badly by his possession(s); the slaves do not know their place. "She" (for "they" are one, in the metaphor as well as in "life" and "history"; they are two of the same kind, they typify "woman"), by attempting to choose her partners actively, is guilty of social, moral, and legal transgressions.

Thus pornography preserves and asserts male social domination through the control of female sexuality. The process is subtle: first a particular case is appealed to, then two, then all is possible, all wives are potential "harlots". It is hardly surprising, then, that pornography is enlisted as a powerful vehicle for the metaphorization of God's relationship with his promiscuous (by definition!) community/"wife".

Feminists recognize that the ultimate *causes* of pornography, beyond the stimulation of desire and its attendant fantasies, hark back to male insecurity and need to affirm and reaffirm gender control in the face of change (Setel). If this is accepted then the utilization of pornography for powerful propaganda in Jeremiah (and Hosea, and Ezekiel) adequately reflects and expresses not only the poet's politico-theological concerns but also his—whoever "he" may be—psychological and social concerns as a male. This is M literature, not just androcentric but truly phallocentric[9] and woman-suspicious—especially wife-suspicious, so much so that the metaphor is expected to function effectively even when delivered by "Jeremiah", a fictive bachelor! Fortunately, sexual derision—like

---

[9] Note once more the phallic preoccupation in the pornographization of males, Ezekiel 23.20 and Jeremiah 5.8a.

sexual jokes—unmasks and exposes sexual dependency, fascination and desire more effectively than it masks them.

Are there non-pornographic representations of "woman" in Jeremiah? Yes, but let us examine some of them.

Jeremiah 31 again has a cluster of metaphorized "women": mother (31.15 onwards), virgin (vv. 4, 21), and daughter (22a). The subject matter of this chapter is an imminent reversal of bad fortune that awaits God's community. Do the female figures undergo a change also?

The archmother Rachel is weeping for her sons. She is a kind mother, totally preoccupied with her (male) children's fate. But she is a dead mother and, as such, a-sexual and a safe object for veneration.[10]

The community has now, miraculously, become a "virgin" after having been a "wife". Poetic license aside, one wonders about (M) stereotyping of the F principle: a nubile but untouched female is deemed better suited for a new beginning than a "wife". Fresh hopes, purity and, once more, a better chance of male control this time? Moreover, is not paternal authority invoked in the "daughter" metaphor? There is no pornography in either of these depictions; however, the preoccupation with male domination, much in evidence in the pornographic passages, reappears here.

Finally, in the last verse of the poem (v. 22b) the speaker announces in exasperation, referring to the "daughter's" antics, Can it be that a female gets round a male (that is, will cause a male so much distress)? This last sentence subverts and deconstructs all the female metaphors in this chapter. It exposes the female images as the product of male concern with legitimate, properly allocated gender roles; and that concern is (unwittingly?) transferred into religious discourse (and see van Dijk-Hemmes 1989d).

Story of O

Let us now consider a modern piece of literary pornography. The *Story of O* was ostensibly authored by a woman, Pauline Rèage (and

---

[10] Jeremiah 20.7-18 is concentrically arranged around two birth images: birth unwanted by "mother" (vv. 7-11) and birth unwanted by "child" (= the speaker, vv. 14-18; see Magonet 1987). The mother image is almost opaque. Hence, it cannot be included in the discussion.

we shall come back to this point later). It was originally published
in French, quickly translated into other languages (including
English), attained great popularity, and made into a film. It has
been acclaimed as a breakthrough in female erotic prose and insight
by some. Yet, and more widely, it is considered a pornographic
novel whose characteristic properties are rendered even more
pronounced by its undeniable literary merits.

O, the focal figure of the narrative, is a young woman in love. She
remains anonymous throughout the book: all the other characters
apart from her, females and males alike, do have names. The story
charts her journey from being a loving person to becoming a naked,
abused sex object whose spiritual or physical death is imminent by
choice. And yet, the literary O—and its authorial parent?—
celebrates her situation. At the end of her story O is a non-person,
a womb controlled by her lovers and open to all, an Orifice—and
by her own testimony she views her condition as the uttermost condition she can achieve this side of death. No matter whether her
death is symbolical, or will be realized shortly. Through an intense
didactic effort on the part of her male mentors, through physical
punishment ranging from beating to group rape to other sadistic
forms of physical and mental violation, she becomes reeducated.
Now naked, with a chain through her genitals for all to see, publicly
displayed as a (positive!) lesson for other nubile females, she has fulfilled her destiny. She has come to realize that the punishment is no
punishment, that the physical marks on her body are no mere tor-
ment marks. They are her masters' stamp, she finally belongs.
Through whoredom she has achieved chastity, through sadomasochism an understanding and fulfilment of her latent female
nature. She is ready. She is to be reborn as a male-acceptable, sub-
missive female who is devoted to the idea/praxis of her gender—the
predetermined bondage of love. In short, she has attained selfhood.

Jessica Benjamin discusses the *Story of O* in a perceptive essay,
"The Bonds of Love: Rational Violence and Erotic Domination"
(1980). Her concern is with the fact that the pornographic fantasy
of rational, or rationalized, violence "mingles love, control, and
submission and also flows beneath the surface of 'normal love' between adults'' (p. 41). Her essay exposes the tension between
differentiation and recognition, and between object and subject.
This tension, whose origins lie in early infancy, is often unsuccess-
fully dissolved (instead of resolved) in our culture into a gender split.

Instead of achieving mutual recognition, inflexible gender roles are parceled out to females and males. False nourishment is then obtained for both genders through the dialectics of master-slave relationships (after Hegel). In the following remarks I shall refer to Benjamin's observations on the *Story of O* and collate them with the relevant biblical passages.

The Story of O and Jeremian Pornography

In the *Story of O* the fantasy of one gender's control and the other gender's reciprocated submission is metaphorized by sadomasochism. The sadomasochism depicted is not mutually inflicted. It is a divided or split sadomasochism. As imaged and mythologized, sadism represents maleness, masochism represents the essence of femaleness and femininity (Caplan 1987). In Jeremiah (and Hosea and Ezekiel, cf. van Dijk-Hemmes and Setel) this fantasy reaches its ultimate. The (male) fantasy of (male) domination is acted out as total through the equation of male power with divine power. The (male) fantasy of (female) submission becomes total and totalitarian through the required recognition of male/divine authority. One can hardly claim that this is just a metaphor, or just a reflection of social norms. As Benjamin shows, the choice of metaphor is deeply rooted in (male) infantile fantasy. One should add, though, that without recourse to female desire and complicity (masochism), this fantasy could not work for its female audience.

This leads us to the next point. The *Story of O* was ostensibly written by a woman. There has been some controversy about that in literary circles. Could it be that a woman composed such an M fantasy? Yes, of course; one gender's fantasy cannot function without the cooperation of the Other's. Whether that cooperation, or reciprocation, derives from one and the same source for either—Is it really a question of (im)pure desire? Is that desire comparable for both parties?—is a separate issue altogether.

The whole point is that O complies with the sadomasochistic procedures she is subjected to *as a subject*: willingly. It is emphasized that she is never overtly coerced into consent. She acquires a partner's position by choosing to internalize and assimilate her masters' value system. The immediate consequences for her are the loss of personal freedom and the emergence of a heightened awareness of her guilt. Is this not what Judah, Jerusalem, Israel, are required to do? They are required to acknowledge their alleged sinful ways, to appropriate their guilt and internalize it. Then they are required to add the restraining forces of shame, repentance, and penance to their repertoire. If they do not, (justified!) violence will be done unto them for their own good.

O is no ordinary victim: to a large extent, she is responsible for her fate through culpability. She becomes convinced by her male mentors' sweet verbal logic that her re-socialization, designed to make her fit into a phallocentric world and conform to its norms, is necessary as well as desirable. Her biblical counterparts are presented as responsible for their so-called deviant behaviour and, eventually and inevitably, for the dismal fate awaiting them. The literary style and the voices differ in each case; verbal violence parading as rational wisdom, social and personal, is discernible in both texts.

O is requested to submit to the rationality and superior reason of her lover(s) after recognizing male superiority. The biblical community is similarly addressed—"she" is to relinquish her judgement in favour of reported divine judgement, to give up "her" sense of independence and well being because a divine/male voice announces that "she" is misbehaving and should therefore undergo a procedure of reeducation.

Among other things, O is guilty of promiscuity—not the promiscuity dictated by her masters, but an active promiscuity generated from within. She is a harlot as well as a whore because she wishes to be sexually active in an independent manner. In order to overcome her guilt, her boundaries are violated again and again. She is stripped, her shame is dramatized into nakedness. Her defenses are taken away. It is emphasized that the sadism practised upon her has a purpose beyond pain and mere punishment—it is educational, it is ostensibly arranged for promoting her own spiritual benefit. The analogy to the biblical communities addressed as "women" is clear. All these things will be/have been done to them, the "prophetic" male voices announce, in the deity's name and for the community's own good.

O becomes a sex object. Her masters, though, retain their subjectivity (and freedom of multiple sexual choice). It is stressed that she is dependent upon them. They, however, maintain their domination by remaining independent of her. In that sense, the Hegelian master-slave relationship receives a different treatment here: the mutuality of victim and oppressor undergoes a shift because of the rigidity of the roles assigned to the respective partners. Similarly, the "woman" Israel and Judah/Jerusalem is depicted as dependent upon her God. He, however, is independent of her. Grieving about her behaviour and strongly affected by it, yes; nevertheless, he remains her absolute master. He was, is, will always be a Subject. Although he desires recognition from his people, God's power is not greatly affected by his failure to receive it. He is separate, different; "she" is not—she is but an extension of him. Like O's lovers, YHWH's domination consists of a declaration of his omnipotence combined with the denial of his "woman"'s separateness.

At the very end of her story, in the final climactic act, O is totally dehumanized and animalized (pp. 152-159). She is without makeup and completely naked, even her pubic hairs are shaved. Like a dog, she is on a leash and chain. She also behaves like an obedient dog: speechless throughout the final scene,

> O searched the crowd, looking for Sir Stephen. At first she did not see him. Then she sensed that he was there... He could see her; she was reassured (p. 158).

Her only masked feature is her face: she wears the tight-fitting mask of an owl.[11] Thus she becomes not just an animal but a fabulous one, an unnatural animal whose parts are natural but not their sum. Such a mythical being—woman/dog/owl—cannot enjoy the independent existence of a human: she becomes "it", an imagined circus animal. It comes as no surprise that her two masters,

> ...had O get up, led her to the centre of the courtyard, detached her chain and took off her mask; and, *laying her upon the table* [emphasis mine, AB], possessed her, now the one, now the other (p. 159).

Thus is female objectification achieved: she is transformed from human to animal to an unnatural animal, then possessed in a manner reminiscent of sacrifice. Be the ambiguities inherent in the male initiative and need to transform her as they may—admiration for O is certainly a manifest component—total control of the female, and her acceptance, depend on the completion of this transformational process. The community's animalization in the Jeremian metaphor

---

[11] The owl, an animal of the night, symbolizes night, death and coldness in many cultures. But, like many other primary symbols, it is ambiguous—see Chevalier and Gheerbrant 1974, vol. 3, 28-29.

does not go that far.[12] Its origins and effect, however, are similar. An animal is inferior, she must be possessed, her judgement is naturally non-existent, she must obey. The two masters-in-the-text, God and his messenger, "naturally" know better (like O's masters).

O sees her experience not simply as an ordeal, but as a spiritual and religious journey: love is transcendence, a devotion to a God. In the biblical passages the opposite obtains: religion is metaphorized and metamorphosed into a certain kind of love. The two perspectives are different enough; and yet, they seem too much like the obverse sides of the same coin for this reader to feel comfortable with either.

In Conclusion

How am I, a woman, an F reader, to respond to O's story? I have two alternatives: to identify with her, for her fantasy—at least up to a point, at least to a certain extent—is my (acquired by education?) fantasy too; or to rebel against the myth of female masochism and the achievement of selfhood through, paradoxically, negation of female independence. I can say, This is carrying things too far; this is the subordination of F fantasy to M fantasy and its complete conquest.

How am I to respond to the biblical passages depicting Israel/ Judah as an objectified spouse, an animalized it-woman, a stereotype, "that kind of woman, you know"? (Or: "Any woman is potentially a harlot, excluding my mother and my sister.") I have two alternatives: to identify with the male/poet/God's viewpoint; or to object to the kind of pornographic/religious pseudotranscendence prescribeded by the metaphor, thoughtlessly if not necessarily unconsciously, for persons of my gender.[13]

---

[12] Nonetheless, at the end of Jeremiah 2.24 we read: "All who seek her [the wild she-ass of the metaphor] will not weary; they will find her in season/heat". It is not natural for a female animal to be in heat continually. Hence, even in Jeremiah, an additional step is taken toward transforming the metaphorized "woman"/community into a fabulous (not just wild) animal.

[13] It is sometimes argued that pornographic presentations are actually beneficial for the consumer because they release desire by supplying a socially tolerated outlet. In other words, what is the fuss about? According to this argument talking, reading, and watching pornography would prevent a desire for its dramatization. This argument probably carries the same weight as opinions discounting the influence of exposure to violence in the media as a factor in the encouragement of

Toward the end of Benjamin's analysis she writes (1980, 66),

> The story illustrates marvelously how the male assumption of mastery
> is linked to the splitting of differentiation and recognition, to both ra-
> tionality and violence...the same psychological issues run through
> both political and erotic forms of domination, for they both embody
> denial of the other subject.

I do not know whether a historical person named Jeremiah (or
Hosea, or Ezekiel) was responsible for the pornographic passages attributed to him. Therefore, I cannot dismiss pornographic religious
propaganda which abuses metaphorized female (and, to a much
lesser extent, male) sexuality on the grounds that it was unfortunately conditioned by "his" private and social circumstances. Instead,
I wish to point out that whoever composed those passages perceived
women and men—not to mention God—and gender relations in a
certain way. That vision, that male fantasy of desire which presup-
poses a corresponding and complementary mythical fantasy of female desire, is pornographic. As a reader, I can resist this fantasy
by criticism and reflection. But I do so against odds, for I myself was
raised and educated to comply with that fantasy and adopt it as my
very own. Like other F readers, I deconstruct myself by having to
fight a wish to reciprocate or even appropriate M fantasy. For
awareness is partial defense only.[14]

---

violence. In fact, a successful presentation whets the appetite and sharpens desire:
it offers the fallacy of a possible acting out. It might indeed serve as defense mechan-
ism against wholesale violation for most people. But even so, pornography corrupts
social norms. Desire might not be acted out in the fashion recommended, but social
attitudes reinforced by it will remain and even become more pronounced. Thus the
influence of pornography, and violence and rape, cannot be measured by their innocent, domesticated practice or extreme criminal consequences alone. Nobody becomes immune to those consequences by consuming or by indulging in pornography.

[14] A shorter version of this study was presented at the Jewish-Christian Bible
Week in Bendorf, Germany, in July 1991. I wish to acknowledge my indebtedness
to those conference participants who responded to my paper after their particular—and varied—fashions.

AFTERWORD

We chose to conclude this book by two discussions of "prophetic" pornography. Our decision was informed by the recognition that the political and personal fantasy of controlling the female body, and female sexuality, is a deep concern of both biblical and Western civilizations; and that pornography radically expresses that concern inasmuch as it legitimizes its "universal" application.

Prophetic pornography metaphorizes female sexuality into a dangerously free, formless, uncontrollable phenomenon. This universalized depiction feeds on male fantasy and male fear. The utilization of this acceptable vision for religious purposes, the fact that female sexuality in it is not a target *per se*, may obscure the vision's origins while, simultaneously, lending it additional weight. Biblical pornography is therefore perhaps more dangerous than modern pornography. Almost imperceptibly we come to identify message and messenger, alleged author and authority—so much so that we have to recall contemporary analogues in order to resist the authority and violent control advocated in order not to be duped by the text's authoritative command. It is not easy to draw a distinction between metaphor and message, and to respond differently to each: the union of content and form in art is seductive.

Exposure is a step towards undermining authority. In this regard, it is helpful to view the biblical vision of female sexuality, as exaggerated by the "divine, faithful husband/(in)human, errant wife" metaphor, as a Utopia of the female body[1] and female sexuality.

In this M biblical Utopia the female body is contained. It is masked and framed by divine male logic, spirituality and religion, be their motivation what it may. Paradoxically, biblical pornography obliterates not only female desire but also female matter in favour of M spirit.

Nead (1992, 12-15) relates Thomas More's map of Utopia, an island whose boundaries/entrance are tricky but whose interior is controlled and tranquil, to representations of woman in art: "...as we suspected all along, it is the anal/vaginal entrance to the bay

---

[1] The term is taken from Nead 1992. We thank Hedva Issachar, of the Israel Broadcasting Authority, for drawing our attention to this article.

which is the key to Utopia" (Nead, 15). The Willendorf Venus of 21,000 BCE, "lumpy and portruding" (Nead, 14), free-floating and ugly(?), transmutates into the contained, idealized forms of Cycladic and later Western art. Thus is woman dealt with: by having her nude shape, that ambiguous matter, transformed into an ideally contoured escape separated from "reality", a nostalgia cum Utopia. Still, the ambiguity inherent in the idealization/separation deconstructs both Utopia and the vision of female nudity.[2]

Not surprisingly, Nead's analysis of female nudity in art is relevant to our analyses of biblical M texts, especially biblical pornography. Woman cannot be ignored; however, her representations are motivated by ambivalence and betray ambiguity. The female principle has to be contained[3] and acculturized. Strict boundaries confine the female body in art (verbal and visual) and its interpretation. Pornography, the visual arts, and biblical literature are so different; yet all reveal similar attitudes towards the F principle in Western culture and society.

---

[2] Nead points out that modern feminist writings reconstruct the female body as an unfinished, fluid, borderless entity. This new Utopia of "feminist aesthetics" (and desire) needs to take female *differences* into account in order to free the female body from its containment in art and society.

[3] In More's Utopia, the island was separated from the mainland by its founder in order to facilitate his task of educating the natives; see Nead.

REFERENCES AND ADDITIONAL BIBLIOGRAPHY

Ackerman, S., "'And the Women Knead Dough': The Worship of the Queen of Heaven in Sixth-Century Judah". In: Day, P.L. (ed.) *Gender and Difference in Ancient Israel*. Minneapolis: Fortress Press 1989, pp. 109-124.

Alter, R., *The Art of Biblical Poetry*. New York: Basic Books 1985.

Anderson, B.W., "The Song of Miriam Poetically and Theologically Considered". In: Follis, E.R. (ed.) *Directions in Biblical Hebrew Poetry*. Sheffield: JSOT Press 1987, pp. 285-296.

Aletti, J.N., "Seduction et Parole en Proverbes I-IX". *Vetus Testamentum*, 27 (1977), pp. 129-144.

Andrew, M.E., *Responsibility and Restoration: The Course of the Book Ezekiel*. Dunedin, New Zealand 1985.

Ardener, E., "Belief and the Problem of Woman" and "The 'Problem' revisited". In: Ardener, S. (ed.) *Perceiving Women*. New York: Halsted Press 1978, pp. 1-27.

Bal, M., *Narratology: Introduction to the Theory of Narrative*. Toronto: The University Press of Toronto 1985.

Bal, M., *Lethal Love. Feminist Literary Readings of Biblical Love Stories*. Bloomington/Indianapolis: Indiana University Press 1987.

Bal, M., *Murder and Difference. Gender, Genre and Scholarship on Sisera's Death*. Bloomington/Indianapolis: Indiana University Press 1988a.

Bal, M., *Death & Dissymmetry. The Politics of Coherence in the Book of Judges*. Chicago/London: The University of Chicago Press 1988b.

Bal, M., *Macht, mythe en misverstand en het recht om verkeerd te lezen. Over Richteren 19 en het interpretatieprobleem*. Amsterdam: KTUA 1989.

Bal, M., Dijk-Hemmes, F. van, Ginneken, G. van, *En Sara in haar tent lachte. Patriarchaat en verzet in bijbelverhalen*. Utrecht: HES 1984.

Barthes, R., *Image, Music, Text*. London: Methuen 1977.

Barthes, R., *S/Z*. Paris: Seuil 1970. English Translation: Miller, R., New York: Hill and Wang 1974.

Barton, G.A., *The Book of Ecclesiastes*. ICC, Edinburgh: T and T Clark 1908 = 1970.

BDB Brown, F., Driver, S.R., Briggs, C.A., *A Hebrew and English Lexicon of the Old Testament*. Oxford: Clarendon Press 1972 (5th edition).

Bekkenkamp, J., *Want ziek van liefde ben ik*. Doctoraalscriptie. Amsterdam: UvA 1984.

Bekkenkamp, J., and others, "Mannenwijsheid". In: *Werkschrift voor leerhuis en liturgie*, 6 (1985) 2, pp. 86-92.

Bekkenkamp, J., "Het Hooglied: een vrouwenlied in een mannentraditie". In: Lemaire, R. (ed.), *Ik zing mijn lied voor al wie met mij gaat. Vrouwen in de volksliteratuur*. Utrecht: Hes 1986, pp. 72-89.

Bekkenkamp, J., Dijk, F. van, "The Canon of the Old Testament and Women's Cultural Tradition". In: Meijer M. and Schaap J. (eds.) *Historiography of Women's Cultural Traditions*. Dordrecht/Providence: Foris Publications 1987, pp. 91-108.

Bendavid, A., *Biblical Hebrew and Mishnaic Hebrew*. Tel Aviv 1971, (in Hebrew) vol II.

Benjamin, J., "The Bonds of Love: Rational Violence and Erotic Domination". In: Eisenstein, H. and Jardine, A. (eds.) *The Future of Difference*. Boston:

G.K. Hall 1980, pp. 41-70. (See also, more recently: *The Bonds of Love*. New York: Pantheon 1988.)

Berlin, A., *The Dynamics of Biblical Parallelism*. Bloomington: Indiana University Press 1985.

Beuken, W.A.M., "I Samuel 28: The Prophet as Hammer of Witches". *Journal for the Studies of the Old Testament*, 6 (1978), pp. 3-17.

Bird, P., "Images of Women in the Old Testament". In: Radford Ruether, R. (ed.) *Religion and Sexism. Images of Women in the Jewish and Christian Traditions*. New York: Simon and Schuster 1974, pp. 41-88.

Bird, P., "The Place of Women in the Israelite Cultus". In: Miller Jr., P.D., Hanson P.D., McBride, S.D. (eds.) *Ancient Israelite Religion. Essays in Honor of Frank Moore Cross*. Philadelphia: Fortress Press 1987, pp. 397-419.

Bird, P., "The Harlot as Heroine: Narrative Art and Social Presupposition in Three Old Testament Texts". *Semeia*, 46 (1989a), pp. 119-140.

Bird, P., " 'To Play the Harlot': An Inquiry into an Old Testament Metaphor". In: Day, P.L. (ed.) *Gender and Difference in Ancient Israel*. Minneapolis: Fortress Press 1989b, pp. 75-94.

Bloom, H., *The Book of J*. Grove, USA: Weidenfeld 1990.

Brenner, A., *The Israelite Woman. Social Role and Literary Type in Biblical Narrative*. Sheffield: JSOT Press 1985.

Brenner, A., "Female Social Behaviour: Two Descriptive Patterns within the 'Birth of the Hero' Paradigm". *Vetus Testamentum*, 36 (1986) 3, pp. 257-273.

Brenner, A., "Job the Pious? The Characterization of Job in the Narrative Framework of the Book". *Journal for the Study of the Old Testament*, 43 (1989a), pp. 37-52.

Brenner, A., *The Song of Songs*. Old Testament Guides. Sheffield: JSOT Press 1989b.

Brenner, A., " "Come Back, Come Back the Shulamite" (Song of Songs 7:1-10). A Parody of the *wasf* Genre". In: Radday, Y.T. and Brenner, A. (eds.), *On Humour and the Comic in the Hebrew Bible*. Sheffield: Almond and JSOT Press 1990, pp. 251-275.

Brooten, B., "Early Christian Women and their Cultural Context: Issues of Method in Historical Reconstruction". In: Collins, A.Y., *Feminist Perspectives on Biblical Scholarship*. Chico, California: Scholars Press 1985, pp. 65-91.

Brueggeman, W., "A Response to 'The Song of Miriam' by Bernhard Anderson". In: Follis, E.R., *Directions in Biblical Hebrew Poetry*. Sheffield: JSOT Press 1987, pp. 297-302.

Bruns, G.L., "Canon and Power in the Hebrew Scriptures". In: Hallberg, R. von (ed.) *Canons*. Chicago 1984, pp. 65-83.

Bücher, K., *Arbeit und Rhythmus*. Leipzig, 1896.

Camp, C.V., "The Wise Women of 2 Samuel: A Role Model for Women in Early Israel". *Catholic Biblical Quarterly*, 43 (1981), pp. 14-29.

Camp, C.V., *Wisdom and the Feminine in the Book of Proverbs*. Sheffield: Almond Press 1985.

Camp, C.V., "Woman Wisdom as Root Metaphor: A Theological Considera-tion". In: Hoglund, K.G. and others (eds.) *The Listening Heart: Essays in Wisdom and the Psalms in honour of Roland E. Murphy*. Sheffield: JSOT Press 1987, pp. 45-76.

Camp, C.V., "Wise and Strange: An Interpretation of the Female Imagery in Proverbs in Light of Trickster Mythology". In: Exum, J.C. and Bos, J. (eds.), *Reasoning with the Foxes: Female Wit in a World of Male Power*. (*Semeia* 42, 1988), pp. 14-36.

Camp, C.V., "What's so Strange about the Strange Woman?". In: Day, P.,

Jobling, D., Sheppard, G. (eds.), *The Bible and the Politics of Exegesis*. New York: Pilgrim Press 1991.

Campbell, E.F., *Ruth*. Anchor Bible VII. New York: Doubleday 1975.

Caplan, P.J., *The Myth of Women's Masochism*. New York: Signet 1987.

Carroll, R.P., *Jeremiah. A Commentary*. London: SCM Press 1986.

Cassuto, U., *Commentary on Genesis I: From Adam to Noah*. Jerusalem: Magnes 1961.

Cassuto, U., *A Commentary on the Book of Exodus*. Jerusalem: Magnes 1967.

Chevalier, J. and Gheerbrant, A., *Dictionaire des Symboles*. Paris: Seghers 1974, vol 3.

Christensen, D.L., "Huldah and the Men of Anatoth: Women in Leadership in the Deuteronomic History". In: *SBL 1984 Seminar Papers*. Chico, California: Scholars Press 1984, pp. 399-404.

Clines, D.J.A., "The Parallelism of Greater Precision: Notes from Isaiah 40 for a Theory of Hebrew Poetry". In: Follis, E.R. (ed.), *Directions in Biblical Hebrew Poetry*. Sheffield: JSOT Press 1987, pp. 77-100.

Collins, A.Y., (ed.) *Feminist Perspectives on Biblical Scholarship*. Chico, California: Scholars Press 1985.

Crenshaw, J., *Old Testament Wisdom: An Introduction*. Atlanta: John Knox Press, London: SCM Press 1981.

Crenshaw, J., "Education in Ancient Israel". *Journal of Biblical Literature*, (1985) 104, pp. 601-615.

Crook, M.B., "The Marriageable Maiden of Prov 31:10-31". *Journal of Near Eastern Studies*, 13 (1954), pp. 137-140.

Cross, F.M., "Early Alphabetic Scripts". In: Cross, F.M. (ed.), *Symposia Celebrating the Seventy-Fifth Anniversary of the Founding of the American Schools of Oriental Research*. Cambridge, Mass.: ASOR 1975

Cross, F.M. and Freedman, D.N., "The Song of Miriam". *Journal of Near Eastern Studies*, 14 (1955), pp. 237-250.

Culler, J., *On Deconstruction: Theory and Criticism after Structuralism*. London: Routledge and Kegan Paul 1983.

Deurloo, K. and Eykman, K. (eds.) *Sjofele Koning. David en Saul in profetisch perspectief*. Baarn: Ten Have 1984.

Doornebal, J., *"Dan geven wij elkaar een naam"*. *Het lied van Hanna*. Doctoraalscriptie. Kampen: Theologische Hogeschool der Gereformeerde Kerken in Nederland, 1984.

Dijk-Hemmes, F. van, "Bezwijk niet voor de schoonheid van een vrouw". In: Hes B. and others (eds.) *Reflecties op Schrift. Opstellen voor Prof.Dr. Gijs Bouwman*. Averbode/Apeldoorn: Altoria 1983, pp. 101-112.

Dijk-Hemmes, F. van, "Een moeder in Israël". *Wending*, 38 (1983) 10, pp. 688-695. And in: *Feministisch-Theologische Teksten*. Gekozen en ingeleid door Denise Dijk, Fokkelien van Dijk-Hemmes en Catharina J.M. Halkes. Delft: Meinema 1985, pp. 52-59.

Dijk-Hemmes, F. van, "Gezegende onder de vrouwen: een moeder in Israël en een maagd in de kerk". In: Dijk-Hemmes, F. van (ed.), *'t Is kwaad gerucht als zij niet binnenblijft. Vrouwen in oude culturen*. Utrecht: HES 1986, 123-147.

Dijk-Hemmes, F. van, "De spiegel van Tamar". *Schrift* (1987) 112, pp. 135-139.

Dijk-Hemmes, F. van, "Als H/hij tot haar hart spreekt. Een visie op (visies op) Hosea 2". In: Alphen, E. van and Jong, I. de (eds.) *Door het oog van de tekst. Essays voor Mieke Bal over visie*. Muiderberg: Coutinho 1988, pp. 121-139.

Dijk-Hemmes, F. van, "Interpretaties van de relatie tussen Richteren 4 en 5". In: Bekkenkamp, J., Dröes, F., Korte, A.M., Papavoine, M. (eds.) *Proeven van*

Vrouwenstudies Theologie. Deel I. IIMO Research Publication 25. Leiden/Utrecht: IIMO/IWFT 1989a, pp. 149-213.

Dijk-Hemmes, F. van, "The Imagination of Power and the Power of Imagination. An Intertextual Analysis of Two Biblical Love Songs: The Song of Songs and Hosea 2". *Journal for the Studies of the Old Testament*, (1989b) 44, pp. 75-88.

Dijk-Hemmes, F. van, "De vrouw als metafoor in profetische beeldspraak". *Tijdschrift voor Vrouwenstudies* (1989c) 38, pp. 221-234.

Dijk-Hemmes, F. van, "Betekenissen van Jeremia 31:22b". In: Becking, B., Dorp, J. van, Kooij, A. van der (eds.), *Door het oog van de profeten*. (Utrechtse Theologische Reeks 8) Utrecht: Faculty of Theology, National University 1989d, pp. 31-40.

Dijk-Hemmes, F. van, "Tamar and the Limits of Patriarchy: Between Rape and Seduction". In: Bal, M. (ed.) *Anti-Covenant. Counter-reading Women's Lives in the Hebrew Bible*. Sheffield: Almond Press 1989e, 135-156.

Dijk-Hemmes, F. van, "Sporen van vrouwenteksten in de Hebreeuwse Bijbel". In: Bekkenkamp, J., Dröes, F., Korte, A.M., Papavoine, M. (eds.), *Proeven van Vrouwenstudies Theologie*. Deel II. IIMO Research Publication 32. Leiden/ Utrecht: IIMO/IWFT 1991, pp. 161-238.

Dijk-Hemmes, F. van, *Sporen van vrouwenteksten in de Hebreeuwse bijbel*. Faculteit der Godsgeleerdheid. Universieit Utrecht 1992.

Eichrodt, W., *Der Prophet Hezekiel*. ATD 22/2. Göttingen 1966.

Exum, J.C., "Murder they wrote. Ideology and the Manipulation of Female Presence in Biblical Narrative". In: Alice Bach (ed.), *Ad Feminam. Union Seminary Quarterly Review* 43. New York 1989, pp. 19-39.

Falk, M., *Love Lyrics from the Bible. A Translation and Literary Study of the Song of Songs*. Sheffield: The Almond Press 1982.

Fokkelman, J.P., *Narrative Art and Poetry in the Books of Samuel*. Vol. I. Assen: Van Gorcum 1981.

Fontaine, C.R., "A Heifer from Thy Stable. On Goddesses and the Status of Women in the Ancient Near East". In: Bach, A. (ed.), *Ad Feminam. Union Seminary Quarterly Review* 43 (1989), pp. 67-92.

Fox, M.V., *The Song of Songs and the Ancient Egyptian Love Songs*. Madison: University of Wisconsin Press 1985.

Fox, M.V., *Qohelet and his Contradictions*. Sheffield: Almond Press 1989.

Freedman, D.N., "Pottery, Poetry and Prophecy: An Essay on Biblical Poetry". *Journal of Biblical Literature*, (1975) 96, pp. 5-26.

Gevirtz, S., *Patterns in the Early Poetry of Israel*. Chicago: University of Chicago Press 1963.

Ginsberg, H.L., *Qohelet*. Tel Aviv 1961 (in Hebrew).

Ginsburg, C.D., *The Song of Songs and Coheleth*. New York: Ktav 1861 = 1970.

Goitein, S.D., "Women as Creators of Biblical Genres". *Prooftexts* (1988) 8, pp. 1-33. (Translation from: "Nasim k'yoṣrot Sugēy Sifrut Bammiqra" in: *Iyyunim Bammiqra*. Tel Aviv: Yavneh Press 1957, pp. 248-317.)

Gordis, R., *Koheleth—The man and His World*. New York: Schocken 1968.

Goulder, M.D., *The Song of Fourteen Songs*. Sheffield: JSOT Press 1986.

Granquist, H., *Child Problems among the Arabs*. Helsingfors/Copenhagen 1950.

Gray, J., *The Canaanites*. Aylesbury 1964.

Gunkel, H. *Genesis*. Göttingen 1910.

Hacket, J.A., "In the Days of Jael: Reclaiming the History of Women in Ancient Israel". In: Atkinson, C.W., Buchanan C.H., Miles, M.R. (eds.), *Immaculate and Powerful. The Female in Sacred Image and Social Reality*. Boston, Beacon Press 1985, pp. 15-38.

Hallo, W.W., "Women of Sumer". In: Schmandt-Besserat, D. (ed.), *The Legacy of Sumer: Invited Lectures on the Middle East at the University of Texas at Austin*. Bibliotheca Mesopotamica IV: 1976, pp. 24-40.

Haran, M., "On the Diffusion of Literacy and Schools in Ancient Israel". *VT Supplement*, 40 (1988).

Herzberg, H.W., *Die Samuelbücher übersetzt und erklärt*. ATD 10. Göttingen 1956.

Hoftijzer, J., "David and the Tekoite Woman". *Vetus Testamentum*, 20 (1970), pp. 419-444.

Janeway, E., "Who Does What to Whom?": The Psychology of the Oppressor". In: Bach, A. (ed.), *Ad Feminam: Union Seminary Quarterly Review* 43 (1989), pp. 133-144.

Jastrow, M., *A Dictionary of the Targumim, the Talmud Babli and Yerushalmi, and the Midrashic Literature*. New York: Judaica Press 1903 = 1975.

Jong, S. de, *Onvruchtbare moeders. Een feministische lezing van Genesis*. Boxtel/Brugge: KBS/Tabor 1989.

Katona, I., "Reminiscence of Primitive Division of Labor between Sexes and Age Groups in the Peasant Folklore of Modern Times". In: Diamond, St. (ed.) *Towards a Marxist Anthropology*. Den Haag: Mouton, 1979, pp. 377-383.

Keel, O., *Die Welt der Altorientalischen Bildsymbolik und das Alte Testament. Am Beispeil der Psalmen*. (3d edition) Neukirchen: Vluyn 1980.

Kikiwada, I., "Two Notes on Eve". *Journal of Biblical Literature*, (1972) 91, pp. 33-37.

Kraemer, R.S., Women's Authorship of Jewish and Christian Literature in the Greco-Roman Period". Paper read at the Rome meeting of the Society of Biblical Literature, August 1991.

Kugel, J., *The Idea of Biblical Poetry. Parallelism and its History*. New Haven: Yale University Press 1981.

Lakoff, G. and Turner, M., *More than Cool Reason: A Field Guide to Poetic Metaphor*. Chicago and London: University of Chicago Press 1989.

Landy, F., *Paradoxes of Paradise: Identity and Difference in the Song of Songs*. Sheffield: Almond Press 1983.

Lemaire, A., *Les écoles et la formation de la bible dans l'ancien Israël*. Fribourg, Suisse/Göttingen: Éditions universitaires/ Vandenhoeck & Ruprecht 1981.

Lemaire, R., "Vrouwen in de volksliteratuur". In: Lemaire, R. (ed.), *Ik zing mijn lied voor al wie met mij gaat. Vrouwen in de volksliteratuur*. Utrecht: HES 1986, pp. 11-42.

Lemaire, R., *Passions et Positions. Contributions à une sémiotique du sujet dans la poésie lyrique médiévale en langues romanes*. Amsterdam: Rodopi 1987a.

Lemaire, R., "Rethinking Literary History". In: Meijer, M. and Schaap, J. (eds.) *Historiography of Women's Cultural Traditions*. Dordrecht/Providence: Foris Publications 1987b, pp. 180-193.

Lemaire, T., "Antropologie en schrift; aanzetten tot een ideologiekritiek van het schrift". In: Lemaire, T. (ed.) *Antropologie en ideologie*. Groningen: Konstapel 1984, pp. 103-124.

Levine, A.J. (ed.), *Women Like This: New Perspectives on Jewish Women in the Greco-Roman World*. Atlanta, GA: Scholars Press 1991.

Levy, L., *Das Buch Qohelet*. Leipzig 1912.

Lloyd-Jones, H., *Female of the Species. Semonides on Women: The first Satire on Women in European Literature*. London: Duckworth 1975.

Loader, J.A., "Qohelet 3.2-8—A 'Sonnet' in the Old Testament". *ZAW*, 81 (1969), pp. 240-242.

Loader, J.A., *Polar Structures in the Book of Qohelet*. Berlin: De Gruyter (BZAW 152), 1979.

Loader, J.A., *Ecclesiastes: A Practical Commentary*. Grand Rapids: Eerdmans 1986.

Lord, A.B., *The Singer of Tales*. Cambridge, Mass.: Harvard University Press 1960.

Maarsingh, B., *Ezechiël*. Deel II, POT. Nijkerk 1988.

Magonet, J., "Jeremiah's Last Confessions: Structure, Image and Ambiguity". *Hebrew Annual Review* 11 (1987), pp. 303-317.

Marks, H., "The Twelve Prophets". In: Alter, R. and Kermode, F. (eds.), *The Literary Guide to the Bible*. Cambridge, Mass.: Harvard University Press 1987.

McKane, W., *Proverbs: A New Approach*. London: SCM Press 1970.

Meer, W. van der and Moor, J.C. de (eds.) *The Structural Analysis of Biblical and Canaanite Poetry*. Sheffield: JSOT Press 1988.

Meijer, M., *De lust tot lezen. Nederlandse dichteressen en het literaire systeem*. Amsterdam: Sara/Van Gennep 1988.

Meyers, C., "Gender Imagery in the Song of Songs". *Hebrew Annual Review*, 10 (1986), pp. 209-223.

Meyers, C., *Discovering Eve. Ancient Israelite Women in Context*. New York/Oxford: Oxford University Press 1988.

Meyers, C., "Of Drums and Damsels". *Biblical Archeologist*, March 1991a, pp. 16-27.

Meyers, C., "'To Her Mother's House': Considering a Counterpart to the Israelite Bet 'ab". In: *The Bible and the Politics of Exegesis*. New York: Pilgrim Press 1991b.

Millard, A.R., "An Assessment of the Evidence for Writing in Ancient Israel". In: Biran, A. (ed.), *Biblical Archeology Today: Proceedings of the International Congress on Biblical Archeology*. Jerusalem: Israel Exploration Society 1985, pp. 301-312.

Naveh, A., "A Paleographic Note on the Distribution of the Hebrew Script". *Harvard Theological Review*, 61 (1968), pp. 71-72.

Nead, L., "Framing and Freeing: Utopias of the Female Body". In: *Radical Philosophy*, 60 (Spring 1992), pp. 12-15.

Newsom, C.A., "A Maker of Metaphors: Ezekiel's Oracles against Tyre". In: Mays, J.L. and Achtemeier, P.J. (eds.), *Interpreting the Prophets*. Philadelphia: Fortress Press 1985, 188-199.

Newsom, C.A., "Woman and the Discourse of Patriarchal Wisdom. A Study of Proverbs 1-9". In: Day, P.L. (ed.) *Gender and Difference in Ancient Israel*. Minneapolis: Fortress Press 1989, pp. 142-160.

Noth, M., *Das zweite Buch Mose. Exodus*. ATD 5. Göttingen 1965.

Ogden, G. *Qohelet*. Sheffield: JSOT Press 1987.

Ohler, A., *Frauengestalten der Bibel*. Würzburg: Echter Verlag 1987.

Ong, W.J., *Orality and Literacy. The Technologizing of the Word*. London/New York: Methuen 1982.

Pardes, I., "Beyond Genesis 3". *Hebrew University Studies in Literature and the Arts* 17 (1989), pp. 161-187.

Parry, A, (ed.) *The Making of Homeric Verse: the Collected Papers of Milman Parry*. Oxford 1971.

Patai, R., *The Hebrew Goddess*. New York: Avon Books 1978.

Polzin, R., *Samuel and the Deuteronomist. A Literary Study of the Deuteronomic History: I Samuel.* San Francisco: Harper & Row 1989.
Pope, M.H. *The Song of Songs. A New Translation with Introduction and Commentary.* The Anchor Bible, Garden City, New York: Doubleday 1977.

Rabin, Ch., "The Song of Songs and Tamil Poetry". *Studies in Religion*, 3 (1973/1974), pp. 205-219.
Rasmussen, R.C., "Deborah the Woman Warrior". In: Bal, M. (ed.) *Anti-Covenant. Counter-Reading Women's Lives in the Hebrew Bible.* Sheffield: The Almond Press 1989, pp. 79-94.
Reage, P., *Story of O.* London: Corgi 1972.
Reed, W.L., *The Asherah in the Old Testament.* Forth Worth, Texas: Texas Christian University Press 1949.
Rollin, S., "Women and Witchcraft in Ancient Assyria". In: Cameron, A. and Kuhrt, A. (eds.), *Images of Women in Antiquity.* London & Canberra: Croom Helm 1983.
Russell, L.M. (ed.), *Feminist Interpretation of the Bible.* Philadelphia: The Westminster Press 1985.

Sancisi-Weerdenburg, H., "Vrouwen in verborgen werelden". In: Dijk-Hemmes, F. van (ed.), *'t Is kwaad gerucht als zij niet binnenblijft. Vrouwen in oude culturen.* Utrecht: HES 1986, pp. 11-35.
Sasson, J.M., *Ruth: A New Translation with a Philological Commentary and a Formalist-Folkorist Interpretation.* Baltimore 1979.
Sasson, J.M., "Ruth". In: Alter R. and Kermode, F. (eds.) *The literary Guide to the Bible.* Cambridge, Mass.: Harvard University Press 1987, pp. 320-328.
Schüssler Fiorenza, E., *In Memory of Her. A Feminist Theological Reconstruction of Christian Origins.* New York: Crossroad 1983.
Schweickart, P., "Reading Ourselves: Toward a Feminist Theory of Reading". In: Flinn, A. and Schweickart P. (eds.), *Gender and Reading: Essays on Readers, Texts and Contexts.* Baltimore and London 1986, pp. 31-62.
Scott, R.B.Y., *Proverbs and Ecclesiastes.* Anchor Bible, Garden City, New York: Doubleday 1965.
Selms, A. van, "Hosea and Canticles". *Studies of the Books of Hosea and Amos. OTS-WA 7/8.* Potchefstroom: Pro Rege pers 1965, pp. 85-89.
Setel, D.T., "Prophets and Pornography: Female Sexual Imagery in Hosea". In: Russell, L., *Feminist Interpretations of the Bible.* Philadelphia: Westminster Press 1985, pp. 86-95.
Showalter, E., "Feminist Criticism in the Wilderness". In: Showalter, E. (ed.) *The New Feminist Criticism. Essays on Women, Literature and Theory.* London: Virago Press 1986, pp. 243-270.
Skinner, J., *Genesis.* I.C.C. Edinburgh: T and T Clark 1910.
Smelik, K.A.D., *Behouden Schrift. Historische documenten uit het oude Israël.* Baarn: Ten Have 1984.
Sternberg, M., *The Poetics of Biblical Narrative. Ideological Literature and the Drama of Reading.* Bloomington: Indiana University Press 1985.
Sternberg, R.J., "A Triangular Theory of Love". *Psychological Review* 93 (1986), pp. 119-135.
Sternberg, R.J., "Liking versus Loving: A Comparative Evaluation of Theories". *Psychological Bulletin of the American Psychological Association*, 102 (1987), pp. 331-345.

Toy, C.H., *The Book of Proverbs.* (I.C.C.), Edinburgh: T and T Clark 1899.

TWAT Botterweck, G.J. and Ringgren, H. (hrsg.) *Theologisches Wörterbuch zum Alten Testament*. Stuttgart/Berlin/Köln/Mainz, 1970 ff.

Toorn, K. van der, *Van haar wieg tot haar graf. De rol van de godsdienst in het leven van de Israëlitische en de Babylonische vrouw*. Baarn: Ten Have 1987.

Toorn, K. van der, "Female Prostitution in Payment of Vows in Ancient Israël". *Journal of Biblical Literature*, 108 (1989) 2, pp. 193-205.

Trible, Ph., *God and the Rhetoric of Sexuality*. Philadelphia: Fortress Press 1978.

Trible, Ph., *Texts of Terror. Literary-Feminist Readings of Biblical Narratives*. Philadelphia: Fortress Press 1984.

Trible, Ph., "Bringing Miriam out of the Shadows". *Bible Review*, (February 1989), pp. 14-34.

Vaux, R. de, *Hoe het oude Israël leefde. De instellingen van het Oude Testament*. Deel I en II. Roermond/Maaseik: J.J. Romen & zonen 1961.

Wacker, M.Th., *Der Gott der Männer und die Frauen*. Düsseldorf: Patmos Verlag 1987.

Wacker, M.Th., "Hulda—eine Prophetin vor dem Ende". In: Schmidt, E.A. and others (hrsg.) *Feministisch gelesen*. Band I. Stuttgart: Kreuz Verlag 1988, pp. 91-99.

Wagenaar, J., " 'Is tegen de rivieren uw toorn ontbrand?' Het principe van profetische mythologie in Exodus 15, Jesaja 51 en Habakuk 3". *Amsterdamse Cahiers voor exegese en bijbelse theologie*, (1986) 7, pp. 55-69.

Watson, W.G.E. *Classical Hebrew Poetry. A Guide to its Techniques*. Sheffield: JSOT Press 1984.

Wenham, G.J., "A Girl of Marriageable Age", *Vetus Testamentum*, 22 (1972), pp. 248-252.

Whybray, R.N., *Wisdom in Proverbs: The Concept of Wisdom in Proverbs 1-9*, London: SCM Press 1965.

Whybray, R.N., *The Book of Proverbs*. The Cambridge Bible Commentary, Cambridge: Cambridge University Press 1972.

Whybray, R.N., *Ecclesiastes* (OT Guides), Sheffield: JSOT Press 1989.

Whybray, R.N., "Some Literary Problems in Proverbs I-IX". *Vetus Testamentum*, 16 (1966), pp. 482-496.

Whybray, R.N., "The Identification and Use of Quotations in Ecclesiastes". *Vetus Testamentum* Supplement, 32 (1981), pp. 435-451.

Whybray, R.N., " 'A Time to Be Born and a Time to Die'? Some Observations on Ecclesiastes 3:2-8". In: *Near Eastern Studies Dedicated to H.I.M. Prince Takahito Mikasa on the Occasion of his Seventy-Fifth Birthday*. (MECCJ V), 1991.

Willis, J.T., "The Song of Hannah and Ps. 113". *Catholic Biblical Quarterly*, 35 (1973), pp. 139-154.

Winter, U., *Frau und Göttin. Exegetische und ikonographische Studien zum weiblichen Gottesbild im Alten Israel und in dessen Umwelt*. (2d edition) Göttingen: Vandenhoeck & Ruprecht 1987.

Yadin, Y., *Warfare in Biblical Lands in the Light of Archeological Discoveries*. Ramat Gan 1963 (in Hebrew).

Yee, G.A., " 'I have Perfumed My Bed with Myrrh': The Foreign Woman ('issa zara) in Proverbs 1-9". *Journal for the Study of the Old Testament*, 43 (1989), pp. 53-68.

Zakovitch, Y., *The Pattern of the Numerical Sequence Three-Four in the Bible*. Unpublished Ph.D. dissertation. Jerusalem: The Hebrew University 1977 (in Hebrew).

Zimmerli, W., *Ezechiël*. BKAT XIII, 1-2. Neukirchen-Vluyn 1969.

Zimmermann, F., *The Inner World of Qohelet*. New York 1973.

INDEX OF ANCIENT SOURCES

BIBLICAL PASSAGES CITED

(On Gendering Texts)

OTHERS